COUNSELING AND DEVELOPMENT SERIES
Allen Ivey, Editor

Narratives in Action: A Strategy for Research and Analysis
STANTON WORTHAM

The African Unconscious: Roots of Ancient Mysticism and Modern Psychology
EDWARD BRUCE BYNUM

Gili's Book: A Journey into Bereavement for Parents and Counselors
HENYA KAGAN (KLEIN)

Constructivist Thinking in Counseling Practice, Research, and Training
THOMAS L. SEXTON & BARBARA L. GRIFFIN, Editors

Research as Praxis: Lessons from Programmatic Research in Therapeutic Psychology
LISA TSOI HOSHMAND & JACK MARTIN, Editors

The Construction and Understanding of Psychotherapeutic Change:
Conversations, Memories, and Theories
JACK MARTIN

Narratives in Action

A STRATEGY FOR RESEARCH AND ANALYSIS

STANTON WORTHAM

Foreword by Kenneth J. Gergen

Teachers College, Columbia University
New York and London

Published by Teachers College Press, 1234 Amsterdam Avenue,
New York, NY 10027

Library of Congress Cataloging-in-Publication Data

Wortham, Stanton Emerson Fisher, 1963–
    Narratives in action : a strategy for research and analysis / Stanton
  Wortham ; foreword by Kenneth J. Gergen.
        p. cm.— (Counseling and development series)
    Includes bibliographical references and index.
    ISBN 0-8077-4076-4 (alk. paper)—ISBN 0-8077-4075-6 (pbk. : alk.
    paper)
    1. Autobiography—Psychological aspects. 2. Discourse analysis,
    Narrative. 3. Identity (Psychology). 4. Self. I. Title. II. Series.
    CT25 .W67   2001
    808'.06692—dc21   00-053272

ISBN 0-8077-4075-6 (paper)
ISBN 0-8077-4076-4 (cloth)

Printed on acid-free paper
Manufactured in the United States of America

08 07 06 05 04 03   8 7 6 5 4 3 2

Contents

Foreword *by Kenneth J. Gergen* — vii
Acknowledgments — ix
Introduction — xi

1. **Narrating the Self** — 1

   Jane — 1
   The Representational Power of Autobiographical Narrative — 5
   The Interactional Power of Autobiographical Narrative — 7
   Enacting the Self — 9
   Interrelations between Representation and Enactment — 13
   Analyzing Narrative Discourse — 14

2. **A Dialogic Approach to Discourse** — 17

   Monologic and Dialogic Approaches to Language Use — 18
   An Actual Encounter — 24
   Mediation — 35
   Voicing — 38
   Emergence — 40
   Chunking: Poetic Structure — 44

3. **Dialogue, Mediation, and Emergence in Narrative** — 47

   A Sample Narrative — 48
   Mediation — 57
   Emergence — 59
   Two Bakhtinian Concepts — 62

4. **Dialogic Analysis of an Autobiographical Narrative** — 76

   Overview of Jane's Life — 76
   Jane Enacts Her Passive Voice — 81

Jane Enacts the Transition from Passive to Active   *101*
Jane Enacts Her Assertive Voice   *119*

5. **Narrative Self-Construction and the Nature
    of the Self**   **136**

The Stable Psychological Self   *138*
The Narrated Self   *140*
The Dialogic Self   *144*
The Enacted Self   *149*
The Multilayered Self   *153*

6. **Implications**   **157**

Studying Interactional Positioning in Other Contexts   *158*
A Dialogic Approach   *160*

Notes   **163**
References   **171**
Index   **179**
About the Author   **185**

Foreword

Deliberations on the nature and significance of narrative now sweep across the intellectual landscape. Literary theorists join linguists, phenomenologists, hermeneuticists, legal theorists, feminist scholars, theologians, therapists, gerontologists, developmental psychologists, social workers, and others in viewing narrative as a pivotal feature of the meaning-making process. Narrative is not only a chief means by which the individual self is defined, but it also exerts a formative influence on our understanding of the world about us. Yet the vast share of this work also concurs in its presumption that narrative structures primarily serve a representational function: They function so as to portray, reveal, or illuminate self or surrounds. The relationship of primary interest is that holding between the narrative and the subject matter to be narrated. Herein lies the primary epistemological drama of recent years: the portraying device absorbs and obliterates that which is ostensibly portrayed. In contrast, precious little attention has been directed to the relationship between the narrating agent and the audience to which the narrative is directed. It is precisely at this point that the present volume enters the dialogue.

Stanton Wortham turns our attention to narratives in action. Through the sophisticated lens of linguistic pragmatics, Wortham invites us to see the function of narrative within the unfolding relationships among people. Narratives not only define the narrator, but the relationship between the narrator and his or her audience. Most fascinating in the present analysis, however, is the line that Wortham draws between the representational and the pragmatic function of narration. With keen sensitivity, Wortham enables us to see ways in which narrative content may parallel the performance of the telling. The narrator may subtly enact characters portrayed in the story being told. In these conjunctions of stories told and stories lived, the narrator creates and embodies a self for the listener.

The possibility that one is essentially thrust into being during the narrative telling is of substantial importance, both theoretically and practically. From Wortham's perspective the narrative is no longer a private possession of the individual; nor is it simply a pawn to the preceding narratives to which one has been exposed. Rather, narratives are best understood in terms of a Bakhtinian dialogic. They are utterances that acquire their significance in the relationship between narrator and audience. On the practical level we also see how narrative tellings might function therapeutically. As narrative enactments define both the teller and the audience, they may also reveal characteristic patterns of reverberating significance. And with the exploration of alternative tellings, the door is open to the creation of new forms of being.

These are exciting ideas and represent a significant entry into contemporary dialogues on narrative. They now invite exploration into such issues as the significance of discrepancies between stories told and lived, the relationship among narrations of self to disparate audiences, and the active part played by the audience in the shaping of the narrator's identity. Wortham's story is thus to be prized as a contribution that both reveals and simultaneously leaves us in keen anticipation of the next.

Kenneth J. Gergen

Acknowledgments

I would like to thank various institutions and colleagues who have made this work possible. The National Academy of Education and the Spencer Foundation awarded me a postdoctoral fellowship that provided time for writing the initial manuscript. Both Bates College and the University of Pennsylvania provided crucial financial and administrative support. Ken Gergen and John Shotter made useful suggestions and showed confidence in the book early in the writing process, and Ken has generously written the foreword. Michael Locher has collaborated with me in joint work on Bakhtin for many years, work that provided essential background for this book. Michael Lempert and Teresa Wojcik have done outstanding jobs as my research assistants at the University of Pennsylvania, and they contributed both substantive insights and logistical support to this project. Dan McAdams first inspired me to work on autobiographical narrative, especially through his books (1985, 1993), and he has generously shared his expertise throughout the project. My mother, Judith Robbins, read an early draft and provided extensive and useful suggestions. Ageliki Nicolopoulou read a later draft and provided many insightful comments. Participants in my seminar on Narrating the Self at the University of Pennsylvania in 1999 read the manuscript and provided useful feedback. Ruth Ebert has provided invaluable help in editing and typing the manuscript several times, and Carol Collins of Teachers College Press has been a skillful editor. I would also like to thank other friends and colleagues for their comments and support: Michael Bamberg, Mark Freeman, Doug Glick, Victoria Johnson, Emily Kane, David Kolb, Jay Lemke, Kathy Low, Bob Neimeyer, Rick Shweder, Michael Silverstein, Stacy Smith, and Greg Urban.

Introduction

Telling a story about oneself can sometimes transform that self. Sitting with friends and describing recent experiences, a narrator often reinforces and sometimes re-creates what sort of person he or she is. Sitting with a therapist and narrating their life's experiences, clients can sometimes realize who they are and who they want to be. Noting such transformative acts of narration, many have proposed that auto-biographical stories do more than describe a preexisting self. Sometimes narrators can change who they are, in part, by telling stories about themselves.

But *how* does this narrative self-construction happen? Most explanations rely on the *representational* function of autobiographical discourse: That is, most accounts claim that an autobiographical narrative can shape the self of the narrator by *describing* him or her as a particular type of person. When talking with friends, therapists, or other audiences, autobiographical narrators represent themselves as particular sorts of people—as people who engage in characteristic activities and relate to others in characteristic ways. By describing past events in which she overcomes exploitation and takes control of her life, for instance, a narrator can reinforce or even create a more active, assertive self. If this narrator had, instead, consistently represented herself as passive and victimized in telling her story, she might have become a more passive, victimized person.

Although this representational account of narrative self-construction may be plausible, it is nevertheless incomplete. Autobiographical narratives also have *interactional* functions: That is, autobiographical narrators *act* like particular types of people while they tell their stories, and they relate to their audiences in characteristic ways as they tell those stories. In this book I show in detail how narrator and audience can position themselves interactionally through the telling of an autobiographical narrative. While representing herself as overcoming exploitation, for instance, a narrator might also act active and assertive with respect to the audience in the storytelling event. I argue that this kind of interactional positioning helps explain how autobiographical narration can partly construct the self. While telling their stories, autobiographical narrators often enact a characteristic type of self, and through such performances they can become that type of self.

In the following chapters I develop a systematic account of how narrative speech can simultaneously represent the self and position the narrator interactionally. Speech, in general, and autobiographical speech, in particular, contain types of linguistic constructions that systematically carry information about the interactional positions of the speaker and the audience. I draw on and extend concepts developed by the philosopher and literary critic Mikhail Bakhtin, in order to provide a detailed account of how autobiographical narrative discourse positions people "dialogically" with respect to others' "voices." In the process, I show the empirical utility of often-cited but slippery Bakhtinian concepts.

Scholars and practitioners in psychology, women's studies, education, anthropology, and cultural studies are becoming increasingly interested in a dialogic approach to the human sciences. According to such an approach, the meaning that experience has for people cannot be understood if people are considered to be isolated individuals. Instead, one must study how social, cultural, and relational contexts play a central role in producing the meaningfulness of experience. The social constructionist critique in recent years has made it clear that such a relational approach to the human sciences is needed (K. Gergen, 1994, 1997; Shotter, 1993a, 1993b). This book provides, in empirical detail, one vision of what a constructionist approach might look like in practice. Drawing on Bakhtin, I provide a systematic account of how relational context is, in fact, crucial to the transformative power of autobiographical narrative.

This book makes two primary contributions, one conceptual and one methodological. First, it offers a detailed account of how narrative self-construction happens. I argue that the self can be partly constructed through the *interrelationship* of represented content and enacted positioning in autobiographical narrative, as narrators enact characteristic interactional positions while telling their stories. This account of narrative self-construction involves both a thorough account of narrative discourse and an extensive discussion of the self. Second, the book offers a systematic methodological approach to analyzing narrative discourse. I give a detailed, concrete description of how narrative discourse can simultaneously represent the self and accomplish interactional positioning. The methodological approach is explained with detailed analyses of several different types of discourse—an extended autobiographical narrative (Chapter 4), a classroom discussion (Chapter 2), and a television newscast (Chapter 3).

The book is written for two types of audiences: academic audiences interested in narrative self-construction and in the representational and interactional functions of narrative discourse, and professional psychologists and educators interested in autobiographical narrative and self-identity. By providing a specific account of *how* autobiographical narrators use language both to represent the self and to enact interactional positions, the book can contribute to anthropological, educational, linguistic, and psychological accounts of narrative and self. For practitioners in education and psychology with applied interests in narrative and self, the book provides examples of detailed analysis that will be useful for conceptualizing everyday work with clients and their stories, even though most practitioners will only occasionally do that sort of analysis themselves.

Readers may notice one irony in the book. While my account focuses on the relational context within which autobiographical stories are told, my own analytic voice maintains scientific distance throughout the book. My intent is to provide a set of analytic tools for studying interactional positioning in narrative performances, including complex emotional and relational patterns. I hope that this sort of work can support a more human, relationally embedded account of discourse in narratives, classrooms, and elsewhere—as opposed to accounts focused solely on rational action and the cognitive content of talk. Thus I am working against purely cognitive, objectivist approaches to human nature.

Nonetheless, some advocates of a reflexive or relational social science would argue that my scientific stance undermines the dialogic approach I advocate in the book—that the analysis should, instead, be as much about my role in the research process as about the subject (e.g., Bloom, 1998). I agree that we can benefit from research that pushes dialogicality into the research process itself (e.g., Lather, 1991). But we can also gain conceptual clarity and methodological rigor from research that backgrounds the researcher's voice and studies relational and emotional patterns systematically. This book provides such clarity and rigor for studying the process of narrative self-construction. I hope that such a systematic approach will yield information useful to people who are ultimately interested in understanding, celebrating, or intervening in relational and emotional patterns. Such an approach may also provide legitimacy for the ongoing project of making the human sciences more humane (i.e., less focused on rational economic actors and purely cognitive minds).

Chapter 1 presents the central argument—that the self can be partly constructed in autobiographical narrative because of interrelationships between the representations of self and the interactional positioning that narrators accomplish through their stories. Chapters 2 and 3 present a systematic account of how narrative discourse can position narrators interactionally and how the interactional and representational functions of autobiographical narrative can interrelate. Chapter 2 provides conceptual and methodological tools for a dialogic approach to speech in general, by defining the central concepts of *dialogue, mediation*, and *emergence* and by applying these concepts to an extended example. Chapter 3 applies these tools to narrative discourse and extends Bakhtin's account of narrative, developing a more precise dialogic approach to narrative discourse.

Chapters 4 and 5 apply this dialogic approach to narrative discourse, analyzing an extended autobiographical narrative and exploring the process of narrative self-construction. Chapter 4 applies the tools developed in Chapters 2 and 3 to analyze an extended autobiographical narrative, and Chapter 5 develops a dialogic theory of self that can account for the interactional patterns found in the narrative. Chapter 5 thus completes the argument that the systematic conceptual and methodological tools developed in this book illuminate how the self can be partly constructed by interactional positioning in autobiographical narration. Chapter 6 considers how these tools, and the more precise dialogic approach they facilitate, can illuminate other important issues in the human sciences.

Narratives
in
Action

CHAPTER 1

Narrating the Self

How can we explain autobiographical narratives' power to transform or construct the self? Almost all answers to this question have relied on the representational power of narrative discourse. Autobiographical narrators represent themselves in recognizable story lines. A narrator might, for instance, represent herself as moving from passive victim to agent of social change. By representing herself as an agent, the narrator might come to think of herself as, and ultimately come to act like, a more active and assertive person. Depending on how it is articulated, this representational account of self-construction in autobiographical narrative can be plausible. But a solely representational account ignores how autobiographical narratives position the narrator in an ongoing dialogue with other speakers. Narrative discourse functions not only to represent characters and events but also to establish relationships between the narrator and the audience in the interactional event of storytelling. This book describes how autobiographical narratives can partly create the narrator's self by interactionally positioning the narrator in salient ways with respect to others.

   This chapter has three goals: (1) to make plausible the notion that the self might get partly constructed in autobiographical narrative; (2) to argue that any full account of self-construction in autobiographical narrative must attend to the interactional positioning accomplished in narrative discourse; and (3) to describe how any analysis of self-construction in autobiographical narrative will require precise methodological tools for studying narrative discourse. I begin with a discussion of an excerpt from one autobiographical narrative in order to illustrate how narrative can contribute to self-transformation.

JANE

   The narrative introduced here, and analyzed in detail in Chapter 4, was told by a woman whom I will call Jane.[1] She was interviewed in the early 1990s when she was 57 years old. Jane had responded to an

ad requesting adult subjects for a psychological study. The interviewer
was a female graduate student training to be a clinical psychologist,
and the interview took place in a research lab at a university psychology department. The autobiographical narrative was the first compo-
nent of the interview, and lasted about 50 minutes. In those 50 minutes, the interviewer prompted Jane only with the request that she tell
the story of her life as if it were a novel divided into chapters.

Jane begins with the setting for her story: her mother was a writer,
an Armenian American; her father was a businessman, and Episcopalian; her maternal grandparents disapproved of the marriage from
the start, and it ended in divorce when Jane was 7. After the divorce
her mother needed to work full-time and did not know what to do
with her child. For some reason she consulted with a local adminis-
trator and went along with his recommendation to send Jane to a
boarding school. Jane refers to this chapter in her life as "the institutionalization of a human being." She was ostracized because of her
Armenian background. She was beaten and humiliated by the staff
at the school. She spent 5 "horrendous" years there, seeing her mother
only occasionally. Jane still vividly recalls the happy day on which
she left this school, much as a prisoner might recall the moment of
leaving jail after serving a long sentence.

Her mother took Jane out of the boarding school in order to return to her parents' home in Louisville. After a brief time in which Jane
had trouble adjusting to her grandparents' Armenian neighborhood,
Jane's mother decided to "institutionalize" her again. Her mother again
took advice from someone, but she apparently did not realize the nature of the institution, because Jane was sent to a boarding school for
"delinquents" and "street people." There she was beaten up, her belongings were stolen, and she was made miserable. At age 16, she ran
away from the school and "blackmailed" her mother by calling home
and refusing to tell her mother where she was until her mother promised not to send her back to the school.

Her mother acquiesced, and Jane moved with her mother into an
apartment near her grandparents. This was a more pleasant period for
Jane than the two institutionalizations, but there were still problems.
They lived in a predominantly Armenian neighborhood where Jane was
ostracized because she was considered Episcopalian. The schools were
good, but district boundaries dictated that she had to attend a lower-
class high school where she again felt out of place. She did well in school
nonetheless, and despite a lack of encouragement from her mother and
grandparents—who expected young women simply to get married—

she went on to college afterward. But after a year she dropped out and went to work.

In her early 20s, Jane had what she describes as an "affair" with a man from her neighborhood, and she got pregnant. Because of her relatives' discomfort with the prospect of single parenthood, she decided to give the child up for adoption. So when her son was born, she brought him to an orphanage in downtown Louisville. In the following excerpt from the interview transcript, Jane describes her experience at the orphanage.[2]

I was being heavily *press*ured by, so*ci*ety, my own *thoughts*, by Robert [the baby's father], by my *m*other, to give the child up. (pause) on the night of April 5, I went into *labor*, went into the *hos*pital, and at *two* o'clock in the morning on April 6, 1956, I gave birth to a, *beau*tiful
5   baby boy. (pause) *while* I was in the hospital, I called, *a*gain by recommendation the city *or*phanage. (pause) at the time, there was a *shor*tage on *good white ba*bies. (pause)

and a *very vile wo*man at the city orphanage, a*greed* to take my baby until I could make a decision. So I took my, my *dar*ling Kenny (pause)
10 um (pause) (crying) (voice quivering) to the orphanage on Thirteenth Street (pause) and *left* him there for *two* weeks. (pause) two of the *hard*est weeks of my life. (long pause) and when the *two* weeks were up (pause) I went *down* there, and this horr*end*ous person had these *pap*ers out for me to *sign*. she had a *fam*ily all lined up. (pause) There
15 was a (pause) there was a *shor*tage of, like I say, in *those* days (pause) a *nice good white ba*by was a, *short* coming. a good *heal*thy baby. (Sniff) She handed me the *pen* (pause) and I *could*n't do it. (pause) I said, "*bring* me my *ba*by." (pause)

I want you to know this woman *yelled* at me (pause) and tried to *guilt*-
20 trip me. she said, "how *dare* you do this to me! I made *place* for your baby. *I* helped you out. you *have* to sign these papers!" I said, "I don't have to do anything of the *sort*. I want my child!" and at first she re*fused* me. And I said, "I want my *ba*by." And she practically threw a *tem*per tantrum right there in the office of the orphanage, and
25 was *scream*ing at me because she had made *room* for my baby and she *want*ed my baby. they brought, my *dar*ling baby to me, who had (pause) his *skin* on his *feet* and his *legs* was totally *scaled* (pause) I think they *left* him a*lone* for two weeks.

This represents a pivotal moment in Jane's life story. Note the parallel between this event and her mother's decision to institutionalize her as a child. Jane herself points to this parallel early in the excerpt (line 6), when she says "again by recommendation"—which points back to the man who recommended boarding school for Jane herself at age 7. At the orphanage in Louisville Jane finds herself about to do to her son what her mother did to her. Will she, like her mother, allow her own life to run along the lines recommended by others? Or will she break out of this pattern?

Jane the narrator skillfully represents her experience at the orphanage, in a way that answers these questions. In this orphanage episode she represents herself as changing from a passive victim to an active, assertive woman. The first segment of the excerpt (lines 1–7) describes the events leading up to the orphanage episode. The second segment (lines 8–18) describes her passively acquiescing to the recommendations made by society. Here she is a victim of Robert's neglect, of society's prejudices against single mothers, and of the orphanage woman's desire for her baby. In the third segment (lines 19–28), however, Jane breaks out of the passivity that characterized her mother's life. She asserts her rights and takes on the responsibility of caring for her son.

Note that Jane herself, while telling this story, also recovers her composure at the same point that she describes how she took control at the orphanage. Throughout the first two segments, she pauses often, her voice breaks, and she even cries at one point. But in the third segment she speaks much more fluently. These cues, and others described in the more extensive analysis of this narrative given in Chapter 4, indicate that in this event of autobiographical narration she does more than describe apparently transformative events. While *describing* her transformation from passive to active at the orphanage, Jane herself *enacts* an analogous shift in her projected relationship with the interviewer. Thus, while telling her narrative, she shifts from being passive and vulnerable to being active and assertive in the storytelling event itself. As documented in Chapter 4, she changes her interactional position with respect to the interviewer, from being rather passive and asking for the interviewer's sympathy early in the interview to actively asserting how she in fact has more life experience than the naive interviewer.

This excerpt from Jane's autobiographical narrative represents a pivotal moment in her life and captures a central theme of that life, her development from passivity to agency. The act of narrating this event also seems to allow Jane herself, in the interview, to recover a sense of control. As described in much more detail in Chapter 4, the narrative not only represents a central unifying theme of her life but also helps her recover an active, assertive position in her interaction with the interviewer.

This short excerpt by itself illustrates how Jane's autobiographical narrative might have the power partly to construct or transform her self. By narrating herself with this story of triumph and transformation, either on a few pivotal occasions or many times, Jane might become a more active, assertive woman. By telling this triumphant story of her life, she might come to understand herself—and to act in her relations with others—as an active, assertive woman. But, if this were to happen, how could we explain the narrative's transformative power? Would the *representation* of herself as active and assertive be central to constructing Jane's self? Or would her *enactment* of an active, assertive role in her interaction with the interviewer be crucial? Or could the representation and the enactment *interrelate* in some way so as to shape Jane's self?

THE REPRESENTATIONAL POWER
OF AUTOBIOGRAPHICAL NARRATIVE

The predominant explanation for autobiographical narratives' power cites their representational functions. Telling the story of his or her life gives the narrator an opportunity to redirect that life when the narrator tells a coherent story that foregrounds a certain perspective or direction (Anderson, 1997; Cohler, 1988; Kerby, 1991; M.White & Epston, 1990). The portion of Jane's autobiographical narrative presented and summarized above, for instance, foregrounds her agency and her triumph over adversity. According to the predominant explanation, it is her representation of herself as triumphant that might transform Jane's self. As described in detail in Chapter 4, her life could be represented in more than one way. She has triumphed over serious adversity, but she has also experienced decline or regression. An autobiographical narrative can have power by foregrounding one particular description, despite other possibilities. Note that this explanation for autobiographical narratives' power need not rely on one pivotal telling of the story. The same story can be repeated on many occasions, in order to reinforce a particular sense of oneself. In Jane's case, for instance, it might well be that she has on many occasions used this triumphant construal of her life to encourage herself to be active and assertive in everyday life. In some cases, a single telling of an autobiographical narrative can be truly transformative, but more often a narrator constructs himself or herself through repeated tellings of similar autobiographical narratives.

In the predominant view, then, Jane's autobiographical narrative has the power partly to construct her self because it represents her as an active, assertive woman who has triumphed over adversity. When an autobiographical representation becomes compelling enough, the narrator sometimes acts in accordance with the characteristics foregrounded in the narrative. Jane's narrative might provide an example of this when her own demeanor in the interview becomes more controlled and assertive as she tells the story of her triumph at the orphanage. Jane's enactment of the transformation from passive to active, in her interaction with the interviewer, might show that Jane has been transformed sufficiently so as to act like her new self.

This representational explanation of autobiographical narratives' power has been advanced in several fields. Anderson (1997), Cohler (1988), M.White and Epston (1990), and other clinicians have presented autobiographical narrative as a therapeutic tool. Therapy, they argue, involves the reshaping of a patient's life story so as to foreground a more healthful direction. The Personal Narratives Group (1989), Rosenwald and Ochberg (1992), Zuss (1997), and others have argued that autobiographical narratives provide a powerful vehicle for resisting oppressive social orders. People can construct their life stories against the grain of accepted patterns, to overcome oppression and to foreground alternative directions for their own and others' lives. Cain (1991), Stromberg (1993), and others have described how life stories can play a central role in the development of religious identity. People can tell the stories of their lives, often by highlighting a conversion experience, so as to foreground their faith and their relation to a religious community. Finally, Cohen (1996), Witherell and Noddings (1991), and others have argued that autobiographical narratives' power can be used to improve education as well. In telling stories about themselves, teachers and students can foreground more educationally promising characteristics and free themselves from less productive story lines.

Despite various differences, work in all these disciplines relies primarily on a representational explanation for narrative self-construction: Autobiographical narratives redirect lives by *representationally foregrounding* more productive characteristics and by inspiring people to enact those more productive characteristics. But how exactly do autobiographical narratives do this foregrounding? Gergen and Gergen (1983), Polkinghorne (1988), and others explain foregrounding in terms of *emplotment:* An autobiographical narrative selects some from among the many events of a life and places them in a sequence that leads toward an ending or resolution. The orphanage episode, for example, shows Jane facing adversity and then triumphing over it. Because the story moves toward and ends with her triumph, Jane emerges from this version of her narrative looking assertive and mature. As described in Chapter 4, the story could have presented Jane moving in a less triumphant direction and regressing to her earlier passivity. This more tragic plot would have foregrounded different characteristics and relationships for Jane, and it might have constructed a different kind of self for her.

THE INTERACTIONAL POWER
OF AUTOBIOGRAPHICAL NARRATIVE

Work in many fields argues that people can construct and sometimes transform themselves by telling coherent autobiographical narratives that representationally foreground certain characteristics—and by subsequently acting in terms of the characteristics thus foregrounded. Although this representational, plot-based explanation remains popular, it oversimplifies the process of narrative self-construction. Two important modifications have recently been suggested. The first comes from feminist and postmodern theorists who challenge a univocal model of the self. Some feminists have argued that men tend to emphasize (and perhaps experience) idealized, harmonious, universalist descriptions of human life—that are appropriately described in epic form—while women experience life as more fragmented and particularistic (e.g., Bloom, 1998; M. Gergen, 1994; Jelinek, 1980). The universalist, masculinized self is presented as heroic or otherwise idealized; it is more likely to compete against others than build relations with them; and it tends to manifest itself in a more systematic, orderly way. Stewart (1996) makes a similar argument about the experience of rural, working-class Americans in Appalachia—both women and men. She evokes the fragmented and particularistic character of their experience by describing the complex, divergent stories they tell about themselves. Bloom, M. Gergen, Jelinek, and Stewart argue that, at least for some people, the self should be conceived in terms of various contradictory and overlapping tendencies.

From this perspective, autobiographical narratives have power not because they foreground one coherent set of characteristics, but because they help narrators express and manage multiple, partly contradictory selves and experiences. Many feminist and postmodern theorists have argued that the genre of autobiographical narrative is well-suited to represent the fragmented, contradictory character of the self (e.g., Davies, 1993; M. Gergen, 1994). Autobiographical narratives can present various past selves and diverse evaluations of these selves within the same story. Furthermore, many of these theorists argue that people should preserve the open, fragmented character of their selves (Stewart, 1996; Zuss, 1997). In doing so, they can resist universalizing narratives of the self that might obscure the experiences and perspectives of various groups, and they can increase their ability to grow past unforeseen challenges.

Seen in this light, Jane's triumphant autobiographical narrative seems oversimplified. The detailed analysis in Chapter 4, however, shows that the narrative is in fact more complicated than the brief analysis in this chapter has indicated. Jane and other autobiographical narrators represent various aspects of themselves, and no one set of these necessarily captures all of their important characteristics. The predominant explanation for autobiographical narratives' power must be amended to include the possibility that such narratives can foreground multiple selves and the possibility that multiplicity can be liberating.[3]

The predominant explanation for autobiographical narratives' power also oversimplifies in a second way, by relying on representation—the fact that narrators describe themselves as particular kinds of people—as the key to self-construction. Like many feminists, Grumet (1987) wants to resist the objectification of self that a univocal autobiographical narrative can create. She argues that people should use the power of autobiographical narratives without allowing them to close off new possibilities. Thus she agrees with the first modification described above, that autobiographical narratives can and should create multiple possibilities for the self. Her explanation for how this might work relies on a pragmatic approach to the language used in autobiographical narrative. She argues that autobiographical narratives are not simply plots that representationally foreground certain characteristics of the narrators, but are also interactional events between narrators and audiences. Autobiographical narratives are open to revision and multiplicity because they are part of ongoing negotiation between the narrator and the audience.

K. Gergen and Kaye (1992) and K. Gergen (1994) make a similar argument. In the predominant view, narrators first use the representational power of language to describe a particular version of themselves; then they act in accordance with this represented version. Gergen and Kaye argue that this account inappropriately privileges the representational function of language. They argue that a more adequate expla-

interactional positioning

nation for the power of autobiographical narrative will cite the *inter-actional positioning* that autobiographical narrators and audiences accomplish while telling and discussing stories. The act of telling an autobiographical narrative is a performance that can position the narrator and audience in various ways. In Jane's narrative, for instance, when she describes a horrible experience and then cries and pauses, she positions herself as someone who has been victimized and could appropriately receive sympathy from the interviewer. Gergen and Kaye suggest that autobiographical narratives might have power because of how they position narrators interactionally, not just because narrative discourse represents certain characteristics of the narrator.

Grumet, and Gergen and Kaye sketch an alternative explanation for autobiographical narratives' power. Autobiographical narratives do more than represent events and characters; they also presuppose a certain version of the social world and position the narrator and audience with respect to that social world and with respect to each other. Thus, narratives not only represent states of affairs but also accomplish social actions, as I will describe in detail in Chapter 3. In the excerpt from her autobiographical narrative given above, Jane not only represents a triumphant version of herself but also comes to act as a more assertive person in the interactional event of storytelling. Perhaps autobiographical narratives foreground certain versions of a self in substantial part because of their power to position the narrator's self interactionally. Autobiographical narratives might construct or transform the self in part because, in telling the story, the narrator adopts a certain interactional position—and in acting like that kind of person becomes more like that kind of person. In other words, autobiographical narratives may give meaning and direction to narrators' lives and place them in characteristic relations with other people, not only as narrators represent themselves in characteristic ways but also as they enact characteristic positions while they tell their stories. Jane, for instance, might construct herself as an active, assertive woman in part because she enacts that role while she narrates her transition from passivity to activity at the orphanage.

ENACTING THE SELF

This view of narrative self-construction gains plausibility in light of recent work on how autobiographical narratives can position narrators interactionally. Telling a story about oneself can transform the interaction between narrator and audience in various ways. Harding

(1992), for instance, describes an autobiographical narrative in which a Baptist minister invites his audience (Harding herself) to step into and, as it were, complete his story. As part of Harding's ethnographic project, the minister had agreed to an interview in which they discussed the Bible and Baptist doctrine. Harding describes this interactional event as partly an interview conducted by her and partly an attempt by the minister to convert her. During this interview the minister tells the tragic story of how he accidentally killed his son. As Harding shows in her analysis of imagery and Bible references, this story takes the canonical form of two great biblical sacrifice stories—Abraham and Isaac, and God and Jesus.

Harding insightfully shows how the minister uses this story to set up a parallel between himself and the great biblical fathers who were willing to sacrifice their own sons. The minister alludes to three roles in the biblical sacrifice stories: for example, *God* sacrifices his *son* for the sake of *humanity*. He then describes the analogous event in which he himself accidentally killed his own son. This event contains only two of the three roles established in the biblical stories, however. For whom did the minister sacrifice his son? Harding argues that he did it for her. It was not planned in the same way as God's sacrifice of Jesus, of course, but in the interview situation itself the minister tells the story of killing his son in order to convert Harding. He thus turns the tragedy of killing his own son into a story of redemption. In telling the story of his tragedy and how Jesus helped him through it, he shows Harding the power of what Jesus has done in dying for all of us. In a sense, then, the minister's son died so that he could tell this story to Harding and offer redemption to her. Thus the minister's autobiographical narrative had the potential to transform Harding's identity and his relationship with her, if he had succeeded in positioning her as a convert.

Cain (1991) uncovers a similar interactional pattern in her study of autobiographical narratives used by Alcoholics Anonymous members. She describes how AA members cultivate a potential member over time and choose the right moment to tell the novice their own life stories. The AA members' life stories follow a set pattern: Before they joined AA, problem drinking damaged their lives, but they blamed others. When they first came to AA, they refused to acknowledge their problem and resisted the organization. Then continued drinking did serious damage to their lives. Finally, they "hit bottom" and recognized their own powerlessness in the face of their addiction. Since they accepted AA, they have managed to control their addiction and improve their lives.

The primary characters in such a typical story are the past alcoholic self who denied the problem and the present alcoholic self (the narrator) who takes responsibility for his problem. Cain insightfully analyzes the implications these stories have for the interaction between narrator and audience. In telling their autobiographical narratives, AA members position themselves as enlightened by their experiences of hitting bottom and by their acceptance of the AA message. In their interaction with new AA recruits, they offer their own lives as a model or icon for the developmental process that the novice could initiate in the storytelling interaction itself. That is, the AA member offers the event of telling *his* life story—the ongoing interaction between member and novice—as a pivotal point in the *novice's* own life story. Just as someone stepped in and offered to help that AA member take responsibility for his addiction—an act that allowed the AA member to become enlightened and live an improved life—the AA member tells his life story at this moment in order to transform the novice's life in an analogous way. The AA member thus hopes that the novice will step into the narrated life story, as it were, and will enact a transformation analogous to the one being narrated.

Both these cases illustrate how autobiographical narratives can transform relationships in the interaction between narrator and audience. Harding's minister does more than *describe* the sacrifice of a son; he *enacts* the role of sacrificer in his interaction with Harding and makes a bid to transform his own and her own self. Had she accepted Jesus because of his story, he would have turned the death of his son into a sacrifice, himself into a sacrificer, and Harding into the beneficiary of the sacrifice. Just as Jane might be constructing herself by enacting the role of an active, assertive woman, Harding's minister tries to construct himself by enacting the role of sacrificer. Similarly, Cain's AA members do more than *describe* how they have controlled their alcoholism; they also *enact* the transformative moment in the novice's own life story by telling their own. In the cases described by both Harding and Cain, ignoring the interactional positioning that can be accomplished through the narration would lead an analyst to miss the transformative potential of the narratives.

This sort of interactional positioning in autobiographical narrative supports an alternative to the predominant explanation for narrative self-construction. Autobiographical narrators might construct themselves in part as they position themselves in characteristic ways in events of storytelling. Jane might become less passive and more active in part as she positions herself that way in her interaction with the interviewer. In this alternative view, a self can emerge through the interactional positions a narrator habitually takes. In Jane's case, if Jane regularly positions herself as active and assertive she can become active and assertive.

This interactional account of narrative self-construction coheres nicely with constructionist accounts of the self. Contemporary work in feminist theory (Butler, 1990; Flax, 1990; Joy, 1993), social psychology (K. Gergen, 1994, 1997), sociology (Gubrium & Holstein, 1994; Somers, 1994), and anthropology (Crapanzano, 1992; Csordas, 1994; Stewart, 1996) has converged on an account of the self as constructed by habitual positioning in everyday practice. All these accounts criticize "essentialist" theories of self—ones that present the self as a stable, coherent entity relatively impervious to context. Instead, these theorists offer what Butler (1990) calls a "performative" account of self. A self emerges as a person repeatedly adopts characteristic positions, with respect to others and within recognizable cultural patterns in everyday social action. Because the positioning that partly constitutes the self depends on social contexts that shift over time, and on the unpredictable counterpositioning of others, the self is an ongoing, open-ended, and often heterogeneous construction. As described in Chapter 5, such a performative account need not present the self as unreal (as "just" a construction), nor as hopelessly fragmented.

The convergence of theories in all these disciplines on a performative, constructionist account of self lends further support to the claim that interactional positioning in autobiographical narratives plays an important role in explaining their power to construct the self. Please note that I do not claim here, or in Chapter 5 to offer a definitive argument for a performative and against an essentialist account of self. Showing how the self gets interactionally positioned in autobiographical narrative cannot prove that no underlying self exists, although Chapter 5 provides reasons to be skeptical about underlying selves. I have two, more modest aims. First, this book illustrates and extends performative, constructionist accounts of self through detailed demonstrations of *how* interactional positioning happens in verbal practice. Performative accounts of self all name verbal practice as a central site for the interactional construction of self, but none adequately explains how language actually positions narrator and audience in interactional events of narration. Second, by documenting how autobiographical narrators can enact complex interactional events, this book offers a piece of evidence that any theory of narrative self-construction should explain. I suggest in Chapter 5 that performative theories of self can convincingly integrate such interactional patterns into a more complete account of narrative self-construction.

INTERRELATIONS BETWEEN REPRESENTATION AND ENACTMENT

Jane's autobiographical narrative contains two patterns, either of which might explain its power. Perhaps she constructs her self by representing herself as active and assertive. Or perhaps she constructs her self by acting active and assertive while telling her story. The choice between these two interpretations raises many venerable philosophical oppositions—between cognitive and performative, rational and practical, and so on. This book argues that, instead of becoming mired in such oppositions, an empirically adequate account of self-construction in autobiographical narrative must acknowledge that narrative discourse both represents the narrator's self and positions the narrator interactionally. Furthermore, I argue that autobiographical narratives' power often comes from complex relations *across* the represented and enacted worlds they create. The book describes how the representational and interactional functions of autobiographical narrative can interrelate so as partly to construct the self.

Any autobiographical narrative involves a *doubling of roles* for the narrator's self—the narrator has at least one role in the represented content of the story and one role in the ongoing interaction between narrator and audience. For instance, in telling a story about themselves the AA members represent a past, narrated self who was in denial about alcoholism. Their stories also represent the transition to a more responsible self, who is the narrator in the present. AA narrators evaluate their life trajectories as a development from denial and misery to responsibility and stability, and they position their present selves firmly on the side of responsibility and the AA program. In the interactional event of storytelling, the potential AA member occupies a position analogous to the narrator's past, irresponsible self. The AA narrator takes advantage of the doubling of roles in autobiographical narrative to offer his own redemption as a model for the development that the initiate might accomplish through AA, starting right now in the moment of storytelling. The transformative power of the story, then, involves an interrelation between the narrator as represented character and the narrator and audience as interactional participants. Only by representing themselves in certain ways can AA narrators invite potential members to step into and enact an analogous story of their own.

It turns out that the power of Harding's minister's story, Cain's AA narratives, and Jane's narrative depends on more than the doubling of roles. It also depends on *parallelism* across represented and enacted patterns in autobiographical narrative. Jane's autobiographical narrative and those described by Harding (1992) and Cain (1991) involve a parallel between the set of roles represented by the autobiographical narrative and the set of roles enacted by narrator and audience. Jane's transition from passive and victimized to active and assertive at the orphanage parallels her shift from vulnerable to assertive in her relation with the interviewer. Similarly, the transition from irresponsible alcoholic to responsible AA member, facilitated by AA intervention, parallels the AA narrator offering himself as a model and a catalyst for the novice AA member's development. In some important respects, then, the content represented in these autobiographical narratives mirrors the interactional positioning made possible by those autobiographical narratives. As described in Chapter 4, the mirroring or parallelism in autobiographical narratives like Jane's can get much more intricate than what has been discussed so far.

In cases that involve such parallelism, *we need not choose* between the predominant representational explanation and the interactional explanation of autobiographical narratives' power. In such cases, the autobiographical narrative *both* provides a represented template *and* facilitates transformative interactional positioning. This yields a third account of narrative self-construction: the *interrelations* between representations of self and the interactional positioning accomplished while representing oneself can underlie autobiographical narratives' power. Autobiographical narrators can (re-)create their selves when they both represent and position themselves in analogous ways. Although not all autobiographical narratives involve a parallel between representation and enactment, many autobiographical narratives (and other types of discursive interaction) involve more extensive parallels between representation and enactment than one might expect (Wortham, 1994, 2001). This book focuses on complex parallelism, like that in Jane's narrative, in order to demonstrate how the interrelation between representation and enactment can facilitate narrative self-construction.

ANALYZING NARRATIVE DISCOURSE

In order to explain the construction of self in autobiographical narrative, then, one must analyze not only the separate representational and interactional functions of autobiography but also their interrelations. Such an account will require methodological as well as theoretical advances. Despite the proliferation of methods for narrative analysis, few offer empirically adequate analyses of how narratives position

narrators interactionally. Many analysts who study interactional positioning in autobiographical narrative ironically use methodologies that
rely primarily on the representational functions of language. Although
they can be useful in some contexts, I claim that such approaches cannot fully explain how interactional positioning gets accomplished
through autobiographical narratives. Precise accounts of how autobiographical narratives partly construct the self require conceptual and
methodological tools adequate to the task of analyzing the interactional
positioning accomplished through narrative discourse.

Any interactional or pragmatic approach to language faces a basic
question: How do the linguistic (and paralinguistic) cues in an autobiographical narrative position the narrator and audience interactionally?
Cues in the utterances that compose an autobiographical narrative
communicate various things, which together enable the autobiographical narrative to position the narrator and audience in types of relationships and events recognized within a given society. But how do such
cues communicate what they do? Cain (1991) and Harding (1992) rely
primarily on propositions, imagery, and allusions. Although these types
of cues can be important, contemporary work has uncovered many
other types of cues that speakers use to enact roles. As I will argue in
Chapters 2 and 3, any analysis of interactional positioning in autobiographical narrative that does not go beyond propositions, imagery, and
allusions will fail to capture how these narratives position narrators
interactionally as they do.

A few analyses of autobiographical narrative have begun to attend
more systematically to other kinds of cues. Gerhardt and Stinson (1994)
study autobiographical narratives' use of discourse markers to convey
implicit evaluations. O'Connor (1994) traces the interactional presuppositions of personal pronouns in life stories. Hensel (1996), Ochs and
Capps (1996), and Stromberg (1993) all attend, to some extent, to other
sorts of cues in autobiographical narrative. But much of this work is,
as Gerhardt and Stinson themselves say, "exploratory." It indicates that
other cues do seem to play an important role in signaling interactional
positioning in autobiographical narratives, but this work offers no
systematic account of what types of cues exist and how they might
work. Furthermore, in the details of the analyses much of this work
actually depends in large part on propositional cues, often under the
rubric of studying "symbolic," "thematic," or "topical" patterns.

This book provides a more systematic approach to the interactional
positioning accomplished through autobiographical narrative, by drawing on Bakhtin's "dialogic" approach to language use and on contem-

porary work in linguistic anthropology. In order to fully understand how autobiographical narrators can construct themselves, one needs conceptual and methodological tools that can capture how language positions speakers interactionally and how this interactional positioning interrelates with the content represented in narrative discourse. Chapter 2 begins to develop these tools by introducing a dialogic approach to language use.

CHAPTER 2

A Dialogic Approach
to Discourse

Narrators do more than represent themselves in autobiographical narratives. They also act out particular selves in telling those stories, and in doing so they can construct and sometimes transform themselves. An adequate analysis of this process requires a more systematic approach to studying the interactional positioning that can be accomplished through narration. This chapter and the next describe in detail how narrative discourse positions narrators and their audiences interactionally. In addition to describing a methodological approach to analyzing narrative, these chapters also provide resources for understanding how the representational and interactional functions of narrative can interrelate.

In this chapter I begin to develop a systematic approach to studying interactional positioning, by articulating and elaborating Bakhtin's dialogic approach to discourse. Any given utterance can position speakers in various ways, depending on the particulars of the context it appears in. In trying to explain how an utterance comes to position speakers in particular ways, Bakhtin claims that dialogic context is essential. Thus positioning accomplished by an individual speaker's utterance depends on the utterances and perspectives of other speakers. I will also combine Bakhtin's account with more contemporary theories in order to develop a more adequate dialogic approach to analyzing interactional positioning in speech.

Linguistic analysis of the details of narrative discourse might at first seem irrelevant to understanding the construction of self through narrative. Why must one study how particular utterances come to position speakers in particular ways in order to understand larger scale phenomena like narrative and self? I offer three answers to this question. First, all theories of narrative and most theories of self-construction presuppose some account of how language use positions speakers and hearers in particular ways. Most do so without reflecting systematically on how this process works. As Chapters 3 and 5 show in detail, such

17

theories often import implausible assumptions about narrative and self along with their implausible, tacit theories of language use. This book takes the opposite approach, by developing a systematic approach to language use that complements its account of narrative self-construction. Second, detailed consideration of interactional positioning will help articulate what Bakhtin and others might mean by a "dialogic" approach to narrative and self. The dialogic aspects of narrative and self will be clearer against the background of a dialogic approach to interactional positioning in general. Third, a systematic approach to interactional positioning yields conceptual and methodological tools that will allow more precise analyses of narrative and self. This chapter defines the central concepts of dialogue, mediation, and emergence, which I will use throughout the book to analyze narrative and self. These analyses will show that the precision required by detailed study of actual language use yields insights into larger scale phenomena like narrative and self.

By emphasizing the dialogic aspects of utterance meaning, Bakhtin encounters an important problem: If meaning essentially depends on more than one person's words and intentions, how can people ever attribute a clear meaning to particular utterances? That is, how do participants and analysts know which (of an indefinite number of) other speakers' utterances and perspectives are relevant to understanding a given utterance? In order to sketch an answer to this question, I introduce the central concepts of mediation and emergence that have been developed in contemporary accounts of language use. Chapter 3 applies this approach to narrative discourse in particular.

MONOLOGIC AND DIALOGIC APPROACHES TO LANGUAGE USE

Most approaches, Bakhtin argues, treat language use as "monologic." Monologic discourse is "the word of no one in particular" (1935/ 1981, p. 276); it acts as if the social position of the speaker is irrelevant to its meaning. Monologic approaches to language use assume that participants and analysts can understand a speaker's meaning with reference only to the structure and content of that speaker's utterance, independent of the speaker's relations with others. Consider the following example: A government spokesperson or briefer, reporting events in an ongoing war, says that "there was some collateral damage yesterday." A monologic approach would focus on the content this utterance represents. "Collateral damage" is a military euphemism for 'unintended civilian casualties,' so the spokesperson is acknowledging civilian casualties suffered the day before.

Bakhtin would argue that, in order to understand what the speaker means by the utterance, an analyst must understand what position the briefer is taking up with respect to the military and potential critics. Does the speaker use this phrase in a straightforward, referential way, as military personnel generally do? If so, how would the speaker respond to those who decry such usage as a euphemism for the intolerable evils of war? Does the speaker use the phrase instead in a mocking or ironic way, and thus place herself against politicians and soldiers who use the phrase merely referentially? These questions describe a rudimentary dialogue opened by the use of that one phrase. In order to understand the meaning of the phrase as uttered by this particular speaker, participants and analysts must understand where the speaker is placing herself interactionally with respect to members of those other groups—as if the speaker were entering a dialogue with those other people.

For Bakhtin, monologic approaches capture some aspects of meaning, but they can never suffice. "The expression of an utterance can never be fully understood or explained if its thematic content is all that is taken into account. The expression of an utterance always *responds* to a greater or lesser degree, that is, it expresses the speaker's attitude toward others' utterances and not just his attitude toward the object of his utterance" (1953/1986a, p. 92). Thus, while an utterance does always represent an object, it also always contributes to the speaker's position with respect to others—and this interactional positioning is essential to the meaning of the utterance.

Bakhtin's point here will become clearer with reference to a central distinction between what Jakobson (1957/1971) calls the "event of speaking" and the "narrated event." I will modify this terminology slightly, and refer to the event of speaking as the storytelling event. The *storytelling event* is the interactional context within which the speaker utters something, whether this be a government briefing, a classroom conversation, a family quarrel, or whatever. The *narrated event* is the event described by the utterance, like the "collateral damage" in the example above. In the excerpt from Jane's narrative introduced in Chapter 1, the narrated event is the encounter at the orphanage between Jane and the orphanage employee. The storytelling event is the interaction between Jane and the interviewer, as Jane tells her story. Note that the narrated event represents a past interaction, whether between two people at an orphanage or two warring forces on a battlefield. Most narratives presuppose at least two interactional events: one described as part of the narrated event and one enacted in the event of storytelling itself. But these two types of interactional events must be sharply distinguished for analytic purposes. Bakhtin's point about dialogue, put simply, is that participants and analysts can understand neither the narrated content represented by an utterance nor the interactional positioning accomplished by that utterance without taking into account various aspects of the storytelling event in which the utterance occurs.[1]

Figure 2.1 depicts this distinction between storytelling and narrated events in the example of the government briefer. The larger rectangle signifies the storytelling event, within which the briefer is speaking. The embedded rectangle signifies the narrated event. A monologic approach would focus only on the narrated event, note that "collateral damage" refers euphemistically to civilian casualties, and stop the

FIGURE 2.1 Storytelling and Narrated Events

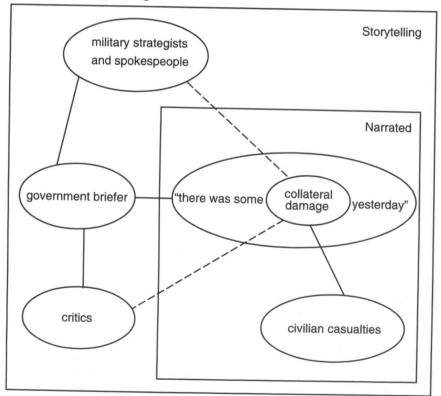

interpretation there. Bakhtin, on the other hand, is interested in "the speaker's attitude toward others' utterances." In this case, he would note first that "collateral damage" is a phrase associated with certain types of speakers—particularly those connected to the military, who often present dead civilians as an unintended but inevitable consequence of war. Because speakers in this recognizable social role characteristically use this phrase, the phrase now indexes or points to military personnel and aficionados. The figure marks this connection with the dotted line connecting "collateral damage" to military strategists and spokespeople. Note that this group is placed in the storytelling event. They need not be physically present in the briefing room because they are part of the social world known and inhabited by everyone in the storytelling event. Also included in the storytelling event are potential critics of military action that endangers civilians. These too—even if they are not actually present in the briefing room—are indexed by the phrase "collateral damage," as a group opposed to the military's acceptance of civilian casualties.

For Bakhtin, then, every utterance contains "two texts" (1961/1986b, p. 107). That is, people cannot interpret represented or narrated content alone. Interpretation of an utterance also requires construal of a second, interactional level, because the words used in any utterance have been spoken by others. Particular utterances or configurations of utterances are often associated with particular social groups because certain types of speakers characteristically use a particular type of utterance. So utterances often open a rudimentary dialogue with particular types of people. Interpreters must attend not only to the represented content of speech but also to the position taken by the speaker in saying what he or she says.

Bakhtin summarizes this point in his description of speech as "a word about a word addressed to a word" (1963/1984a, p. 266; cf. also 1953/1986a, p. 88). Note the three aspects of this description. Speech is in part a (monologic) word, the represented content typically carried by the word. Speech is also "a word about a word." The speaker says something about past words that have been spoken about the same issue, and thus he or she takes a position with respect to those other speakers and their positions—as the hypothetical government briefer must take a position with respect to the military personnel typically associated with the phrase "collateral damage." Bakhtin claims that any utterance must take some position with respect to past words. "The speaker is not the biblical Adam, dealing only with virgin and still unnamed objects" (1953/1986a, p. 93). Speakers must use words already used by others because all words have been. As Bakhtin sometimes puts it, all words "echo" with the "voices" of others, and, as interpreters, we try to understand the speaker's position with respect to the others who characteristically speak this way. The speaker enters into dialogue with those past speakers, such that part of the current speaker's meaning and part of what he accomplishes interactionally through speech involves his relationship to prior speakers' positions. "Discourse is directed toward an ordinary referential object, naming it, portraying, expressing, and only indirectly striking a blow at the other's discourse, clashing with it [or affirming it], as it were, within the object itself" (1963/1984a, p. 196). Bakhtin's dialogic approach to utterance meaning does not eliminate the ordinary represented values of words.[2] Instead, it adds consideration of the speaker's position within the storytelling event—such that the represented content communicated and the interactional position established cannot be separated from each other.

In the third aspect of Bakhtin's formulation, an utterance is also addressed to future words. The speaker not only takes a position with respect to past speakers' utterances on the topic, but also anticipates future speakers' responses. The government briefer thus speaks in a situation where critics of military action (e.g., some members of the press corps) may well respond, and these potential responses can shape the utterance's meaning as the speaker adjusts her interactional position in anticipation of these critics. For Bakhtin, then, dialogue does not only look toward the past. For any utterance, "its beginning is preceded by the utterances of others, and its end is followed by the responsive utterances of others" (1953/1986a, p. 71). In discussing "collateral damage," the briefer takes a position with respect to past users of the phrase and also anticipates what future speakers will say about her use of the phrase. Knowing that some might mock the phrase, a speaker intending to use it in a straightforward way might insert some hedge in order to head off subsequent speakers' responses. The speaker "does not expect passive understanding that, so to speak, only duplicates his own idea in someone else's mind. Rather, he expects response, agreement, sympathy, objection, execution, and so forth" (1953/1986a, p. 69). Full understanding of the utterance requires an analyst to understand the speaker's position with respect to these anticipated subsequent speakers as well.

However, if the represented content and interactional positioning accomplished by any utterance depend in part on the speaker's relation with both past and future speakers, the meaning of the utterance would seem to be ultimately indeterminate. There are an indefinite number of prior and future speakers that the current speaker might be responding to or anticipating, and the speaker's position with respect to these others can change as different speakers become relevant. The government spokesperson might be mocking typical military briefings by uttering "collateral damage," but also ironically distancing herself from certain overly earnest peace activists—and an indefinite number of further inflections on the positioning are possible. Thus interactional positioning accomplished by an utterance could forever be reinterpreted, as subsequent speakers recall or anticipate other possible positions and the speaker's relation to them.

Bakhtin himself accepts this indeterminacy. For him, an utterance is never a completed whole. It can always be reopened, and this is simply the nature of our verbal life. He refers to this openness as *unfinalizability*, and he believes that it is a positive aspect of the human condition (creativity, for instance, would be impossible without it; cf. Morson & Emerson, 1990). Unfinalizability does raise an analytic problem, however, which Bakhtin himself does not adequately address: If the interactional positioning accomplished by an utterance depends on the speaker's relation to other speakers, and if an indeterminate number of other speakers might be relevant to understanding that speaker's position, why do utterances often have clear meanings in practice? For instance, various types of interactional positioning might be going on in the storytelling event between Jane and the interviewer. When Jane breaks down and cries, she might be positioning the interviewer as a potential therapist and herself as a client in emotional distress. When Jane recounts her triumph at the orphanage she might be positioning herself as a mature adult, who has more experience with life's challenges than the young interviewer, and thus she might be positioning herself as an advisor to the interviewer. Or Jane might be trying to act like a reliable subject in a psychology experiment, by providing the interviewer with clear and unbiased data. Any of these three interpretations, and likely others as well, could plausibly describe the storytelling event that takes place between Jane and the interviewer. So how do participants and analysts know which type of event is actually going on?

This is a central problem—one related to the broad problems of "the hermeneutic circle" (Heidegger, 1927/1962), the problem of "relevance" (Sperber & Wilson, 1986), or the "indeterminacy of contextualization" (Silverstein, 1992)—and it will reappear throughout this chapter and the next. An adequate dialogic account must explain how meaningful utterances do in most cases position speakers in apparently unambiguous ways despite the ultimate indeterminacy of the dialogues that shape that positioning. The rest of this chapter develops the concepts of mediation and emergence, two central concepts that help address this problem.

AN ACTUAL ENCOUNTER

In order to develop the concepts of mediation and emergence, the rest of this chapter draws on a richer example of interactional positioning. This section describes an interaction that took place during a half hour of classroom conversation. Various utterances from this example will be cited in the conceptual discussion that follows. I provide considerable detail here because any adequate account of interactional positioning through speech must face the complexity of actual encounters. Too many theorists rely on contrived examples, or examples torn from context, and produce unrealistically simple theories. Despite the detail given here, space limitations prevent a full description and analysis of this classroom interaction (for a fuller analysis, see Wortham, 1994, 2001).

At first glance it might seem odd to have an extended analysis of classroom discourse in a book on autobiographical narrative. I include this analysis in order to introduce the central conceptual and methodological tools of my approach and in order to show the broad applicability of that approach. The tools developed here can be used to uncover the interactional positioning that goes on in various types of discourse. In this chapter and in Chapter 3 and 4, I demonstrate the power of these tools through extended analyses of three types of discourse (classroom, media, and autobiographical narrative), and thus I show how this dialogic approach to interactional positioning can contribute to work across the human sciences. The classroom and media examples do pose a danger, insofar as they raise various questions about the particular content of these examples—for example, about the reproduction of social power relations in classrooms or about the media's claim to objectivity—questions that I cannot pursue in this book. But in relevant spots below, I refer to other work in which I analyze these examples in more detail and in which I do explore these other questions.

The conversation that will serve as an example for this chapter happened in a ninth-grade history class in an urban American public school. Two white teachers are running this class session. There are 15 students: 10 black girls, 2 black boys, 2 white girls, and 1 white boy. In preparation for the class session students have read selections from Plutarch's *Life of Lycurgus* (taken from Bailkey, 1987). This text describes the Spartan political system, in which the welfare of the whole society was generally placed above the welfare of the individual. Sparta was ruled by a committee of elders, called "Ephors," who made decisions on behalf of the community. In this classroom conversation the students object strongly to one particular Spartan practice: When a citizen had a baby, she had to bring the baby to the Ephors for judgment; if they felt the child was sickly, such that it would likely be a burden on the society, the mother was forced to leave the baby outdoors to die of exposure.

The students react so strongly to this Spartan practice, in part, because they have internalized American values that favor the individual more than the collective. But the classroom discussion also raises the question of whether a society should support disadvantaged members, or whether those members should be sacrificed for the good of the whole. This section analyzes the students' and teachers' utterances dialogically—with respect to the interactional positions they are themselves adopting in the storytelling event and with respect to the larger political issues raised by their discussion—and shows that the relationship between disadvantaged and more privileged members of society plays an important role in the relationship between teachers and students in the classroom itself.

The students' argument against Sparta's treatment of unhealthy infants begins with the following excerpt, the first of four from this class session. The participants in the class discussion are: "JAS" Jasmine, one of the students; "T/S" Mr. Smith, one of the two teachers; "T/B" Mrs. Bailey, the other teacher; "ST" unidentified student; "STS" more than one student; "CAN" Candace, another student; "CAS" Cassandra, another student; "MR" Martha, another student. Transcription conventions are given in Figure 2.2

```
     T/S:  [ and if you bring someone in=
     JAS:  [[ 3 syll ]
     T/S:  =there that isn't going to do their share as the wall
           of Sparta. you're giving that- that person, something
  5        that could be used better bu- by someone else. I- I
           sort of think that's perfectly right [      if a baby=
     JAS:                                        [that's not-
     T/S:  =can't hack it you get rid of it. that's going to be a
           problem in the future.=
  10 JAS:  they- they not equal if- if shead a baby and hers
           lived and I had a baby and mine didn't. we not equal.
     T/B:  yeah you're right. you didn't produce a healthy baby.
     T/S:  that's [right
     JAS:         [how do you kno that. they just say that one
  15        ain't healthy. and then lookit. mine probably grew up
           to be taller and [ stronger
     T/S:                   [because they're the Spartan Ephors
           [ who make a decision. the Ephors know what makes a=
```

FIGURE 2.2 Transcription Conventions

-	abrupt breaks or stops (if several, stammering)
?	rising intonation
.	falling intonation
___	(underline) stress
(1.0)	silences, timed to the nearest second
[	simultaneous talk by two speakers, with one utterance represented on top of the other and the moment of overlap marked by left brackets
=	interruption or next utterance following immediately, or continuous talk represented on separate lines because of need to represent overlapping comment on intervening line
[. . .]	transcriber comment
:	elongated vowel
°. . .°	segment quieter than surrounding talk
,	pause or breath without marked intonation
(hh)	laughter breaking into words while speaking

JAS: [and [5 syll]
20 *T/S:* =good Spartan because they're sixty years old and
they've seen an awful lot. and they know what makes a
good soldier. they've been in it from the time they
were seven.

   This passage gives the flavor of the positions taken by teachers and students, with the teachers playing devil's advocate by defending Sparta and the students objecting strongly. It also introduces the example that will remain central to the discussion for about a half hour. Jasmine introduces herself as a hypothetical Spartan mother in lines 10–11. She also nominates another student as a second hypothetical Spartan mother (according to my fieldnotes from the interaction, "she" refers to another student named Erika).

   Figure 2.3 shows the structure of this conversation after the introduction of the example. There are two narrated events in play: the text,

FIGURE 2.3 The Example of Jasmine's Baby

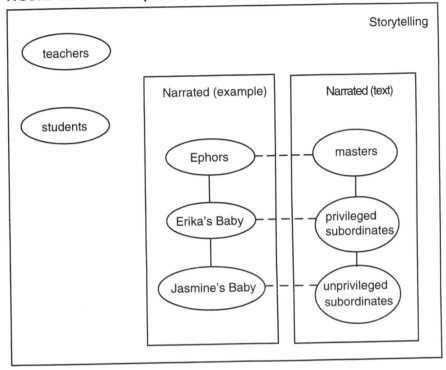

which describes Spartan society, including relations among Ephors and citizens; and the example, which describes the two students' hypothetical babies and how the Ephors might treat them. The example describes two types of relationships. First is the relationship between the two hypothetical Spartan mothers, one of whom must leave her unhealthy-looking child to die of exposure, while the other gets to keep her child; this is a relationship between the out-of-favor and the favored, or between the unprivileged and the privileged. The second relationship is between the mothers and the Ephors; this is a relationship between the subordinate and the powerful.

A monologic account would focus only on these two narrated events. It might explore the relationship between the conceptual structure set up in the example and that in the text, to see whether the example did (or could) help students better grasp the thematic contents of the text. But it would not attend to the storytelling classroom conversation among teachers and students. In a dialogic account, participants and analysts cannot fully understand the teachers' and students' utterances without also attending to the types of people who might make similar utterances and to the implications of these utterances for teachers' and students' own interactional positions.

The example of Jasmine's baby includes some of the speakers participating in the storytelling event itself (Jasmine and Erika, so far), and it is thus a *participant example*. This sort of example makes salient the implications that represented content can have for interactional positioning because such examples double the roles of certain participants. Jasmine, for instance, now has two identities in this classroom conversation: a student participating in class discussion and a hypothetical Spartan mother. As illustrated by the rest of the analysis, and as described at length elsewhere (Wortham, 1994), speakers can make comments about participants' *hypothetical* characters within a participant example and implicitly comment on *actual* participants. In this case, comments about Jasmine's character within the example have implications for the interactional position and perhaps the more enduring identity of the student Jasmine herself. A dialogic analysis of this conversation will explore how the conversation establishes teachers' and students' own interactional positions.

The following excerpt, which occurs soon after Jasmine gives her example, begins to show the implications that the example has for the storytelling event.

```
      JAS:  if she had a baby and- and hers lived and mine died
            we not equal. and if they want it to be- everybody to
            be equal then I [ should've got to kept ] mine too.
      T/B:  what- wait a second. your baby's going to grow up and
 5          be this unhealthy runt. [        her baby's going to grow=
      STS:                          [hahaha
      T/B:  =up and be: healthy
      JAS:  I'm equal to her then
      T/B:  yeah you're equal. but you know take it twenty years in
10          the future. her baby's going to have to do what for
            your baby. your baby's going to do what. lay around.
      ST:   hahahaha drinking beer
      STS:  haha [haha         haha    hahaha         haha
      T/B:       [drinking beer. eating their- their bean soup.
```

Analyzed solely for its contribution to the represented content, the students and teacher here are simply elaborating the pro-Spartan argument. They articulate the Spartans' reasoning, by imagining how an unhealthy baby would become a burden on the society. Examined for its interactional implications, however, a more disturbing pattern starts to emerge in this passage. What sort of person would stereotypically say "your baby's going to do what? lay around . . . drinking beer"? More evidence is needed to make firm conclusions (see Wortham, 1994), but this accusation might index or point to the recognizable social group of welfare critics, who often decry the alleged laziness of the welfare recipients whom taxpayers support. This particular index has the potential to influence and complicate the storytelling interaction among teachers and students, because the students come from a social group often stereotyped as lazy welfare recipients (lower-class black Americans).

The passage above represents the beginning of a pattern in which the students' own position becomes analogous to that of unprivileged Spartans. Through this analogy, teachers' and students' utterances position the students as being like underprivileged welfare recipients. In the classroom and in contemporary America, just as in Sparta, there are privileged and unprivileged people as well as powerful and subordinate types of people. Like Spartan mothers who must submit their children to be judged, students must submit to teachers' judgments. And, as Spartan society did to unhealthy babies, American society often turns its back on the students' social group (lower-class blacks). Jasmine, in both her hypothetical and actual roles, is unprivileged and subordinate. This analogy begins to develop in the passage above (lines 11–14), when Mrs. Bailey characterizes Jasmine's baby as naturally inferior (an "unhealthy runt"), unproductive ("laying around"), and intemperate ("drinking beer"). Although Mrs. Bailey is explicitly talking about the hypothetical example, her characterization of Jasmine's hypothetical baby as a lazy drunkard begins to sound like the contemporary American stereotype for some lower-class black welfare recipients.

I emphasize at this point that the teachers are still either teasing the students or playing devil's advocate to defend the Spartan political system, but the implications of their discussion are developed as the classroom conversation proceeds. The following excerpt occurs a few minutes later.

```
    T/B:        yeah but see you're- you- but that's the
        [    hitch isn't it? you've got this baby that's not=
    JAS: [I'm sayin'-
    JAS:              [I know. so [ 3 syll ]
5   T/B: =healthy      [and you're afraid's going to go in the army,
        [breathless inhalation] and why should the rest
        of us [ s-    support your baby.
```

> *STS:*   [hahaha
> *ST?:* are you saying=
> 10 *JAS:* if they wanted them to be <u>e</u>qual then even if my child
>   was re<u>tard</u>ed or whatever he should go into the army <u>too</u>

Examined for clues about interactional positioning in the story-telling event, one utterance in this passage stands out: Mrs. Bailey's question, "why should the rest of us support your baby?" (lines 6–7). Note Mrs. Bailey's use of *us* in this utterance. For the first time, Mrs. Bailey includes herself in the example, in a group opposed to Jasmine's. She attributes a definite social identity to Jasmine's baby: He is an unproductive freeloader. Mrs. Bailey and her social group—whoever is included in *us*—are taxpayers forced to support such people. Here Mrs. Bailey puts herself, and implicitly Mr. Smith and other taxpayers, into a position analogous to the Ephors'. In both the text and the example the Ephors refuse to expend resources on unhealthy babies. Analo-gously, in the storytelling event Mrs. Bailey herself seems to resent spending tax money on "unproductive" children.

Two aspects of this passage make it seem unlikely that Mrs. Bailey is simply teasing Jasmine here. First, Mrs. Bailey raises an issue that is particularly charged in the contemporary United States: the use of workers' tax payments to support nonworking people. It would have been safer to use a more hypothetical or less sensitive issue if she were simply teasing. Second, paralinguistic cues seem to indicate Mrs. Bailey's commitment to the issue: Both the tempo and volume of her speech increase markedly in this passage. These cues support my interpreta-tion that discussion of the example is becoming an implicit commen-tary on taxpayers (like the teachers) and welfare recipients (like some of the students).

Figure 2.4 depicts the storytelling and narrated events at this point. Included are utterances from the last two excerpts, in which the teacher describes Jasmine's hypothetical baby. These utterances sound like the arguments of welfare critics, a group that both teachers and students rec-ognize from their own society. Given this, the question becomes, where do the actual teachers and students stand with respect to this presupposed group? The last passage indicates that in the storytelling event Mrs. Bailey aligns herself with the welfare critics, as an irate taxpayer. The fact that most of these students are lower-class blacks makes it possible that they themselves are being positioned—through the too-common U.S. stereo-type—with Jasmine's hypothetical unproductive baby.

This latter connection becomes more robust as the conversation proceeds. By the time of the following excerpt, which occurs at the end

FIGURE 2.4 Echoes within the Example

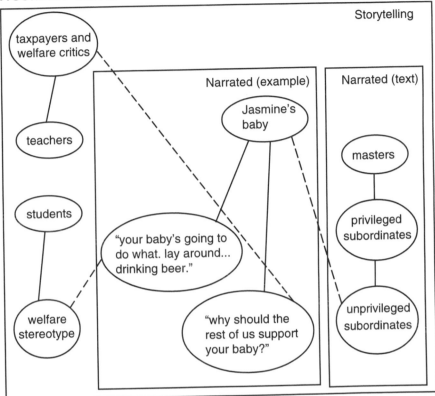

of the 30-minute classroom discussion of this example, the topic has shifted from the example to contemporary America. The class is discussing how U.S. society might be strong like Sparta yet still humane to the underprivileged.

    T/B: yeah prosperity is <u>mo</u>ney <u>rich</u>es wealth. Okay how do- how
         do we become a <u>rich</u>, nation. a <u>p</u>owerful nation.
    CAN: work hard? <u>work</u> for it.
    T/B: you've got [to <u>work</u> for it.
5   CAS: [[4 syll] good education
    T/B: you've got to have a good edu<u>ca</u>tion. why.
    MR: like some um, like some of them <u>A</u>sian women are taking
         over 'cause they are <u>smart</u>.
    STS: Asians Asian girls hnh

10   T/B: because they work hard?
      STS: [2 sec overlapping comments]
      T/B: they just don't <u>work</u> harder than you do.
      MR: they work <u>hard</u> but they <u>smart</u> too.
      JAS: they have to be smart to learn all them <u>signs</u>.
15   STS: hahaha [[overlapping comments and laughter]
      T/S: [if- if <u>that's</u> the case Martha. if <u>that's</u>- if
            <u>that's</u> the case because they're <u>smart</u> and they work
            <u>hard</u>, then because you're <u>not</u> smart you <u>don't</u> work hard
            maybe [we should throw you in the glen early to give=
20   ST?:   [[6 syll]
      T/S: =<u>them</u> the benefit?
      ST?: [2 syll] that smart
      CAN: there's this- there's this <u>boy</u> I know he just came
            from- India and stuff and I swear °you know° he- he
25   learned how to speak <u>English</u> in about a <u>month</u>. like
            <u>this</u>. [snaps fingers] smart.
      T/S: so why should we waste time with <u>you</u>. I think we'd best
            go to <u>him</u> and work with <u>him</u>. and he'll be our best
            future <u>citizen</u>.=
30   T/B: make them the <u>Hel</u>ots.
      STS: [hnhhnh
      T/S: [that's right. I <u>like</u> that idea.

Analyzed just in terms of represented content, this final passage further articulates the concept of privileged, productive members of a society. It does so by establishing a third realm of narrated content, one drawn from contemporary U.S. society. Asians in the United States, like Erika's healthy baby, will work hard and contribute to the society. Less talented and diligent students will not work as hard and will not contribute as much.

Analyzed for its contributions to interactional positioning, it becomes clear that more is happening here. The passage contains several clues that the students' and teachers' own social positions—and, more generally, issues surrounding race relations and welfare programs in contemporary America—are also at issue here. In lines 16–29, Mr. Smith clearly connects the relationship between these students and Asian students to the relationship between Jasmine's and Erika's hypothetical babies. He does this, for example, by talking about throwing these students "in the glen" (line 19). Plutarch uses the same phrase, saying that unfit Spartan babies were left outside "in a glen" to die. Mr. Smith makes clear that students like Jasmine are less well endowed: Asian students are smart and they work hard; other students are dumb and lazy. He also follows Lycurgus in claiming that society should turn its back on underendowed children.

Mrs. Bailey's comment at line 30—"make them the Helots"—captures and summarizes the implications of this discussion for the storytelling event. This comment also presupposes another piece of background information. The Helots were serfs or slaves who farmed the land around Sparta, allowing Spartan citizens a life of leisure. Helots outnumbered Spartans by a ratio of approximately ten to one, so citizens always feared a revolt. The reading describes two ways Spartan citizens reduced the threat: They periodically snuck out of the city at night and murdered Helot men; and they invited strong, eloquent Helots into the city on the pretense of honoring their talents, then killed them.

Figure 2.5 includes this information in its depiction of the (narrated) discussion about the text. The class discusses three social groups in Sparta: those in power (Ephors), the privileged (citizens), and the unprivileged (Helots). The figure makes clear that the example of Jasmine's baby, and the briefer discussion of Asian students, set up analogous three-part sets of social groups. All of this would be captured by a thorough monologic analysis of the represented content. But understanding the interactional implications of teachers' and students' utterances also requires analysis of the other social groups that are indexed by those utterances. The figure includes this in the storytelling event and shows that the teachers and students themselves occupy roles analogous to those in Sparta and the example. In discussing how society should treat the underprivileged, teachers and students are not only discussing past and hypothetical events, they are also positioning themselves with regard to contemporary questions about how powerful and privileged people (like the teachers) should treat underprivileged people (like some of the students). As shown in the figure, in the storytelling event the teachers end up siding with welfare critics and discouraging overinvestment in the underprivileged.

Mrs. Bailey summarizes this whole pattern of interactional positioning when she proposes making the students Helots. She casts white teachers and Asian students as superior to black students, in the same way that Spartan Ephors and citizens were superior to Helots. This both points out black students' subordinate position and provides a potential justification for it in terms of inferior capacities. Expressed bluntly, the teachers' interactional positioning communicates the following messages to the students: Productive people like us are tired of paying taxes for freeloaders like you; you are members of a parasitic social group

FIGURE 2.5 Interactional Implications of the Example

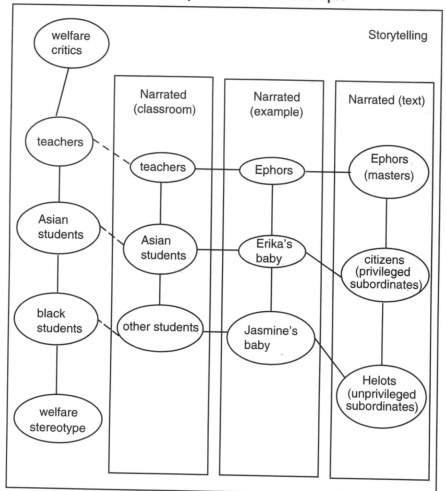

that does not deserve equal rights; those in power like us will decide which of you are potentially productive and deserve to enjoy the benefits of society.[3]

In summary, then, note what it has taken to understand the interactional positioning accomplished by utterances like "why should the rest of us support your baby?" and "make them the Helots." An understanding of represented content has been necessary but not sufficient. We cannot understand these utterances' interactional implications without understanding the narrated content of the discussion, including the analogies between the text and the example. But a purely monologic analysis would miss the other social groups presupposed in the discussion, and it would miss the positioning of teachers and students with respect to these groups. A full analysis of these utterances, then, must be dialogic.

But what type of account could explain the interactional positioning accomplished through language in such a complex case? Mrs. Bailey's "make them the Helots" can only be understood with respect to presupposed social groups from the larger society (the larger social context) and with respect to textual patterns that develop in the conversation itself (the discourse context). Given the many potential aspects of social and discourse context that might potentially be relevant—that is, given all the others whose utterances and perspectives might enter the dialogue—how can one analyze the interactional positioning that these utterances accomplish? An adequate answer will rely on two central concepts: mediation and emergence.

MEDIATION

What particular cues in the teachers' and students' speech about Sparta let participants interpret or react coherently to what was going on in the interaction? The intuitive answer, articulated by early speech act theory (Searle, 1969), proposes *rules* that connect particular linguistic cues to types of interactional effects. For instance, under normal conditions calling someone an "idiot" counts as an insult, and comparing someone to members of a subordinate group counts as a put-down. But it turns out that rules alone cannot explain how speech accomplishes interactional positioning.

To see why, consider the Spartan babies class. What rules could explain the interactional effects of Mrs. Bailey's utterance "make them the Helots"? As described above, on my reading this utterance has the force of a put-down or insult. It also carries an analogical message about the students' social position, something like "people like you deserve your underprivileged status." Is there a rule that connects "make them the Helots" to this complex meaning? What cues would signal the interactional positioning accomplished with this utterance? In Mrs. Bailey's utterance about the Helots, "them" (line 30) refers anaphorically to the same group as Mr. Smith's "you" (line 27), namely the black students, who are being compared unfavorably to Asians. Her utterance positions the black students interactionally because of the implicit analogy between blacks and subordinate Helots, Asians and more privileged Spartans. To establish this analogy, the utterance indexes two conceptual structures. One covers social organization in Sparta, which teachers and students have read about and discussed earlier. The other has emerged during the conversation, as teachers and students mention and reinforce parallels between subordinate, unprivileged Spartans (and Helots) and the black students themselves. Over time the organization of Sparta comes to provide an implicit relational map of the classroom interaction itself, with the black students cast as unproductive and subordinate.

This reliance on a contingent, emergent interactional pattern suggests that rules alone cannot fully explain the interactional positioning accomplished by Mrs. Bailey's utterance. In general, rules cannot suffice to explain interactional positioning because of the indeterminacy of relevant context (Goffman, 1976; Havránek, 1932/1955; Levinson, 1981). Later in the Spartan babies class, for example, someone might have revealed that Mrs. Bailey and her children received government aid, or that the Helots ultimately slaughtered the Spartans: Contextual information like that might change my interpretation of Mrs. Bailey's utterance. So, because the positioning accomplished by any utterance can be refigured if different aspects of context become relevant, the question becomes: How do certain aspects of the context become relevant, such that an utterance comes to accomplish a particular kind of interactional positioning for the speaker and hearers?

The concept of *mediation* helps answer this question. Something more flexible than rules mediates between the cues in an utterance and the interactional positioning that utterance accomplishes. That is, instead of a two-stage account—with types of cues connected by rules to types of verbal acts—we need a three-stage account of interactional positioning through speech. The concept of "contextualization cues" (Gumperz, 1982, 1992) or "indexicality" (Garfinkel & Sacks, 1970; Peirce, 1897/1955; Silverstein, 1976) captures this mediating step. A *contextualization cue* is some aspect of an utterance that indicates how its context should be construed. Hearers first attend to (sometimes conflicting) cues in utterances, on the basis of which they next select aspects of the context as relevant, and they then apply rules (or presupposed regularities) to determine what positioning is going on.

This sort of mediated account, with an intermediate construal of context between the utterance and interactional positioning in the storytelling event, would help explain Mrs. Bailey's "make them the Helots." Certain aspects of the context have been made salient prior to this utterance: the teachers are white taxpayers; most of the students are black, and many are lower-class welfare recipients; these groups in some cases have a social relationship analogous to certain groups in ancient Sparta. To catch the interactional positioning accomplished by the utterance, the context must be construed as a juxtaposition of these two groups. This requires an appreciation of the analogous structures set up earlier—the unprivileged/privileged and subordinate/master relationships present both in the example and in the classroom—and the fact that these structures apply not only in the represented content but also in the interactional positioning. By construing the context in this way, hearers can catch the teachers' implicit complaint about unprivileged and allegedly unproductive people like the students. Note here that *some regularities are presupposed*, such as knowledge about racial stereotypes in the contemporary United States. These enter the interpretive process only through a mediating construal of the context, but hearers must nonetheless have some conventional knowledge about race and power to understand the utterance. Analysts, then, must know something about the ethnographic context in order to interpret interactional positioning.

Thus the relationship between an utterance and the interactional positioning it accomplishes is mediated by participants' construal of the context. Mediation is the first crucial concept in an adequate dialogic approach to interactional positioning in speech. Note that, on this sort of account, two questions must be answered: (1) How do the linguistic and nonlinguistic cues that compose an utterance make certain aspects of the context salient? and (2) How does a set of cues and salient contextual features establish the particular interactional positioning being accomplished by this utterance?

Gumperz (1982), Silverstein (1976), and others have provided an answer to the first question. Verbal cues signal indexically, to point out and sometimes create aspects of the context. Silverstein (1976, 1992, 1993) provides an account of indexical signaling to describe the types of cues central to mediation. This work describes how cues in an utterance highlight relevant aspects of the context. An *indexical sign* or cue points to an aspect of the content as its object (Peirce, 1897/1955). The linguistic form *I*, for example, refers by indexing to the individual uttering the sign. A weathervane indexes the direction of the wind. Use of the French *vous* to refer to an addressee indexes a more formal or deferential relationship between speaker and addressee. Indexicals do most of the work in making aspects of the context salient. Bakhtin uses the concept of "voice" to describe one way that indexical cues highlight relevant context.

VOICING

Sophisticated analysts of interactional positioning now largely agree that a mediated account is required and that indexicals will be an important part of such an account. Bakhtin begins to provide such an account in his discussions of "voicing." *Voice* is a central concept throughout Bakhtin's work. He begins his definition of voice by observing the internal stratification of language, which he also calls heteroglossia (1935/1981, p. 263). Heteroglossia refers to the natural state of language, where any given language contains within itself forms that index a wide variety of social groups.

> Language has been completely taken over, shot through with intentions and accents. . . . All words have the "taste" of a profession, a genre, a tendency, a party, a particular work, a particular person, a generation, an age group, the day and hour. Each word tastes of the context and contexts in which it has lived its socially charged life. (1935/1981, p. 293)

The social world is composed of many, overlapping social groups—religious groups, family groups, ethnic groups, and so on. These groups can be defined by social position and by ideological commitments. "Certain features of language take on the specific flavor" of particular groups (Bakhtin, 1935/1981, p. 289). *Dude,* for instance, would not normally be a word used by elderly Episcopalians. Speakers inevitably use words that have been used by others, words that "taste of" or "echo with" the social locations and ideological commitments carried by those earlier uses (1953/1986a, p. 88).

Speaking with a certain voice, then, means using words that index some social position(s) because these words are characteristically used by members of a certain group. Novelists represent certain voices by using words that index particular social positions for certain characters. Everyday narrators do the same with the characters they describe. In the Spartan babies class, for instance, when Mrs. Bailey says, "why should the rest of us support your baby?" she speaks with the voice of a welfare critic. When the teacher and students describe Jasmine's baby "laying around" and "drinking beer," they may be voicing the baby as a stereotyped welfare recipient.

Bakhtin describes various types of cues that can index particular voices. In particular, he follows[4] Vološinov (1929/1973) in attending to quoted speech. When narrators put words into a character's mouth, it gives them the opportunity to index a certain voice for that character—that is, the voice of those in the social world who typically speak in the same way that the narrator makes the character speak. By making a character's utterances consistently sound like those who occupy a particular position from the larger society, a narrator can make that character speak with a definite voice. Voices form an indefinitely large set, because there are as many voices as there are recognizable types of people in a society. This set changes over historical time.

This account of voicing however, sounds in some ways like a rule-based theory. Isn't Bakhtin proposing rules that connect types of cues to types of voices, without much attention to the particular context? I argue that he does not. Some analyses of voice, including my own in places (Locher & Wortham, 1994; Wortham & Locher, 1996), have presented voicing as too decontextualized a process. But Bakhtin himself makes clear that participants and analysts cannot compute a character's voice by applying rules that associate types of words and expressions with certain social types. He makes this point by describing the "living" character of voices. Complex novelistic characters are not "some manifestation of reality that possesses fixed and specific socially typical or individually characteristic traits." Instead, characters embody "a *particular point of view on the world and on oneself* . . . the position enabling a person to interpret and evaluate his own self and his surrounding reality" (1963/1984a, p. 47; emphasis Bakhtin's). A living voice is not simply a static social position. The voice does speak from some position, but it does so in the midst of an ongoing process of self-definition. The social position represented by a voice changes as it enters dialogue with other voices. So a voice represents not just a static social role, but a "whole person" or an "integral point of view" who speaks from some position but is not fully defined by that position (1963/1984a, p. 93). Any living voice—the type represented by great novelists—defines itself through dialogue with others, not simply by occupying a preestablished social slot.

As I interpret it, this means that Bakhtin's concept of voice is compatible with a mediated account of interactional positioning in narrative. Stratified language and corresponding social positions do exist in the world prior to any particular storytelling event. Both novelists and everyday narrators presuppose these regularities as they describe others. But in general these regularities do not suffice to explain how particular characters come to speak with particular voices. As Bakhtin puts it, voices get articulated through dialogue. I take this to mean, in part, that hearers identify particular voices only by attending to how language highlights particular aspects of the context as relevant.

Characters' voices get articulated through dialogue with other voices represented in the novel in an ongoing process that provisionally stops only when a pattern of indexical cues and relevant context solidifies and allows participants and analysts to understand or react coherently to the types of voices speaking. A participant or analyst cannot conclude, solely with reference to rules that connect "laying around" and "drinking beer" to stereotyped welfare recipients, that Jasmine's baby is in fact being voiced as a social parasite. Instead, participants and analysts infer from the pattern of indexical cues and relevant context that the baby might be getting assigned this voice. Over the larger segment of conversation that includes these utterances—as more cues index this same voice for the baby and Jasmine, and as the teachers speak in ways that index the complementary voices of welfare critics—this set of cues and relevant context solidifies in such a way that Jasmine and her baby do indeed seem to be speaking with the voice of parasitic welfare recipients.

Bakhtin's concept of voice, then, supports a mediated account of how cues in narrative can establish socially relevant positions for narrated characters. In describing others, narrators inevitably presuppose voices for the people they describe. This process of voicing invokes positions and ideologies from the larger social world, as the characters described come to speak like recognizable types of people. As described further in Chapter 3, this process of voicing also provides the raw material that narrators use to position themselves interactionally. Narrators articulate their own voices, and thus adopt their own social positions, by juxtaposing themselves against the various voices established in their narratives. Before discussing Bakhtin's account further, however, we need to understand the other concept central to an adequate account of interactional positioning: emergence.

EMERGENCE

Any given utterance can potentially echo with many voices. "Laying around" and "drinking beer" might index the voice of a fraternity brother, or a typical American male on a Sunday afternoon during football season, instead of a welfare recipient. But increasingly, as the classroom discussion of Jasmine's example proceeds, teachers and students presuppose that welfare recipient is the most relevant voice in this storytelling event. Given that many voices might potentially be relevant, how do people ever know what kind of interactional positioning is actually going on?

The fields of ethnomethodology (Garfinkel, 1967; Garfinkel & Sacks, 1970) and conversation analysis (Schegloff & Sacks, 1973) have developed an answer to this question: the concept of *emergence*, which captures how subsequent utterances can transform the implications of prior ones. The conversation analysts argue that other participants' responses to an utterance can change the interactional positioning accomplished by an earlier utterance. Without knowing what responses followed an utterance, participants and analysts often cannot know what interactional positioning the utterance signaled.

Along with mediation, emergence is central to an adequate dialogic approach to interactional positioning. This concept describes how an utterance's interactional functions depend on how subsequent utterances cohere with it. An utterance contributes to particular interactional positioning in the storytelling event, ultimately, because of the effect it comes to have in the interaction. Cues in an utterance establish its interactional positioning only as subsequent utterances indicate that those cues have been taken in a certain way.

In the Spartan babies class discussed above, Mrs. Bailey's question, "why should the rest of us support your baby?" might have seemed at the time part of a rational academic discussion about ancient Sparta. The teachers had been defending Spartan practices against students' objections, and perhaps Mrs. Bailey's question was another piece of their argument. As the analogy between underprivileged students and unprivileged Spartans developed, however, Mrs. Bailey's utterance began to contribute to another kind of interactional positioning beyond that of teachers and students engaged in a dispassionate academic discussion. In my interpretation this utterance turns out to be an implicit complaint about stereotyped black welfare recipients. Teachers and students did not know at the moment of utterance what kind of interactional positioning this utterance would eventually contribute to. Only later, as the analogy between unproductive Spartans and contemporary American welfare recipients became clear, did this positioning coalesce. Subsequent context was required to establish the positioning accomplished by the earlier utterance.

An utterance comes to position speakers and hearers as it gets recontextualized by subsequent interaction or as a pattern of relevant context emerges over time. By this reasoning, in order to interpret or react to an utterance, participants and analysts must attend not only to the moment of utterance but also to some later moment when subsequent context has helped the meaning of the utterance solidify. At the moment of utterance the relevant context often has not yet emerged. Before Mrs. Bailey's utterance, teachers and students knew some relevant things about the prior context—about social organization in Sparta, about the example of Jasmine's baby, and about the different social worlds that the teachers and students come from. If the interaction had been interrupted at this point, they would likely have interpreted the utterance as part of the teachers' argument supporting Spartan practices. By the time Mrs. Bailey says "make them the Helots," however, more relevant context has emerged. This context includes at its center the analogy between lower-class black students and unprivileged Spartans. With respect to this analogy, analysts can now see— and participants now themselves presuppose—the association between the white teachers and welfare critics and the relevance of this interactional positioning for relationships in the classroom. Teachers and students have been separated as different social groups with different interests. The concept of emergence allows an adequate explanation of how subsequent context became integral to understanding the interactional positioning accomplished by the earlier utterance.

Bakhtin agrees with the conversation analysts that, in general, utterances accomplish identifiable interactional positioning only as they get contextualized. Bakhtin emphasizes the unfinished character of the implicit dialogues with others that partly constitute interactional positioning through speech. Because these dialogues can always be reopened, the interactional positioning accomplished by utterances must always be open to recontextualization. Instead of being fixed by rules, Bakhtin argues that the interactional positioning an utterance accomplishes will depend on contingent social reality. The positioning an utterance accomplishes "does not inhere in the word itself. It originates at the point of contact between the word and actual reality, under the conditions of that real situation articulated by the individual utterance" (1953/1986a, p. 88). The "real situation" Bakhtin speaks of is partly the subsequent context emphasized by conversation analysts. And this openness to subsequent context makes an utterance's interactional implications inexhaustible, "like a spring of dialogism that never runs dry—for the internal dialogism of discourse is something that inevitably accompanies the social, contradictory, historical becoming of language" (1935/1981, p. 330).

Many analysts of language, in Bakhtin's time and ours, resist such open-ended accounts of interactional positioning. Subsequent interpreters might bring new readings of an utterance, but surely the speaker meant something that could be determined at the time of utterance or else speakers and interpreters would be completely at sea. Both Bakhtin and the conversation analysts resist this desire for a closed account. As Bakhtin notes, "it is much easier to study the *given* in what is created (for example, language, ready-made and general elements of world view, reflected phenomena of reality, and so forth) than to study what is *created"* (1961/1986b, p. 120). Reducing interactional positioning to something largely computable through rules outside of context would make analysts more comfortable, because it does not open up the inexhaustible possibilities of recontextualization. But such an approach misses the essentially open character of interactional positioning through speech.

As Morson and Emerson (1990) describe, Bakhtin had extreme patience for plurality and the details of particular contexts. He was willing to forgo the security of closed interpretations, knowing that further examination of context might yield new insight into the interactional positioning that was actually accomplished in a particular case. He also recognized the danger of closed interpretations, which he called "finalized." A finalized utterance has no more potential for meaning, because it has been closed off from any subsequent context. Such an utterance "cannot be reborn, rejuvenated, or transformed" (1961/1986b, p. 115). For Bakhtin, a finalized account of the world, whether of art or people or language, eliminates the possibility for growth. To him, "all that is finished and polished" (1965/1984b, p. 3) represents stagnation and death. The breakdown of finalized structure and an openness to connection with other voices in dialogue allow growth. So Bakhtin happily tolerated the indeterminacy that comes with adopting the concept of emergence, because the alternative eliminates the possibility of creativity.

Like Garfinkel and the conversation analysts, then, Bakhtin celebrates what he called "unfinalizability," the ultimate openness of relevant emergent context. In a related expression, he claims that all utterances contain a "loophole"—"the possibility for altering the ultimate, final meaning of one's own words" (1963/1984a, p. 233). As much as anyone, Bakhtin revels in what Silverstein (1992) calls the "indeterminacy of contextualization." Bakhtin's book on Rabelais (1965/1984b) expresses this most fully. But his love for unfinalizability does not keep him from acknowledging the importance of structure. Every utterance is subject to forces of both "centralization and decentralization" (1935/1981, p. 272; he also calls these forces "centripetal and centrifugal"). Words and expressions do have regular meanings—for example, certain types of utterances do usually presuppose certain voices—and particular concrete utterances are shaped by these regular meanings. Speakers often use language in routine ways, and in such cases the interactional positioning accomplished by an utterance can be clear at the moment of utterance and can be described by simple rules. But alongside "unification, the uninterrupted processes of decentralization and disunification go forward" (1935/1981, p. 272).

Other voices always speak through particular words, and this leaves open possibilities for new meaning. Many cases cannot be explained by simple rules applicable at the moment of utterance. In more contemporary terms, this means that a full account of interactional positioning through speech must include the concepts of mediation and emergence.

But what kind of theory can account for the structure that clearly plays a role in establishing interactional positioning, while still acknowledging unfinalizability? How can participants and analysts tell what the relevant later time is, at which interpreters can give an adequate reading of the interactional positioning accomplished by an utterance? If the positioning depends ultimately on subsequent context, the positioning would seem to be indeterminate, because new context is always appearing. How can "make them the Helots" be a sort of put-down, when subsequent context could make this reading implausible? The concept of poetic structure helps answer these questions.

CHUNKING: POETIC STRUCTURE

The interactional event that gets established in a conversation is shaped by the indexical cues in the utterances. But the indexical values also depend on the type of event presupposed at the moment of utterance. In other words, the account described thus far is too linear. In understanding or reacting coherently to interactional positioning, participants and analysts cannot move sequentially from verbal and nonverbal cues, to construals of the context, to interactional positioning. To identify relevant indexes and to construe relevant context, participants and analysts already need some presuppositions about what is going on.

The indexicals in any utterance cannot themselves determine interactional events because participants and analysts can make multiple construals of the indexical values in any utterance. The values of particular indexes in an utterance highlight certain aspects of the context and thus indicate that a particular type of event is likely to be going on, but at the same time prior conceptions about what type of event is occurring influence the values of the indexes. For example, when Mrs. Bailey says, "why should the rest of us support your baby?" is this a complaint by a white taxpayer directed toward the lower-class black students? The group indexed by "us" (i.e., taxpayers) does seem to establish this sort of event, given how the utterance was contextualized by subsequent ones. But other indexical values and other event types could easily have become salient, in many different ways. The utterance could have been ironic, if participants had just finished discussing Mrs. Bailey's own reliance on welfare. Or it could have been a request for commonly accepted information, if they had all just agreed that governments should fund children's programs above all else.

How does a definite type of event ever get established amid this circularity and indeterminacy? This is a problem of *chunking*. Given a stream of speech and indefinite potentially relevant context, how do speakers and analysts know which chunks cohere and have implications for establishing interactional positions? In most conversations, groups of utterances come to cohere as having accomplished particular interactional positioning. For example despite the fact that "laying around" and "drinking beer" could have indexed the voice of a fraternity brother, together with other cues they come to voice Jasmine and her baby as stereotyped welfare recipients. This happens as a *set* of indexical cues *collectively* presuppose that particular voice and as Jasmine gets recruited into that voice. Jakobson (1960) and Silverstein (1992) describe such a set of indexical cues as a particular type of implicit structure, a *poetic structure*. Poetic structure emerges, solidifies, and thus establishes a relevant context and a more plausible set of interpretations for a series of utterances.

Sometimes particular interactional positions get established when speakers explicitly describe them, as in utterances like, "I'm in charge here" or "I just insulted you, you idiot." But in many cases, as in the Spartan babies class, implicit poetic structures of indexical cues collectively establish the interactional positioning that must be going on, because those indexes make certain context relevant (like Jasmine's race and social class). The concept of poetic structure also establishes that isolated indexical cues generally do not suffice to establish a plausible account of relevant context and interactional positioning. Rather, *patterns* of indexical cues, in utterances made by various participants over an interaction, come collectively to presuppose certain context as most relevant. Once such cues solidify, such that an organized poetic structure of them presupposes one interpretation or another, analysts and participants can infer that particular interactional positioning must have been going on in the interaction. The brief analysis of the Spartan babies class touches on a few components of the poetic structure— the indexical presuppositions and entailments of utterances like "what's your baby going to do . . . lay around drinking beer?" and, "why should the rest of us support your baby?" and "make them the Helots." As this structure of mutually presupposing indexicals emerges, it supports the complex set of analogies depicted in Figure 2.5.

Silverstein (1992, 1993, 1998) provides a detailed account of poetic structures and how indexical patterns constitute them. Although these details are essential to a full account of interactional positioning in speech, they are beyond the scope of this chapter. This chapter and the next aim only to describe the central concepts of dialogue, mediation, and emergence, so that we can analyze interactional positioning in autobiographical narrative. For this purpose it is enough to see that indeterminate context gets (provisionally) limited as a contingent structure of indexical cues emerges in a conversation.

The concept of poetic structure helps explain how interactional positioning gets established through a mediated and emergent process. Utterances position speakers and hearers because indexes in those utterances point out aspects of the context relevant to interpreting or reacting to them. Certain indexical values and not others become salient because speakers and hearers already presuppose various regularities that make some aspects of the context more salient. As the interaction proceeds, subsequent utterances establish the context that must have been relevant to interpreting prior utterances. At some point, a structure of mutually presupposing indexes and relevant contextual features solidifies in such a way that the utterances in that segment have clearer interactional implications. As mentioned above, some everyday utterances that position speakers in routine and predictable ways do not require such an elaborate account. But many autobiographical narratives are not routine and predictable, so explanations for the interactional positioning that they accomplish will require an approach based on the concepts of dialogue, mediation, and emergence. The next chapter sketches such an approach to interactional positioning in narrative discourse.

CHAPTER 3

Dialogue, Mediation, and Emergence in Narrative

In recent decades narrative has been studied more than any other verbal genre. The term narrative indexes many different intellectual projects, from metaphysical claims about human nature or the nature of particular subgroups to methodological claims about appropriate social scientific research, to empirical work on a certain verbal genre. I do not attempt a comprehensive review here (cf. Mishler, 1995). Instead I focus on theories that will help answer a particular question: How do the verbal signs that largely compose a narrative position the narrator interactionally?

In Chapter 2 I showed that, in general, the interactional positioning accomplished by an utterance depends on segments of the conversation beyond the utterance itself. An utterance's implications for interactional positioning become clear to participants and analysts when a structure of indexical cues and relevant context emerges in the conversation in such a way that a particular interpretation of or coherent reaction to the utterance becomes plausible. Mrs. Bailey's question, "why should the rest of us support your baby?" for instance, has clear implications for the interaction between teachers and students only after a structure of indexical cues and relevant contextual factors emerges in the classroom conversation. Two central concepts underlie an adequate account of this process: Indexical cues in an utterance *mediate* participants' construal of the utterance. These indexicals presuppose relevant aspects of the context, and these relevant aspects *emerge* over some segment of conversation such that participants and analysts can coherently interpret the utterance. Exactly what cues in an utterance will be relevant to the interactional positioning often cannot be established ahead of time, because this depends on contingent aspects of each particular conversation. There are, of course, relatively formulaic utterances and segments, and when speakers use these the relevant context can be predicted in advance. However, an adequate approach must account for the creative as well as the routine cases.

In this chapter I use the concepts of dialogue, mediation, and emergence to sketch an account of how storytelling can position narrators interactionally. Like the last chapter, this one begins with an extended example of narrative discourse that will be used throughout the chapter. Then the chapter describes what a dialogic, mediated, and emergent approach to narrative discourse looks like. The final sections of the chapter elaborate concepts from Bakhtin's account of narrative, in order to provide a working account of how storytelling interactionally positions narrators.

A SAMPLE NARRATIVE

Like accounts of interactional positioning in speech, accounts of narrative too often rely on overly simple examples and generate overly simple theories as a result. This section presents a complex narrative that I will use as an example throughout this chapter. As with the example of the Spartan babies, I have analyzed this case more extensively elsewhere (see Wortham & Locher, 1996). The narrative comes from network news coverage of the 1992 U.S. presidential campaign. This particular narrative is unusual, in that it has more than one narrator and the audience cannot respond directly. The multiple narrators and the overall complexity of the narrative make this a good example for my purposes because an adequate account of interactional positioning in narrative should be able to explain hard cases.

This story was broadcast on October 30, 1992, four days before the presidential election that included as candidates the elder George Bush, Bill Clinton, and Ross Perot. On this day a special federal prosecutor released notes written in 1986 by Caspar Weinberger, who had been Ronald Reagan's secretary of defense. The notes were released as part of an indictment, alleging that Weinberger had lied to Congress in an attempt to hide the fact that both President Reagan and Vice President Bush—in 1992 the incumbent president seeking reelection—knew about beforehand and approved of the secret 1986 U.S. sale of missiles to Iran. The notes were a lead story because they apparently contradicted Bush's repeated statements that he did not know of the arms sale ahead of time. The *CBS Evening News* reported the story in about thirteen hundred words, organized into the following seven sections:

1. Introduction by the anchor, Dan Rather
2. Law correspondent report of the facts, including clips from journalists and Bush himself

3. Anchor introduction of campaign correspondents
4. Bush campaign correspondent, including clips from Bush and his campaign staff
5. Clinton campaign correspondent, including clips from Clinton and his campaign staff
6. Perot campaign correspondent, including clip from Perot
7. Anchor report of poll on public trust of Bush and Clinton

This report contains several narratives, some embedded within others and some in sequence. Here I present and analyze the complex narrative developed in Sections 1, 2, 3, and 7. (For an analysis of Sections 4–6 see Wortham and Locher, 1996).

In the introductory "teaser" before the opening titles for the *CBS Evening News*, which briefly summarizes the top stories of the day, the first words spoken by Dan Rather are: "A secret arms deal with Iran. A grand jury sees evidence contrary to what President Bush repeatedly has said . . .". After the titles, Rather begins the newscast as follows:

> Dan Rather reporting. There is <u>new</u> <u>writ</u>ten evidence tonight concerning <u>what</u> President Bush <u>knew</u> and <u>when</u> he knew about the <u>se</u>cret deal that sent some of America's <u>best</u> missiles to the <u>A</u>yatollah Khomeini. The <u>grand</u> jury evidence raises <u>new</u> questions about whether Mr. Bush is telling the truth. CBS News law correspondent Rita Braver has de<u>tails</u> on this dra<u>ma</u>tic turn of events.

This provides what Labov and Waletsky (1967) call an "abstract" of the story to come, and it also gives some of the setting. Note that there are already two narrated events in play here: Bush's conduct and knowledge in the 1986 U.S. sale of missiles to Iran; and Bush's position at the time of the newscast (specifically, how the release of the Weinberger notes is affecting his chances in the closing days of the 1992 presidential campaign). Rather's short introduction also provides some information about how the story might be positioning Dan Rather in the storytelling event: Rather—and later the other CBS narrators—frame the events as very serious new questions about whether Bush has been telling the truth. Several cues support this interpretation. Note first the emphasis on "new" evidence: Rather uses this word twice, and other correspondents use it several times in their stories. At the end of this passage Rather labels the Weinberger notes a "dramatic turn of events." Later on, CBS correspondents use the terms "bombshell" and "revelation" to describe the notes. All these terms presuppose that Bush now faces a serious challenge from the newly publicized notes. In addition,

Rather portrays the 1986 sale as a terrible mistake. It was a "secret deal," the sort of arrangement criminals make. It sent our "best missiles," not just generic armaments. And it sent them to the hated "Ayatollah Khomeini." Many Americans particularly detested Khomeini for his role in kidnapping U.S. hostages a decade earlier. Rather could have said we sent missiles to "Iran"—one imagines, after all, that the Ayatollah did not accept delivery of the missiles personally—but he singles out the most hated figure as a metonym for the country of Iran.

Figure 3.1 depicts the narrative so far. There are two narrated realms, one embedded within the other. The foregrounded story, which Rather describes in the present tense, involves the release of Weinberger's notes and the questions they raise for candidate Bush's credibility on October

FIGURE 3.1 Rather's Introduction of the Narrative

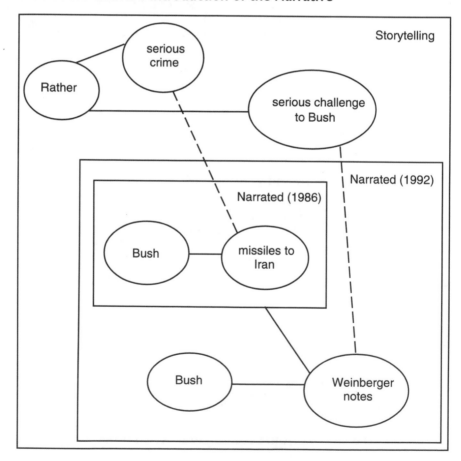

30, 1992. The notes themselves describe events surrounding the 1986 sale of missiles to Iran, which indicate that Vice President Bush may have approved the sale ahead of time. Thus the narrated content represents one story, a story which contains one incident embedded within another. To understand the interactional positioning accomplished in the storytelling event, as represented in the outermost rectangle, participants and analysts must ask what position Rather himself takes in the storytelling event. The cues mentioned above indicate that Rather takes both the 1986 crime and the 1992 challenge to Bush's credibility very seriously. Rather positions himself as a serious critic of Bush, though this is not the only positioning possible (Wortham & Locher, 1996).

After Rather's introduction, Rita Braver (the CBS News law correspondent) presents the details of the story, including clips of earlier statements made by Vice President Bush, and by Anthony Lewis, a *New York Times* correspondent speaking on tape (dates appear in lower right corner of the picture).

> *Braver:* An em<u>ba</u>rrassing revelation for George <u>Bush</u>. Evidence released for the <u>first</u> time to<u>day</u> <u>con</u>tradicts his previous <u>state</u>ments that he was <u>out</u> of the loop on the Reagan administration's <u>deal</u> to ship arms to Iran in exchange for American <u>host</u>ages. New charges returned in the ongoing <u>case</u> against former defense secretary Casper <u>Wein</u>berger <u>de</u>tail Weinberger's <u>hand</u>written <u>notes</u> of a meeting George Bush at<u>ten</u>ded January 7, 198<u>6</u>. Weinberger writes that President Reagan decided to ap<u>prove</u> a scheme to release <u>host</u>ages in return for the sale of 4,000 TOW missiles to Iran by Israel. Weinberger op<u>posed</u>. Others, in<u>clu</u>ding Vice President Bush, <u>fa</u>vored the deal.
>
> *Lewis:* This is <u>further</u>, <u>very</u> strong evidence that George Bush knew all about the trading of arms for hostages, which he has consistently <u>denied</u>.
>
> *Braver:* For <u>years</u>, over and over a<u>gain</u>, Mr. Bush claimed neither <u>he</u> nor President Reagan knew the <u>de</u>tails.
>
> *Bush* [12/3/86]: The President is <u>abso</u>lutely convinced. (1.0) that he <u>did</u> not swap arms for <u>host</u>ages
>
> *Braver:* President Bush has changed his story several <u>times</u>, and in fact earlier this <u>month</u> appeared to admit that he knew something about the deal.
>
> *Interviewer* [10/13/92]: You knew about the arms for hostages.
>
> *Bush* [10/13/92]: <u>Yes</u>. And I've said so all along.
>
> *Braver:* But in that same interview the President <u>also</u> denied being at <u>key</u> meetings, including the one in the note released to<u>day</u>, where

> Weinberger opposed the trade. *New York Times* columnist An-
> thony Lewis, who's been tracking the President's Iran-Contra
> connection, says it's ironic George Bush is trying to make Bill
> Clinton's truthfulness an issue.
> *Lewis:* It's the President of the United States deliberately, knowingly,
>   forcefully telling you an untruth, year after year, month after
>   month. That's going to destroy our faith in our political system.
> *Braver:* The independent counsel insists the release of the note was
>   timed to meet the schedule for Caspar Weinberger's trial, not to
>   embarrass the President in the final days of the campaign. Rita
>   Braver, CBS News, Washington.

As shown in Figure 3.2, the narrated content of Braver's story contains
the two events described by Rather and adds two more. The outermost
event is occurring on October 30, 1992, the day of the newscast. George
Bush, the current presidential candidate, has had his credibility threat-
ened by the release of the Weinberger notes. As Rather did, Braver
describes this event using the present tense. Like Rather she also
reports the past events of January 1986—the meeting described in
Weinberger's notes—at which Bush allegedly approved the sale of
missiles to Iran. In exploring the implications of the notes for Bush's
credibility, Braver also describes two other past events. In December
1986 Bush denied that he and President Reagan approved the sale of
missiles, but on October 13, 1992, Bush appeared to admit that he knew
about the sale ahead of time. So Braver presents a complex narrative
about George Bush's credibility, with three embedded episodes describing Bush's past actions.

To uncover the interactional positioning accomplished by this
complex narrative requires, first, an analysis of the voices assigned to
characters in the narrated events and, second, an analysis of how Braver
positions herself with respect to these voices in the storytelling event.
What kind of person does she voice Bush as? And what position does
she herself take up with respect to George Bush and his various past
actions?

Braver's use of the verb "contradict" emphasizes the new evidence
that Bush has been lying. She picks up Rather's use of the term "deal"
to refer to the arms sale, and she also uses "scheme." Both these words
can index criminal acts, and by using these terms to describe actions
that George Bush condoned, she may be voicing him as akin to a criminal in some respects. Several other cues support this voicing. For instance, Anthony Lewis puts the verb "deny" in Bush's mouth. Braver

FIGURE 3.2 Braver's Elaboration of the Narrative

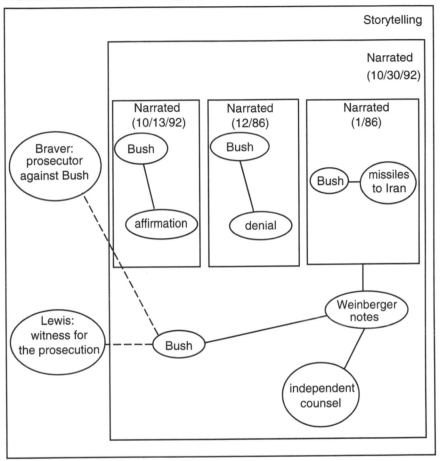

describes Bush's "claims" and how he "has changed his story." She also uses the phrase "the President's Iran-Contra connection." All these terms used to describe Bush are often associated with criminal defendants (see Wortham & Locher, 1996, for further evidence). The use of so many terms associated with criminals begins to voice Bush as a criminal defendant facing serious charges.

Braver's positioning in the storytelling event builds on this voicing of Bush as a criminal. Recall that Braver is the CBS News *law* correspondent. No other newscast that we analyzed uses a legal correspondent for this story. This might presuppose that CBS's investigation of

Bush's actions is legal or judicial. Recall also that Rather introduces the newscast by foregrounding "grand jury" involvement, which might also indicate a quasi-legal frame for the storytelling event. As Rather presents it at the beginning of the newscast, it even sounds as if the grand jury might be indicting Bush himself. The audience does not learn until the third sentence of Braver's report (120 words into the story) that the grand jury is indicting Weinberger and not Bush.

In Braver's report, the presence of Anthony Lewis—a *New York Times* journalist who followed the sale of missiles to Iran closely—leads me to interpret the newscast conversation as a mock trial. Lewis's comments are spliced into Braver's story as if he is conversing with her about Bush's actions and the new evidence. Interactionally, Braver positions herself as a mock prosecutor, and Lewis plays a witness for the prosecution. He indicts Bush bluntly—as one would expect a prosecution witness to do—by claiming that Bush really "knew all about" the deal. After Lewis's "testimony," Braver illustrates Bush's "claims" with Bush's own words. She produces, as an exhibit, a tape of Bush denying that Reagan knew of the swap. Like a good prosecutor, she then produces more evidence, again an exhibit in Bush's own words, that he "has changed his story." The contradiction between the two Bush quotes is blunt, and it leaves the clear impression that Bush must have been lying at some point. Next Braver introduces Lewis, even though he has already spoken once without introduction. Lewis goes on to claim that Bush has been repeatedly lying. He also identifies the victim of the crime: Our political system is losing credibility because of Bush's lies.

So Braver organizes the storytelling event as if Bush is a criminal defendant on trial for lying about his role in the sale of missiles to Iran. She speaks with the voice of a prosecutor, Lewis speaks with the voice of a witness for the prosecution, and they both use descriptions of Bush that index criminal activity and thus voice him as a criminal defendant. At the very end of her report, in just one sentence, Braver mentions that the release of the evidence might have been politically motivated. After the strength of her case against Bush, this possibility is barely in play as she signs off.

In the next utterance Dan Rather ignores this political possibility and himself joins the case against Bush in the storytelling event.

> The grand jury evidence appears to be at variance with what then Vice President Bush said in an interview on this broadcast in 1988. The President sent one of his spokesmen out today to say there is nothing new in the Weinberger note. White House correspondent Susan Spencer is with the President, on the campaign trail in St. Louis. Susan.

Note that Rather reinforces the legal threat that Bush faces by referring to the Weinberger notes as "grand jury evidence" again. He could have simply referred to the notes without mentioning their role in an ongoing criminal proceeding. By mentioning the grand jury—without clarifying that the grand jury was investigating Weinberger and not Bush—Rather leaves open the possibility that Bush himself may be put on trial (and in my interpretation he *is* metaphorically being put on trial in the interactional event being enacted by Rather and Braver). Figure 3.3 depicts the narrative at this point. In his reference to the grand jury evidence Rather presupposes the two narrated events he described before: the credibility question that the Weinberger notes raise for candidate Bush on October 30, 1992; and the January 1986 White House meeting about the sale of missiles. Rather also introduces another narrated event: In 1988, on this very program (the *CBS Evening News*), with Dan Rather himself as the interviewer, Bush made claims that are contradicted by the new evidence from the notes. By introducing this new narrated event from 1988, Rather introduces more evidence that Bush has been lying.

In the storytelling event, then, Rather speaks with the voice of a witness who provides corroborative, eyewitness evidence against Bush. (In control of the broadcast insofar as he allocates speaking turns and mediates the correspondents' relations with the audience, Rather is in some ways the judge at Bush's mock trial. In the passage above, however, Rather steps out of the judge role to give evidence against the defendant, as a witness.) In speaking like a witness, Rather not only strengthens Braver's case but also introduces Bush himself as a quasi-participant in the storytelling event. After Rather's statement, the audience knows that Bush knows Rather personally and that Bush himself has appeared on this very program. This makes Bush's status as a "defendant" in the mock trial more plausible. Figure 3.3 shows this by placing Bush also in the storytelling event, as the target of the case developed by Braver, Lewis, and Rather. Rather's implicit message to the audience in the storytelling event is "Bush lied to me too, and I'm here both to hold him responsible and to warn you about him."[1]

So Rather and Braver present a complex narrative, one which involves the main story (of 10/30/92) and four embedded episodes. In telling the story, they position themselves interactionally by using cues that index the voices of witness and prosecutor at a trial. And they assign Bush the voice of a criminal defendant. Thus the storytelling event can be interpreted as a mock trial. Here I skip over the next three parts of the news story, in which Rather turns to the campaign correspondents for their stories of how the Bush, Clinton, and Perot campaigns reacted to the release of Weinberger's notes.

FIGURE 3.3 Rather's Role in the Storytelling Event

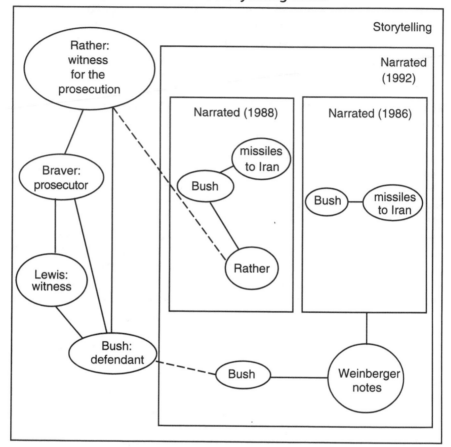

After the campaign correspondents present their stories, Rather introduces another story that seems to have no close connection with the story of the Weinberger notes. This story presents the results of a new poll—a *"full* poll," Rather says, *"not* a tracking poll":

> *Rather:* . . . It <u>in</u>dicates that Governor Clinton may be hanging on to his lead over President <u>Bush</u>. The survey was completed be<u>fore</u> today's weapons for Iran new evidence. . . .
> *Correspondent:* For a <u>Pre</u>sident campaigning on the <u>trust</u> issue, and who's now fighting off another-Iran Contra <u>bomb</u>shell, there are some <u>worry</u>ing numbers in today's CBS News <u>poll</u> about whether

people believe what he <u>says</u>. The issue here is <u>Iraq</u>gate. Mr. Bush has said he didn't <u>know</u> Saddam Hussein was using U.S. <u>aid</u> to build up his military before the Gulf <u>War</u>. But the <u>polls</u> show <u>twice</u> as many people <u>don't</u> believe him as <u>do</u>. That's fewer people than believe Bill <u>Clin</u>ton's version of his Vietnam War draft <u>his</u>tory. Here the public is <u>split</u> between belief and disbelief. . . .

The narrated content here involves the results of a poll. Although this poll does not specifically examine Bush's credibility with regard to the Iran missile sale, its placement at this point in the broadcast makes it seem much like a jury verdict. The public—the implied audience of the newscast, in the storytelling event—finds Bush guilty of lying, by a ratio of two to one. We can only expect, Philips implies, that the new evidence against Bush will make the verdict even more lopsided.

This verdict completes the quasi-legal proceeding that CBS has staged against Bush. They presented a convincing prosecution case from Braver, including firsthand testimony from Rather himself, a feeble defense from Bush, and various witnesses to support the prosecution (Lewis, Clinton, Gore, Perot). Now the public has indicated its belief that Bush is lying. The "sentence" has to wait for the actual election, as the voters are the ones empowered to depose Bush. And this, of course, they did.

As long as participants and analysts have relevant cultural background knowledge about the normal components of a jury trial, they can recognize this mock verdict as the final piece of the interactional positioning accomplished through the news stories. In the storytelling event Rather and his correspondents present Bush speaking with the voice of a criminal defendant, one who is most likely guilty. They position themselves as the prosecution, responsible for making the case against Bush and warning the public. Using this example, the rest of this chapter examines how the concepts of dialogue, mediation, and emergence can be applied to narrative discourse.

MEDIATION

How can an analyst grasp the interactional positioning accomplished when Rather and Braver narrate the various events that involve George Bush? Contemporary accounts of narrative have begun to posit a mediating step between the cues in a narrative and the narrative's overall meaning, a step in which hearers infer the significance of those cues (e.g., Ervin-Tripp & Küntay, 1997; Fludernik, 1993; Georgakopoulou, 1997).

Many early theories found the essence of narrative in the temporal or causal sequence of elements. Others have since pointed out, however, that a mere sequence of events does not in itself constitute a meaningful narrative (e.g., Bamberg & Marchman, 1991; Culler, 1975; Ricoeur, 1980; Toolan, 1988; H. White, 1987). As Polkinghorne puts it, "narrative ordering makes individual elements comprehensible by identifying the whole to which they contribute" (1988, p. 18). One cannot understand a narrative simply by listing the narrated events in temporal order. To grasp the "narrative whole," which involves the overall purpose for putting these narrated events together, participants and analysts infer the meaning of the narrative based on cues in the narrative utterances plus their own knowledge of the context.

Such an inferential process relies on the concept of *mediation*. As described in the last chapter, participants and analysts must infer the meaning of an utterance or a narrative from a pattern of cues. In the analysis of the newscast just conducted, the conclusion that Rather and Braver stage a mock trial of Bush is reached by inferring from several cues: Braver's status as law correspondent, her utterances that sound like the introduction of evidence by a prosecutor, the comments by Anthony Lewis in which he speaks like a witness for the prosecution, various indexes that associate Bush with criminal activity, and so on. It would not make sense to posit a simple rule that when the narrator is a law correspondent, the storytelling event takes the form of a mock trial. This rule would have many exceptions, and each of these would require new rules. An adequate account of narrative meaning will describe how cues make certain aspects of the context relevant, such that participants and analysts can infer the overall meaning of the narrative in particular cases.

Bower and Morrow (1990), in a mediated account of narrative, argue that interpretation of a narrative has two major components: (1) "Translate the surface form of the text into underlying conceptual propositions," then (2) "use . . . world knowledge to identify referents . . . of the text's concepts, linking expressions that refer to the same entity and drawing inferences to knit together the causal relations among the action sequences of the narrative" (p. 44). This type of mediated account comes from a tradition in cognitive psychology, often associated with Johnson-Laird (1983), that posits "mental models." Participants and analysts understand experience in general, including narratives, by building mental models. This is a two-stage process. People first examine the cues in a narrative and then infer from some pattern of these cues what the overall meaning must be. As with the interpretation of particular utterances, this process is not linear. Preexisting mental models lead people to interpret cues and elements in certain ways, then some cues and elements can lead people to revised models, and so on.

This mediated account of narrative resembles Gumperz's (1982) account of utterance meaning in some ways. Both use the key concept of mediation to explain how hearers get from actual speech to an understanding of its meaning. Bower and Morrow, however, are concerned solely with representational values—the "underlying conceptual propositions" that narrative utterances communicate. Narratives have meaning when the hearer mentally *represents* a description of the experiences and events communicated by the narrator, not when an emergent *interactional* positioning emerges for narrator and audience. I argue that, while represented content is almost always relevant to interpreting the interactional positioning accomplished in narrative, it rarely suffices. To understand the interactional positioning accomplished in Braver's narrative, for instance, participants and analysts need to know that she is talking like a prosecutor, and this information is not carried solely by the representational value of her utterances. Various aspects of her utterances, some involving represented content and some not, index a certain type of speaker. Participants and analysts infer from these indexes that she is acting like a mock prosecutor herself in the storytelling event.

It will take more work to apply the concept of mediation to narrative discourse in a dialogic way.[2] Bower and Morrow, and most others who offer mediated accounts of narrative, are not concerned with the position of the narrator in the storytelling event. They are concerned solely with the content represented as narrated events, an approach which fails to explain the interactional positioning accomplished in a narrative such as Rather and Braver's mock trial of Bush. No one *represents* this mock trial at all. The mock trial gets *enacted*: Indexical values of various utterances lead hearers to infer that Rather and Braver are occupying certain positions in the storytelling event. Participants and analysts do, of course, need to understand the represented content in order to understand what Rather and Braver are doing interactionally. But to focus only on narrated events would miss the interactional positioning accomplished by the narrative.[3]

EMERGENCE

A mediated account of interactional positioning in narrative must explain how hearers limit the context in such a way that a narrative comes to accomplish something particular in practice. Many aspects of the context might potentially be relevant to interpreting a narrative, and different configurations of relevant context would support different interpretations. For instance, if Rather and Braver had alluded regularly to the prevalence of lying among all politicians—thus presenting Bush as the same as the rest—participants and analysts might interpret the interactional positioning in their story differently. Despite the indeterminacy of potentially relevant context, however, in everyday practice people often act as if narratives accomplish relatively clear positioning. Most theories of narrative, including those discussed so far, rely ultimately on representational content to limit the relevant context. According to cognitive psychologists, an interpretation of a narrative solidifies because it matches some mental model. But mental structures simply push the indeterminacy back into the mind without examining how structure emerges in actual discourse. According to Polanyi (1989) for example, an interpretation of a narrative solidifies because of the explicit or implicit propositional values of some narrative utterances. But mere propositional values do not account well for the sorts of complex interactional patterns enacted in the Braver and Rather example. The analysis I have given above does summarize the interactional positioning in propositional terms—as a mock trial of Bush. But in the storytelling event itself, this trial was enacted and not propositionally represented. Rather and Braver took advantage of language's ability to presuppose and create interactional patterns, and they enacted the storytelling event of a mock trial.

The conversation analysts' concept of *emergence* provides an alternative here. Their account of positioning in narratives describes how interactional effects can emerge and solidify in practice. Jefferson (1978) is the conversation analyst who has done the most work on narrative, although she gives substantial credit to Sacks (1978; cf. also C. Goodwin, 1984; M. Goodwin, 1990). She analyzes how stories are integrated into ongoing conversation, focusing on how participants negotiate the beginnings and endings of stories so that they fit smoothly into the ongoing storytelling event. What begins as a study of stories' margins, however, elegantly leads to a reconceptualization of their essence.

Jefferson (1978) describes a sequence of units, extending beyond the narrative itself, that is essential for a coherent narrative: The narrator gives a story preface; other participants accept the role of audience in the storytelling event by ratifying the preface (e.g., by saying "that sounds interesting [pause]"); the narrator tells the story; then members of the audience acknowledge the story through their response. Jefferson gives detailed analyses of how speakers fit their talk into this structure, concentrating on how audience members' contributions can facilitate transitions into and out of the story. At any moment, speakers understand what is happening by examining how the most recent utterance fits into the sequence of utterances that have preceded it. Speakers use specific techniques "to display a relationship between the story and prior talk and thus account for, and propose the appropriateness of, the story's telling" (p. 220). In beginning a story, for instance, speakers will often index the element of the prior conversation that triggered the story, and they will also often use a "disjunct marker"— for example, "oh, I just heard a story about that"—which requests the several uninterrupted speaking turns that will be required to tell the story.

As discussed in the last chapter, however, prior sequence alone does not determine the meaning of a given utterance. On the contrary, the interactional positioning accomplished by any utterance or narrative can be revised based on subsequent utterances. Jefferson (1978) gives examples in which the point of a story emerges from subsequent conversation. She argues that the point of a story cannot be determined solely by examining its internal components, but instead emerges from the "sequential implicativeness of the story" (p. 231) or "what the story has amounted to" (p. 233). Thus, although Jefferson started her chapter claiming only to study transitions into and out of narratives, she ends up showing that both the boundaries of a story and its overall interactional effects cannot be fixed by formal rules because boundaries and effects emerge in ongoing conversation.

Jefferson's analysis of how the boundaries of a story themselves can be revised, given subsequent context, helps one interpret Braver and Rather's narrative. Braver's telling of the story puts her into the role of mock prosecutor in the storytelling event. But perhaps she has simply been giving an energetic reading of the day's news about George Bush. This interpretation becomes much less plausible when Rather follows Braver's story with an utterance that positions Rather himself as a witness, offering further "testimony" against Bush. Without any intervening material, Rather offers another incident—parallel to the ones Braver has just introduced—in which Bush contradicted himself while discussing the Iranian missile sale. At this point the interpretation of Braver as a mock prosecutor in the storytelling event becomes more solid. Utterances earlier in the story, as when Braver says "President Bush has changed his story several times," might entail that she is speaking as a mock prosecutor. By the first sentence of Rather's follow-up to Braver, in which he ratifies her role as mock prosecutor by himself stepping for a moment into the role of mock witness, this entailment has become part of the relevant context. This interpretation of the narrative solidifies further when Rather later presents the poll which serves as a mock verdict.

The conversation analysts thus show how a narrative itself may not represent the only conversational segment relevant to understanding the interactional positioning it accomplishes (e.g., Jefferson, 1978; Sacks, 1978). Narratives often cohere only with reference to preceding and subsequent conversation. In such cases the segment of conversation relevant to understanding the meaning of the narrative is larger than the narrative itself. In the CBS News example, one cannot fully appreciate the interactional positioning being accomplished until after the narrative itself is over. In other cases, however, a narrative stands apart as a relatively autonomous segment that can be understood primarily with reference to the narrative itself. How large the segment relevant to understanding a narrative is, is a contingent matter to be decided on a case-by-case basis. In these ways the conversation analysts show how the concept of emergence can be applied to narrative discourse (for emergent accounts of autobiographical narrative in particular, see Gergen & Gergen, 1983; Hermans & Kempen, 1993; Sarbin, 1997; Schafer, 1992).

TWO BAKHTINIAN CONCEPTS

In summary, then, a *mediated approach* analyzes how cues in the narrative establish particular context as relevant to interpreting the interactional positioning accomplished through the narrative, and an *emergent approach* studies how the contextual structures relevant to interpreting a narrative emerge over a conversation, often solidifying after the narrative itself has ended. The next sections describe two Bakhtinian concepts that, together with the concept of voice discussed in the last chapter, can support a mediated and emergent account of narrative.

Double Voicing

Although Bakhtin does not intend to give a systematic account of interactional positioning in narratives, he offers several concepts useful for such an account. The last chapter argued that his central concept of voice can be extended to describe how narrative cues index aspects of the context, aspects which then become relevant to interpreting the interactional positioning accomplished by a narrative. This section and the next describe how the concepts he calls "double voicing" and "ventriloquation" can support an emergent approach to interactional positioning in narrative.

Bakhtin (1963/1984a, 1935/1981) develops the concepts of voice, double voicing, and ventriloquation in his theory of the novel. He claims that novelists, particularly Dostoevsky, focused in particular on the aspects of meaning that come from dialogue—the fact that people communicate not only by representing objects but also by positioning themselves with respect to others who have spoken about the same objects. More than any other literary genre, novels gain their meaning by manipulating the dialogic potential of speech.[4] When they represent characters' speech, novelists portray those characters dialogically commenting on each other. And novelists position or articulate themselves by engaging in dialogue with various characters. That is, novelists often do not explicitly represent their points, but instead they adopt positions by juxtaposing and inflecting the voices of various characters. For this reason novels, and other narratives as well, cannot be reduced to the plot. Novels have plots, but "the plot itself is subordinated to the task of coordinating and exposing languages to each other" (1935/1981, p. 365). Novelists position themselves through the narrative by juxtaposing speakers—including the narrator, others whom the narrator quotes or indexes, and others who speak in the storytelling event—and positioning these speakers with respect to one another.

Authoring, for Bakhtin, is the process of juxtaposing others' voices in order to adopt a social position of one's own (cf. K. Clark & Holquist, 1984). Bakhtin argues that everyday speakers author themselves much as novelists do. As discussed in Chapter 2, he argues that all speakers draw on the many voices present in the social world and that their utterances have meaning only through a dialogue among their own and these other voices. Novelists have more control over how voices get juxtaposed than everyday speakers do, so they can intensify and exploit the dialogic processes that go into making meaning. But everyday speakers do something qualitatively similar. Real-life narrators, like novelists, describe a set of events. In doing so they establish a dialogue among the characters, and they themselves adopt a position with respect to those characters.

As they describe characters who speak with recognizable voices from the social world, narrators speak through these voices and establish their own positions. In the same narrative descriptions, both the narrator's and the characters' voices can get established. Bakhtin refers to this juxtaposition of relevant voices with the concept of *double voicing.* In his seminal work on Dostoevsky, Bakhtin calls double-voiced discourse "the chief subject of our investigation, one could even say its chief hero" (1963/1984a, p. 185). Double-voiced discourse "has a twofold direction—it is directed both toward the referential object of speech, as in ordinary discourse, and toward *another's discourse*, toward *someone else's speech*" (p. 185). In double-voiced discourse the speaker's meaning emerges in part through an interaction with the voice of another, with both voices often speaking through one character's words. In double-voiced discourse "a conflict takes place," as the speaker layers his own intonations over the still live words of another (p. 74).

Bakhtin writes that novels are built around double-voiced discourse. The following illustration comes from Dickens' *Little Dorrit*. In this scene the businessman Merdle admires the dinner that has been laid upon his own table:

> It was a dinner to provoke an appetite, though he had not had one. The rarest dishes, sumptuously cooked and sumptuously served; the choicest fruits, the most exquisite wines; marvels of workmanship in gold and silver, china and glass; innumerable things delicious to the senses of taste, smell, and sight were insinuated into its composition. *O, what a wonderful man this Merdle, what a great man, what a master man, how blessedly and enviably endowed*—in one word, what a rich man! (Book 2, chap. 12; quoted in Bakhtin, 1935/1981, p. 304; emphasis Bakhtin's)

In Bakhtin's analysis, this passage begins with a "parodic stylization of high epic style." The first two sentences might echo the thoughts of Merdle himself—at those moments when Merdle fancies himself as important as royalty. The italicized portion is "a chorus of his admirers in the form of the concealed speech of another." These words echo with the voice of Merdle's hypocritical admirers, who sing his praises only because they want to share in his wealth and fame. Bakhtin calls the last seven words "authorial unmasking." Here Dickens replaces all the earlier praises with the single word "rich," and thus he points to the hypocrisy of Merdle's sycophants.

In this passage Dickens juxtaposes at least three voices: Merdle, his admirers, and those like Dickens himself who appreciate the irony of the situation. Figure 3.4 depicts this account. The narrated event contains Merdle and his fawning admirers. Dickens describes these characters using cues—largely a modified form of quoted speech that represents the thoughts of characters as if they were being spoken—that index certain groups in the socially stratified world of Dickens' time: self-satisfied businessmen and their sycophants. Dickens himself also adopts a position in the storytelling event with respect to those two other groups, by laughing at them and exposing their hypocrisy.[5] Dickens' descriptions in this passage are double voiced because they pre-

FIGURE 3.4 Double Voicing

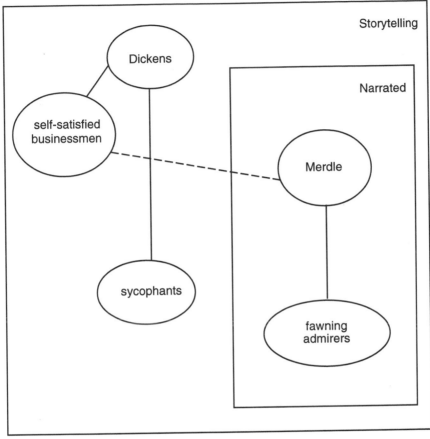

suppose three recognizable types of people from the social world and because they put these voices into a metaphorical conversation, at the level of the social positions and ideologies associated with these voices. In this case the dialogue—the social positioning of narrator and characters with respect to each other—is relatively simple: Self-satisfied businessmen like Merdle sometimes admire themselves for their worldly success; their sycophants admire them for this too; but people like Dickens think this admiration is ridiculous and really a disguise for base materialism. Note that Dickens makes his point in this dialogue by *positioning* himself with respect to others in the storytelling event, not by representing it explicitly. Like Rather and Braver's narrative, Dickens' story gets its full dialogic meaning only implicitly, as it juxtaposes the three voices in a certain way.

Although this is a relatively simple example, analysts cannot compute its meaning with reference only to rules. To interpret the novel requires an inference from the pattern of cues to the voices being represented and then an inference from these voices to the position being taken up by Dickens himself. As argued in Chapter 2, a narrative does sometimes rely on normative cues and accomplish predictable interactional positioning. But interpreters must always be sensitive to relevant context and nonnormative cues, because these often play a role in signaling the interactional positioning accomplished through narration. For example, although Braver voices Bush as a criminal defendant and herself as a prosecutor, Bush could equally have emerged as unjustly maligned as the narrative continues to unfold. The cues in a narrative do not determine some stable relation among the respective voices, because the dialogue is ongoing. In other words, subsequent context might lead participants and analysts to reread the cues and voices as composing a different narrative whole. But how is this indeterminacy ever overcome in practice so that narratives can (provisionally) accomplish clear interactional positioning?

Ventriloquation

The concept of double voicing establishes the dialogic character of Bakhtin's approach, because it describes how narrators articulate their own voices (and thus interactionally position themselves) by juxtaposing themselves with respect to other voices. The concept of double voicing also begins to describe the type of emergent patterns relevant to interpreting the interactional positioning accomplished by a narrative. In the case of narrative, Bakhtin argues, the relevant patterns centrally involve voices that are presupposed by indexical cues in the narrative. Because these voices are drawn from a complex, often conflictual social world, they engage in a dialogue that involves multiple perspectives and often conflicting positions.

As discussed in Chapter 2, Bakhtin is particularly fond of the indeterminacy or unfinalizability of such dialogues. But he acknowledges that in practice narratives do often have relatively clear interactional implications. These get established when the narrator takes up a position within the storytelling event with respect to social positions represented by the characters and others in the storytelling event. But how does this interactional positioning ever get established, given that newly relevant context could always be introduced that would lead hearers to reinterpret cues, voices, and the overall narrative? Bakhtin's answer is similar to the solution sketched in the last chapter. Patterns of cues, voices, and relevant context emerge over the course of a narrative. When a pattern solidifies, participants and analysts can give plausible interpretations of the characters' voices and the position of the narrator in the storytelling event. Braver's narrative, for instance, becomes a mock trial when the subsequent context established by Rather's witnesslike utterance makes clear that she has, in fact, been speaking as a mock prosecutor and Bush has been speaking as a mock defendant.

Bakhtin analyzes these sorts of emergent patterns in large part through his concept of ventriloquation. Novelists, he claims, have "the gift of indirect speaking" (1961/1986b, p. 110). They make their points by positioning themselves with respect to others' voices, not by speaking directly in their own voices. Discourse in the novel thus "serves two speakers at the same time and expresses simultaneously two different intentions: the direct intention of the character who is speaking, and the refracted intention of the author" (1935/1981, p. 324). Narrative language actually contains three layers: (1) It refers to and characterizes narrated objects; (2) it indexes the voices of the characters who are represented; and (3) it establishes a social position for the narrator himself. Bakhtin uses the term *ventriloquation* to describe the process of positioning oneself by juxtaposing and speaking through others' voices. By speaking through or ventriloquating others' voices, narrators can establish positions for themselves. Dickens, for instance, lampoons the sycophants who admire rich people only for their money. Interactional positioning solidifies when hearers can identify the narrator entering the dialogue and positioning himself with respect to the voices established in the narrative.

Bakhtin uses various metaphors to describe ventriloquation. He speaks of how novelists "highlight" and "accent" others' words and of how they bring out various "resonances" in those words (1935/1981, p. 362). In all these metaphors, he describes the relationship of the narrator's voice to those represented in the narrative. Sometimes the narrator harmonizes with a particular represented voice: He "does not collide with the other's thought, but rather follows after it in the same direction." At other times the narrator's voice "clashes hostilely with its primordial host and forces him to serve directly opposing aims" (1963/1984a, p. 193).

Another important metaphor Bakhtin uses to describe ventriloquation is spatial. "The language of the prose writer deploys itself according to degrees of greater or lesser proximity to the author" (1935/1981, p. 299). Some voices can almost directly represent the narrator, although in the novel there is always some inflection. Narrators accent many voices, "humorously, ironically, parodically, and so forth" (p. 299), and thus they establish varying degrees of distance. "Yet another group may stand even further from the author's ultimate semantic instantiation, still more thoroughly refracting his intentions" (p. 299). And some voices are so far from the narrator that he completely reifies them and represents them as objects. In this metaphor, the narrator speaks through others by standing closer or further away from them. Rather and Braver, for instance, place themselves far from George Bush. This metaphor is useful, but still too one-dimensional to capture the diverse ways in which narrators can ventriloquate other voices.

Bakhtin also offers the more complex metaphor of "refraction." This appears in Bakhtin's relatively early book on Dostoevsky (e.g., 1963/1984a, p. 203; the first Russian edition of this book was published in 1929), but Bakhtin elaborates it more fully in the essay "Discourse in the Novel" (1935/1981). Here he describes the narrator's utterance as a ray of light entering a chamber filled with various gases that change its character. "The word, directed toward its object, enters a dialogically agitated and tension-filled environment of alien words, value judgments and accents, weaves in and out of complex interrelationships, merges with some, recoils from others, intersects with yet a third group" (p. 276). Ultimately the light reaches the object of the narrative utterance, which is like a crystal with various facets; depending on how the light was refracted by the various other voices in the preceding chamber, it illuminates certain facets in a particular pattern. If it had encountered different voices in the chamber, the pattern of facets illuminated would have been different.

> The living and unrepeatable play of colors and light on the facets of the image that it constructs can be explained as the spectral dispersion of the ray-word . . . in an atmosphere filled with the alien words, value judgments and accents through which the ray passes on its way toward the object; the social atmosphere of the word, the atmosphere that surrounds the object, makes the facets of the image sparkle. (p. 277)

This image presents perhaps the most complex metaphor for how the narrator's voice emerges only through interactions with various other voices represented in the narrative.

The example of Rather and Braver's narrative can help clarify these metaphors. Ventriloquation is the process through which a narrator adopts a social position in the storytelling event with respect to the types of voices he or she has indexed while describing the narrated event. Dan Rather introduces a story about the recent threat to George

Bush's credibility, and Rita Braver narrates the bulk of the story. Analysts can infer from indexical cues, and from the context that the cues make relevant, that Rather and Braver make Bush speak with the voice of a criminal defendant. But how do they ventriloquate this voice? That is, using the distance metaphor for ventriloquation, how far from Bush do they place themselves? As Braver herself adopts the position of mock prosecutor and Rather the role of mock witness for the prosecution, it is clear that they place themselves far away from Bush—on the other side of the line between right and wrong. They defend the truth, whereas Bush has ignored it.

The more complex refraction metaphor captures the nuances of this ventriloquation better. Rather and Braver do more than distance themselves from Bush. Their words index not only the criminal defendant role but also other positions and ideological struggles associated with Bush's acts. Politicians lie, and different groups in our social world interpret this differently: Some see it as a necessary evil; some decry the erosion of our democracy; some see it as an amusing yet also disgusting game. Rather and Braver's narrative enters this "atmosphere" of social positions and contestation around the question of political lies. The "ray of light" represented by the narrative is intensified by those like Lewis who say politicians' lies take a serious toll on our political system. Rather and Braver's narrative metaphorically reaches "the crystal," the object being described, in this case George Bush's actions. The narrative illuminates this object in part because it establishes certain social positions for the narrators themselves in the storytelling event. Rather and Braver position themselves as earnest public servants, doing the important job of prosecuting Bush and protecting the public.

So the inferential process from cues to voices to interactional positioning gets completed when the narrator adopts a position within the storytelling event with respect to the other voices indexed by the narrative. Bakhtin's metaphors are helpful in analyzing examples like Rather and Braver's narrative, where narrators do not represent the point of their narrative explicitly. It would have been ludicrous for Braver to say in a straightforward way: "I hereby set myself up as a sort of prosecutor, responsible for showing how Bush has deceived us and damaged our political system." Bakhtin explains how this sort of storytelling event can be enacted, without being translated into a representational message, as narrators position themselves with respect to other voices indexed in their stories.

Any narrative contains cues and voices that could establish more than one position for the narrator, however. How do hearers identify such a structure when they come across it, given that cues are often ambiguous and that the rudiments of many such structures might be present in any given narrative? In order to catch the relevant cues and make the right inferences, participants and analysts must know the culture—both the sorts of social groups and interactional events that might be presupposed in this speech community and the cues typically used to index these groups and events. For example, in order to identify Rather and Braver's narrative as a mock trial, participants and analysts must recognize this type of social event. Bakhtin stresses that a culture's stock of such events and cues is broad and diverse, and that it changes over time. Identifying the interactional positioning accomplished by a narrative is a contingent interpretive process: One needs to know the language, know the culture, and pick up the relevant patterns of indexical cues and relevant context as they emerge.

Analytic Tools for Identifying Voicing and Ventriloquation

Bakhtin's concepts of voicing, double voicing, and ventriloquation begin to provide a dialogic, mediated, and emergent approach to analyzing interactional positioning in narrative. Storytelling can position the narrator when a pattern of cues and relevant context emerges to establish a configuration of voices for various characters and a position for the narrator with respect to these various voices. In his description of this process, however, Bakhtin does not adequately specify the types of cues narrators use to accomplish voicing and ventriloquation.[6] Drawing on Silverstein (1993) and others, Wortham and Locher (1996) extend Bakhtin's approach by describing five types of cues that narrators use to index voices and to position themselves with respect to those voices: reference and predication; metapragmatic descriptors; quotation; evaluative indexicals; and epistemic modalization. This is not meant as an exhaustive list, but only as a set of heuristic tools one can use to begin an analysis of interactional positioning in any particular narrative.

Reference and predication. Reference is the picking out of things in the world through speech. Predication characterizes the objects picked out. When narrators refer to and predicate about characters in a narrative, they often identify those characters socially. That is, characters are referred to and predicated of in such a way that they fit identifiable social types. Narrators can also use the linguistic machinery that accomplishes reference and predication to position themselves with respect to those characters.

Reference to characters in a narrated world may be accomplished with the use of proper names, titles, kinship terms, or any of a number of other culturally variable possibilities. The narrator's choice of referring expression inevitably characterizes or voices the referent in some way. Consider these examples:

> <u>Tom</u> promised to take me to a movie this week; now <u>the bastard</u>
> [i.e., Tom] is trying to get out of it.
> That <u>klutz</u> [Sue] spilled coffee on me again today.

In both cases the narrator gives a strongly negative evaluation of the person referred to, primarily by using particular terms to refer to Tom and Sue. Consider another example: A narrator referring to a character as "Mr. Johnson" or "my cousin" puts herself in a particular social relationship to that character and may thereby position herself in a particular social universe with respect to the voice of that character. Some forms of reference strongly entail certain frameworks of relationship between the narrator and another ("my cousin"), while others do this less ("the man").

The use of adjectives and other predicates by the narrator can also voice and evaluate characters. Thus a noun that has little evaluative power by itself ("the man") may be made highly evaluative by adding an adjectival string:

> The surly man dressed in filthy rags
> The kind-faced man in the top hat

With such use of language the narrator places the characters in recognizable social groups and takes an evaluative stance with respect to them; that is, the narrator voices and ventriloquates them. Dan Rather uses this first type of cue, for instance, when he chooses to refer to Weinberger's notes as "grand jury evidence." He could have chosen other terms to refer to the notes. As described above, his choice of terms that index the ongoing legal procedures reinforces the quasi-legal character of the storytelling event.

Metapragmatic descriptors. These centrally include the so-called *verba dicendi*, or verbs of saying, which describe instances of language use. Such verbs are "metapragmatic" because they refer to and predicate about language in use (Silverstein, 1976). Characterizing someone's speech using metapragmatic verbs is a powerful means of voicing and ventriloquation. Consider these alternatives:

Tom spoke.
Tom lied.
Tom hemmed and hawed.
Tom whined.
Tom rhapsodized.

Each of these examples represents an instance of speaking in a particular way, with the narrator limiting the type of voice that the character Tom might have. In using one verb and not the others, the narrator can also provide a moral evaluation of Tom. In the CBS News example, Braver uses this device when she says that Bush "has changed his story" and when she describes him as "admitting" and "denying." These metapragmatic descriptions help establish that Bush speaks with the voice of a criminal defendant.

In English, the verb *to say* is the most value-neutral of the metapragmatic verbs. In most contexts it carries no evaluative presuppositions about the voice of the quoted speaker (cf. Goossens, 1982). On the other hand, a verb like *to filibuster,* meaning 'to deliver a barrage of verbiage intended to keep others from taking the floor in an interactional event,' describes an instance of speaking such that the quoted speaker is most likely someone officious, if not actually an official. Note that narrators can also use nominalized metapragmatic characterization of speech events (*speeches, lies, poems, promises,* and so on). Such terms refer to particular types of speech, and by characterizing the style or content of the speech, the terms can index voices for both narrators and characters. A "keynote address," for instance, is a particular kind of speech normatively delivered on particular kinds of occasions—and not, say, in the middle of a golf course.

Quotation. Quotation combines reference to the quoted speaker, metapragmatic verb, and quoted utterance in order to represent some instance of speaking. Quotation can range from near-absolute mimicry through quasi-direct discourse to indirect quotation (cf. H. Clark & Gerrig, 1990; Vološinov 1929/1973, p. 145). The first possibility attempts to recreate the utterance of the speaker, while the various degrees of indirection involve overt translation into the narrator's words. Consider these examples, with quotations arranged from more to less direct:

Sue (on the phone to the narrator): I'll be there in an hour.
Narrator: Sue said, "I'll be there in an hour."
Narrator: Sue said she'll be here in an hour.
Narrator: Sue said that she's coming soon.

Even in direct quotation, however, the narrator inevitably filters the quoted speaker's message, if only by selecting the quote, choosing the framing material, and using some type of intonation (H. Clark & Gerrig, 1990; Fludernik, 1993; Waugh, 1995). When a novelist puts words in a character's mouth, she has the opportunity to use words that identify the character as a particular sort of person, as a person who speaks with a certain voice. By choosing the quoted speech carefully, the novelist can also ventriloquate the character's words and position herself with respect to the character. Braver uses this device when she says that Bush "appeared to admit he knew something about the deal." The metapragmatic verb *admit* here can presuppose a legal defendant. The term *deal* can also presuppose a criminal scheme, and so it contributes to voicing Bush as a criminal and positioning Braver as a mock prosecutor or at least an earnest friend of the public who is exposing Bush's political lies.

Evaluative indexicals. According to Bakhtin, particular expressions or ways of speaking get associated with particular social groups when members of a group habitually speak in that way. Members of every speech community stereotypically associate certain utterances with certain types of people. These indexicals may be lexical items, grammatical constructions, accents, or any of a number of other linguistic patterns.

Use of such an indexical marks the speaker as being from the social group that characteristically uses that type of utterance, unless other indexes mark the utterance as parody or irony. With their choice of indexical forms speakers may index their occupations, regional origins, genders, and so on. Narrators can make characters speak with particular voices by putting particular indexes into their mouths or by using indexicals in describing them. Consider the following passage from a short story by Thomas Pynchon (1959):

> Presumably intelligent talk flickered around the room with the false brightness of heat lightning: in the space of a minute Siegel caught the words "Zen," "San Francisco," and "Wittgenstein," and felt a mild sense of disappointment, almost as if he had expected some esoteric language, something out of Albertus Magnus. (p. 205)

With the three terms in quotes Pynchon voices a roomful of people. This passage also illustrates ventriloquation. The three terms index particular social types, those who characteristically use words like this. But the narrator also positions himself with respect to these voices or types. His characterization of the talk as "presumably intelligent" expresses his evaluation.

Evaluative indexicals not only index particular voices but also position the narrator with respect to these voices. In the CBS News example, Rather uses evaluative indexicals in his introduction to the story. His first sentence starts: "There is new written evidence tonight concerning what President Bush knew and when he knew about the secret deal . . . ." During the Watergate scandal people used very similar wording to discuss "what the President knew and when he knew it" when referring to the criminal acts committed by the Nixon administration. By using similar wording to describe Bush, Rather indexes the serious crimes committed and serious consequences faced by Nixon, and thus he contributes to voicing Bush as a criminal and positioning himself as a critic of Bush.

Epistemic modalization. Epistemic modalizers compare the epistemological status of the storytelling and narrated events. Narrators can claim to have a God's-eye-view or to be merely participating in a contingent event of speaking. Narrators can also ascribe greater epistemic access to certain narrated characters and less to others. The "calibration" (Silverstein, 1993) of epistemic status across storytelling and narrated events can, for instance, be accomplished through formulae that place the narrated event out of space and time, as in "once upon a time." This work can also be done grammatically, through verb tenses and other types of linguistic forms.

Epistemic modalization contributes both to voicing and to ventriloquation. During the 1992 presidential campaign, for example, the *CBS Evening News* ran a regular segment called "Reality Check" in which reporters assessed the truth of candidates' claims. On many occasions the reporters would claim that candidates had insufficient information to substantiate their accusations about each other. Thus they voiced the candidates, characterizing them as politicians who "spin" limited information into unfounded but self-serving claims. And the reporters presented themselves as reasonable people who had looked up the relevant information and were now objectively presenting all the facts. By giving themselves this privileged epistemological position, the reporters were able to ventriloquate the candidates—the reporters aligned themselves with the public and shook their heads in disgust at the lying politicians (cf. Locher & Wortham, 1994; Wortham & Locher, 1999).

These five types of cues make Bakhtin's concepts of voicing and ventriloquation more empirically useful. In order to analyze the interactional positioning accomplished in narrative discourse, analysts can first study patterns in these five types of cues across a segment of conversation, and then they can use these patterns to infer the voicing and ventriloquation done by the narrator. It should be clear from the discussions of mediation that an analyst cannot mechanically apply these five tools to compute the voicing and ventriloquation in a narrative. The presuppositions of any cue can be changed in a given instance by newly relevant context. And cues establish meaning only as they solidify in some poetic structure. Interpretation of a narrative requires the analyst to identify this contingent structure, a process which cannot be done solely with reference to ready-made rules. But these five types of devices can nonetheless provide an analytic entry into the interpretation of narratives. By identifying instances of these devices, the analyst may be in a better position to identify the voices in play and to interpret the interactional positioning being done through the narrative. The next chapter illustrates this approach by analyzing the interactional positioning accomplished in one extended autobiographical narrative.

CHAPTER 4

Dialogic Analysis of an Autobiographical Narrative

Bakhtin's concepts of voice, double voicing and ventriloquation—as elaborated in a more systematic form in the last chapter—provide tools to analyze interactional positioning in narrative discourse. This chapter uses these tools to analyze the voices represented and the interactional positioning accomplished in Jane's autobiographical narrative.

OVERVIEW OF JANE'S LIFE

The first chapter introduced Jane's story, from her institutionalizations as a child to the episode in which she claimed her baby at the orphanage as a young adult. This section gives an overview of her life story, as she told it to a psychology graduate student as part of a research project. Jane had volunteered for the study by responding to an advertisement. She presumably expected to participate in a scientific study of autobiographical narrative, and the interviewer expected to gather data from a subject. When Jane arrived she was given an informed consent form, which she read and signed. The interviewer had been instructed to speak as little as possible, and she begins by asking "please tell me the story of your life as if it were a novel divided into chapters." Jane proceeds to tell her story for almost an hour with little prompting from the interviewer.

Jane's story includes 36 episodes, plus brief interludes in which Jane stops describing the narrated events and directly addresses the interviewer. The story includes 33 characters—not including the various narrated versions of herself that Jane describes—counting undifferentiated collective groups (e.g., the working-class students at Jane's high school) as 1 character. Of these 33, I would argue that 18 are minor characters; they are mentioned only briefly, and they do not seem to speak with voices salient in the story. The major characters, and their salient voices, will all be described below. Table 4.1 provides a breakdown of the 36 discrete events Jane describes.

Exploring the voicing and the interactional positioning accomplished in this autobiographical narrative, however, will require more than brief descriptions of the narrated events. Some cues as to the voices that might emerge in this narrative are provided by the list of characters represented in each episode. In order to develop a list of the salient voices with which various characters in her narratives speak, however, the following sections provide more detailed analyses of the indexical cues Jane uses while describing these characters.

Table 4.1 also shows that Jane describes various past selves (i.e., Jane as she was in the past) in 34 of the episodes. Inasmuch as some of these narrated selves appear at several points in the autobiographical narrative, in all about 22 distinct past selves are described.[1] Table 4.2 lists these 22 past selves and groups them by type, showing that Jane represents herself as oscillating between a passive, vulnerable voice and an active, assertive one. These two primary types of narrated self, passive and active, appear in two typical types of relationship throughout Jane's story. As she recounts episodes from her life, Jane presents herself as moving, four separate times, from being the passive victim of negligent caretakers and abusive institutions to actively asserting herself and showing the failed caretakers that she can successfully run her own life. Each time she takes this developmental step, however, she confronts a new situation that makes her once again a passive victim.

The central interpretive question for a dialogic analysis of Jane's narrative is to understand how Jane positions her storytelling self with respect to these two types of narrated selves and with respect to the interviewer. How does she ventriloquate the two voices her narrated selves speak with, in order to position herself in the storytelling event as a certain kind of person? It might seem initially that the positioning could be distorted or artificial, given that this was an interview and not a naturally occurring conversation. It would, of course, be helpful also to have recordings of Jane's spontaneous autobiographical narratives. For logistical reasons, that is not possible in this case. The weakness of interview data (i.e., decontextualization) is at least partly offset in these data because it is unusual to find naturally occurring spoken life stories as extensive as Jane's outside of interview or therapy settings. Furthermore, the interaction between life history interviewer and subject involves complex action (Crapanzano, 1984), and interviewees often slip into telling narratives of personal experience much as they would in everyday life (Labov, 1972; Linde, 1993).

In this interview, at least three types of interactional positioning are being enacted. First, and most saliently, Jane is engaged in a research interview. The typical positioning in a research interview involves an

Table 4.1 Episodes and Characters in Jane's Life Story

#	Lines	Events	Characters
1	1–12	setting: parents' situation	father, mother, grandparents
2	13–24	mother institutionalizes J at Academy	mother, McGee, J@7
3	25–55	J spends 5 years at Academy	J@7–12, mother, teachers, others
4	55–64	"normal" early childhood (f)	father, mother, J@0–7
5	64–72	grandparents send for J's mother	mother, grandparents, J@12
6	73–87	leaving the Academy	J@12, mother, neighbor
7	87–103	arriving in Louisville	grandparents, mother, J@12
8	103–114	description of "pathetic" teachers (f)	teachers, priest, J@7–12
9	115–124	being ostracized by Louisville Armenians	J@12, Armenians, grandparents, mother
10	125–130	mother institutionalizes J again	J@15, mother
11	130–139	J runs away from institution	J@16, grandparents, mother
12	139–150	J abused at second institution (f)	abusive girls, J@15–16
13	151–173	mother's first job and illness	J@16–17, mother, women, grandfather
14	174–186	mother's job as an executive	mother, J@16–18, customers, manager
15	187–206	extended review of past episodes	
16	206–228	J's enrollment in high school	J@16, grandmother, black and white students
17	229–260	high school	working class students, J@16–18, Dean, mother, art teacher
18	260–271	no family support for J's education	grandparents, women, mother, J@18
19	272–298	work and night school	J@19, mother
20	298–328	relationship with Robert	J@22, Robert
21	328–352	another job, and pregnancy	J@22–23, boss, mother
22	352–368	contacting Robert about pregnancy	J@23, Robert, Robert's mother
23	368–375	taking the baby to the orphanage	J@23, orphanage woman, baby
24	376–394	retrieving baby from the orphanage	J@23, orphanage woman, baby

(continued)

TABLE 4.1 (*continued*)

#	LINES	EVENTS	CHARACTERS
25	395–403	lying about alleged marriage	J@23, Robert, grandmother, family
26	403–412	raising preschool child	nanny, J@23–28, mother, baby
27	412–428	job and school-age child	J@28–30, son, mother, grandparents
28	429–435	mother's death	J@30, son, mother
29	436–452	changing neighborhoods	J@30, son
30	452–459	J's family not helping her education (*f*)	J-as-child, mother, grandparents
31	459–479	relationships with men, one woman	J@30ff., boyfriends, woman
32	480–532	first abortion (*f*)	J@24, boyfriend, son, Mob woman, pregnant teenager, mother
33	533–547	second abortion	J@34, son, women's organization
34	547–577	becoming active in women's movement	J@40–50, son
35	578–589	child leaves for college	J@43, son
36	589–600	J alone	J@57, son

(*f*) indicates a flashback, in which the episode actually occurred before episodes that have already been narrated. J refers to Jane.
J@7 refers to Jane at age 7.

investigator who maintains scientific distance and a subject who tries to provide accurate data. Second, Jane and this interviewer both act as if Jane could be evaluated on how well her performance matches that of other, cooperative research subjects. Jane seems worried on occasion about whether she is doing a good job in this respect. In this second type of interactional positioning, Jane appears insecure and tries to justify her performance to the interviewer—and at times this spills over into attempts to justify aspects of her life to the interviewer. Third, as a result of telling intimate details of her life to a stranger, one who is not expected to reciprocate with any self-revelation of her own, Jane becomes vulnerable in the storytelling event. At times Jane speaks as if she would like to position the interviewer as a sympathetic friend or even a therapist, instead of as an objective stranger treating her intimate experiences as data.

TABLE 4.2 Jane's Narrated Selves, Showing Oscillation between Passive and Active Voices

TYPE OF NARRATED SELF	EPISODE	NARRATED EVENTS
passive, vulnerable	2	J@7 going to Academy
	3, 8	J@7–12 in Academy
	5, 6	J@12 leaving Academy
	7	J@12 moving to Louisville
	9	J@12 in Louisville
	10	J@15 going to second institution
	12	J@15–16 in second institution
active, assertive	11	J@16 running away
passive, vulnerable	16	J@16 enrolling in high school
active, assertive	13, 14, 17	J@16–18 in high school
	18, 19, 30	J@18 going to college at night
passive, vulnerable	20	J@22, relationship with Robert
	21, 22,	J@22–23, pregnant
	23	J@23 taking baby to orphanage
active, assertive	24	J@23 claiming her son
	25, 26, 29	J@23ff. as good mother
	27, 28	J@23–30 caring for own mother
passive, vulnerable	32	J@24, first abortion
	31	J@30ff. in dead-end relationships
active, assertive	33	J@34, second abortion
	34	J@40–50 as women's activist
the narrating present	35, 36	J@57, alone

These events are arranged in the order of Jane's ages at the time they occurred.

The analyses in the next several sections show that, while all three types of interactional positioning are potentially in play at any point in the storytelling event, Jane's interactional position oscillates between more vulnerable moments in which she tries to position the interviewer as sympathetic listener and more assertive moments in which she tries to justify her performance to the interviewer. This interactional oscillation between vulnerability and self-justification is *in some respects* parallel to the oscillation between vulnerability and self-assertion that Jane represents as the narrated events. In some ways Jane projects the interviewer into the same role as her mother—as someone whom she alternately looked to for support and protection (which, in both narrated and storytelling events, never came) and someone to whom she also tried to assert and justify her own value as a person. There is also another type of partial parallel between the represented content and interactional positioning. Just as Jane's narrated self develops over the course of the story from being more passive as a child to being more assertive as an adult, over the course of the storytelling event Jane more vigorously asserts herself in her interaction with the interviewer.

The detailed analyses in the rest of this chapter show this emerging parallel between represented content and interactional positioning, and the next chapter describes how the parallel might contribute to Jane's narrative self-construction. I am not claiming, however, that this parallel is complete. Self-assertion is parallel to self-justification only in some respects. And the research interview type of interactional positioning, which the interviewer herself sticks to, contributes to the parallelism only in two respects: in its prohibition of emotional support and in the presupposition that a subject might provide better or worse data. The represented content and interactional positioning are not parallel in all ways, but those elements that *are* parallel may be particularly important to Jane's narrative self-construction.

I divide Jane's storytelling interaction with the interviewer into three sections: one in which she often acts passive and vulnerable; one in which she shifts from being passive to being more assertive; and one in which she generally acts assertive with respect to the interviewer. Within each of these three sections, I organize the discussion by analyzing in chronological order the central episodes that Jane narrates. In analyzing the passages, I will proceed by first analyzing the central voices, then analyzing how Jane the narrator ventriloquates these voices, then analyzing Jane's positioning with respect to the interviewer in the storytelling event. For definitions of the various types of cues, see the end of Chapter 3.

JANE ENACTS HER PASSIVE VOICE

First Institutionalization

After giving her name and briefly describing her parents' occupations, Jane begins the first episode of her life story. (In all the narratives reported in this chapter, "J" = Jane, and "I" = Interviewer.)

12 *J:* uh . . . <u>when</u> I was six and a half my parents were divorced. a:nd,
       my mother went into:
13   the <u>mar</u>keting field. and for <u>some</u> reason was talked <u>into</u>, by a
       man I've never
14   forgotten his name, by the name of Mister Mc<u>Gee</u>. uh: that I
       should uh, that <u>she</u>
15   should con<u>sid</u>er uh putting me in school, a <u>boar</u>ding school. and
       he recommended
16   Irish Girls Academy which is in New <u>York</u>.
17 *I:* is-were you <u>born</u> in New York?
18 *J:* I was <u>born</u> in New York, in the city. a:nd uh, she looked <u>into</u> it, and
       the:y had
19   some kind of <u>slid</u>ing scale and even though I was Armenian, the:y
       agreed to take me
20   for- I don't know, <u>fif</u>ty dollars a month, which <u>when</u> I- I remember-
       I don't know <u>why</u>
21   we were fifty dollars a month, but when you look <u>back</u> to, 1940
       fifty dollars a month
22   was a <u>lot</u> of money.
23 *I:* mm<u>hm</u>.
24 *J:* a <u>lot</u>. (2.0) I was there for <u>five</u> years.
25 *I:* so you <u>start</u>ed there when you were si[x
26 *J:*   [seven=
27 *I:* seven years old.=
28 *J:* seven [years old.=
29 *I:*   [and this- you <u>stayed</u> there all the[time?
                                                              [mm<u>hmm</u>.
30 *J:*   [until I was <u>twelve</u>. I saw my
          [mother on, <u>one</u>
31   weekend a month. one long- you know, you'd go home on <u>Fri</u>day
       night and come home
32   on Sunday night. sometimes they were- you were allowed to visit
       with your mother on
33   <u>Sun</u>days only. <u>those</u> <u>five</u> <u>years</u> we:re (1.0) ho<u>rren</u>dous.
34 *I:* mmhm.
35 *J:* the teachers at the Academy, <u>nine</u> out of ten of them came from
       Europe.
36   extra<u>or</u>dinarily oppressed women. I mean, we're talking, I mean
       it- it almost goes
37   without <u>say</u>ing, but <u>unbe</u>lievable. um quite <u>mean</u> and vin<u>dic</u>tive. I
       was <u>beat</u>en, which

38   my mother did not <u>know</u> about. u:m, my mother also, was <u>not</u> of
          good <u>health</u>. she'd
39   had pneu<u>mo</u>nia several times as a child, had a <u>hole</u> in her lung.
          and <u>twice</u> in that five
40   years I remember different people coming to <u>see</u> me, and I found
          out later on that my
41   mother had been near <u>death</u>.
42 I: <u>mm</u>hm.
43 J: and there was con<u>cern</u> for me. (1.0) or for my not finding <u>out</u> or
          pre<u>pa</u>ring me for it,
44 either one, I'm not sure at this point. um, those five years have,
          <u>haun</u>ted me.
45 I: <u>hn</u>mm

This episode contains five characters: Jane at age 7, Jane's mother, Mr. McGee, the teachers, and the friends of Jane's mother. These friends do not reappear in the story, nor do they speak with a voice that plays any important role in the rest of the story. But all four of the other characters do speak with salient voices that recur. Identifying these voices will require an analysis of the indexical cues Jane uses to characterize them.

Jane presents her 7-year-old narrated self as passive and vulnerable. People decided things for her and did things to her. Jane says, for instance, that the Academy "agreed to take me" (line 19). Once at the school, she was subjected to rigid rules—"you were allowed to visit with your mother on Sundays only" (lines 32–33). Jane also presents her 7-year-old self as a victim, who was "beaten" by the abusive teachers. Jane voices these teachers as both oppressed and abusive. They were "extraordinarily oppressed women" and also "quite mean and vindictive" (lines 36–37). On one or two occasions later in the interview she expresses some sympathy for the teachers, presenting them as oppressed women forced to live in a constricted world. But most often she simply presents them as cruel and unjust.

In this passage Jane also voices Mr. McGee and her mother. She characterizes Mr. McGee by using metapragmatic verbs and quoted speech (lines 13–15). As an overall characterization of the verbal interaction between her mother and Mr. McGee, Jane says that her mother "was talked into" institutionalizing her. This characterizes Mr. McGee as actively wanting to get Jane institutionalized and her mother as resisting at first but then yielding. Next Jane uses indirect quotation to represent what Mr. McGee might have said, that her mother "should consider putting me" in the institution. Note the contrast between this quotation and the initial metapragmatic verb "talked into." Saying that an interlocutor "should consider" a course of action seems less forceful than "talking someone into" that action. What is the effect of this mismatch between the metapragmatic verb and the quotation that follows it? In the indirect quotation Jane gives an image of Mr. McGee being relatively nondirective, but she (as the narrator) suggests with her metapragmatic characterization that he was in fact intent on getting her institutionalized. He had an institution in mind, and he "recommended" it immediately. I argue that this contrast between the metapragramatic verb and the quotation makes Mr. McGee seem a smooth, manipulative person. He makes Jane's mother think he is simply recommending something, but in fact he pushes her toward doing what he himself wanted all along.

Two other sorts of evidence support my reading of the voice given to Mr. McGee in this passage. First, a few lines later Jane notes that the fee for her boarding school was a *"lot* of money" (line 22). This provides a motive for Mr. McGee and the Academy—greed. Second, Jane voices her mother as weak. Her mother was the type that someone could "talk into" institutionalizing her child. At other points in the narrative, as we will see, Jane's mother needs to be told what to do by others, and she follows this advice. Jane partly excuses her mother for this by citing her poor health. She presents Mr. McGee as more responsible for her institutionalization than her mother, because he took advantage of her mother's weakness to get what he wanted.

So far Jane has represented four salient voices in her narrative: her mother, a potential caregiver who does not adequately care for her; Mr. McGee, a self-interested person who recommends an abusive institution for her; the teachers, heartless representatives of the institution who abuse her; and Jane herself, a passive, vulnerable victim. These four voices recur at least four times in Jane's narrative. The same people do not always occupy the four roles. In a later episode, for instance, the father of Jane's child speaks with the voice of a potential caregiver who does not adequately care for her and the orphanage employee speaks as a heartless representative of the institution. Figure 4.1 shows these four recurring voices and their characteristic relationships. The arrow from the recommenders to the failed caregivers indicates that the recommenders speak with authority and influence the caregivers' actions toward Jane. The arrow from the abusers to Jane indicates that they have control over her. (The four different shapes used for these voices have no intrinsic meaning, but they identify the recurring voices in subsequent figures.)

　　As described in Chapter 3, narrators do more than presuppose voices for their characters. Narrators also position themselves with respect to, or ventriloquate, these voices. By giving such negative voices to the manipulative and greedy Mr. McGee and to the mean and vindictive teachers, Jane clearly distances herself from these two voices. She is more ambivalent about her mother. Someone who sends her daughter off to such a "horrendous" institution is not appealing, but Jane partly excuses her on medical grounds. What about the relationship between Jane at age 7 and Jane the narrator? There appears to be a strong connection. Jane notes, "I've never forgotten the name" of Mr. McGee (lines 13–14) and "those five years have *haunt*ed me" (line 44). So her experiences as a young child still influence her as an adult.

　　A full account of Jane the narrator's interactional positioning will also describe the relationship between Jane and the interviewer in the storytelling event. In my interpretation, Jane makes an implicit plea

FIGURE 4.1 Four Voices that Recur in Jane's Narrative

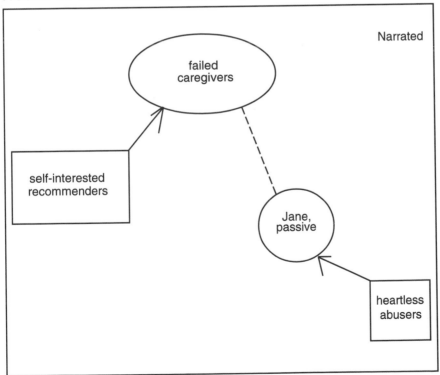

for the interviewer to take a more sympathetic position in the storytelling event, but the interviewer does not do so. After Jane first describes how she was institutionalized as a child, the interviewer could have appropriately responded in the storytelling event with sympathy. But the interviewer responds in a more distanced way, with a request for information (line 17). Jane follows this by answering the interviewer's question, but then she immediately indexes the Academy's greedy motive for institutionalizing her (lines 21–22). This, again, could have been followed by a sympathetic response from the interviewer. But the interviewer again requests information (line 25). Then at line 29 the interviewer finally reacts in a way that might be sympathetic, responding to Jane's statement that as a small child she would only occasionally see her mother by asking, "you stayed there [at the institution] all the time?"

As described in Chapter 2, utterances often only come to have clear meaning in light of subsequent contextualization. The interviewer's question at line 29 might establish a more sympathetic, less-distanced relationship between Jane and the interviewer, but participants and analysts cannot know at the moment of utterance whether it does in fact accomplish this. As the interaction proceeds, Jane ratifies the interviewer's (potential) sympathy in some ways but not in others. She initially distances herself from her experiences as a child, by describing those experiences using the indefinite pronoun *you* (lines 31–32). She might instead have closed the distance between narrated and storytelling events by using *I* throughout this passage, and this would have more strongly presupposed the interviewer's (potential) sympathy. But in other ways Jane does presuppose that the interviewer's comment was sympathetic, when she describes those years as "horrendous" (line 33) and says that they have "haunted" her (line 44). At the end of the passage, then, two distinct types of interactional positioning are in play. Both Jane and the interviewer clearly presuppose that they are engaged in a research interview. But they may also be presupposing that Jane's past continues to affect her emotionally, and this might position the interviewer as someone who could appropriately be sympathetic. A few indexical cues seem to presuppose this second type of interactional positioning, but a pattern of cues has not yet emerged and thus this type of positioning has not yet solidified.

As the storytelling interaction continues, Jane appears to presuppose the interviewer's sympathy more strongly.

46   *J:* I am so against boarding schools. anytime I hear a friend talk about
        putting a child in

47   a- in an institution, uh oh, it's better for the <u>child</u>, o:r, we can get
        on with <u>our</u> life,
48   or I can make more <u>mon</u>ey, or the child will get a good edu<u>ca</u>tion,
        <u>I</u> go into a
49   <u>ti</u>rade.
50   *I:* <u>mm</u>hm.
51   *J:* you <u>cannot</u> <u>put</u> a child in an institution from age seven to twelve o:r
        any age. those are
52   the <u>for</u>mative years. and that has <u>haun</u>ted me. and I can <u>hon</u>estly
        say that I think that
53   that was the <u>mis</u>erable time in my life. and the most <u>help</u>less.
        (1.0) u:m (2.0)
54   *I:* would you <u>say</u> that that- <u>boar</u>ding- those <u>boar</u>ding school years,
        would you- call that
55   the <u>first</u> chapter or?
56   *J:* yes, becau- well, maybe the <u>sec</u>ond chapter. the first chapter was
        (3.0) vaguely
57   remembered because all was quote normal unquote.

For most of this segment Jane moves out of the narrative and draws conclusions from her story that are applicable to present-day practices. She describes how she, as an adult, goes "into a tirade" when others talk about institutionalizing their children (lines 48–49). Then she reiterates that her first institutionalization "has haunted" her, and she calls it the "most helpless" time of her life (lines 52–53). All this reinforces that Jane had a terrible experience which still affects her. Thus Jane seems to presuppose that the interviewer was indeed being sympathetic in her question about conditions at the school (at line 29).

Figure 4.2 depicts both the narrated and the storytelling events together at this point in the narrative. The narrated event—in the embedded rectangle—contains the four recurring voices that Jane represents while describing her first institutionalization. The storytelling event—signified by the outer rectangle—involves Jane and the interviewer. I place Jane below the interviewer to indicate that she acts in a more passive, vulnerable way in the storytelling event at this point. By positioning the interviewer as a sympathetic listener and herself as a victim still affected by horrendous early experiences, Jane might be acting vulnerable in the storytelling event. The double dotted line between Jane in the storytelling event and Jane in the narrated event indicates the parallel between her narrated and storytelling roles (i.e., that she is vulnerable in both).

FIGURE 4.2 The Storytelling Event Early in the Story

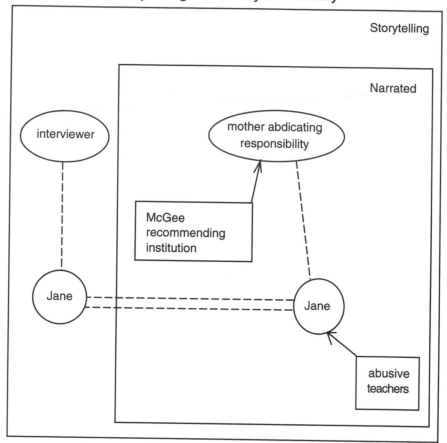

Figure 4.3 presents a key for understanding all the figures in this chapter. I indicate each of the five salient voices with a different shape. (Jane voices her narrated self as active and assertive in later episodes.) The figures also depict the three different types of relationship Jane takes up with respect to the interviewer in the storytelling event. The dotted line between the interviewer and Jane, when Jane positions herself as "vulnerable," indicates that the interviewer does not respond to Jane's positioning of her as potentially sympathetic. The solid line between Jane and the interviewer, when Jane positions herself as a "cooperative research subject," indicates that the interviewer does ratify this positioning. The arrow from Jane to the interviewer, when Jane

FIGURE 4.3 Key for Figures in Chapter 4

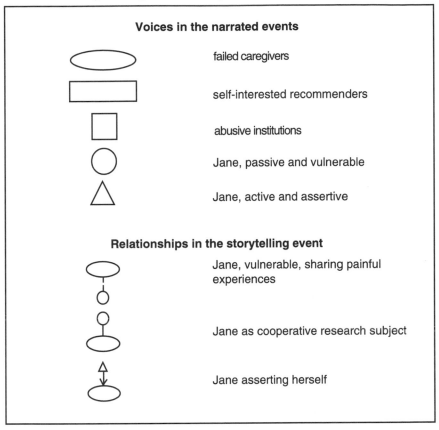

Voices in the narrated events

failed caregivers

self-interested recommenders

abusive institutions

Jane, passive and vulnerable

Jane, active and assertive

Relationships in the storytelling event

Jane, vulnerable, sharing painful experiences

Jane as cooperative research subject

Jane asserting herself

positions herself as "assertive," indicates that Jane asserts herself against the interviewer.

After Jane positions herself as vulnerable when describing her first institutionalization, however, the interviewer goes back to presupposing that they are engaged in a research interview when she asks about the organizational structure of the narrative. By asking about the "chapter" represented by this part of the narrative (lines 54–55), the interviewer indexes her earlier request that Jane break her life story into chapters. Because this request was part of the explicit research protocol that the interviewer read to begin their interaction, her use of "chapter" presupposes that she and Jane are engaging in a research interview where displays of sympathy would be less appropriate.

Note also that the interviewer does not presuppose the same voicing and ventriloquation that Jane uses in her description of the first institutionalization. By using the word "institution," which indexes places like "mental institutions," and by describing herself as passively subjected to the institution, Jane presupposes that she was imprisoned against her will in an unjust and cruel place. But at line 54 the interviewer refers to this place as a "boarding school," not an institution. And at lines 25 and 29 the interviewer casts Jane as grammatically active. She "started there" and "stayed there," as if she had some agency. These cues, in addition to her question about the "chapter," show the interviewer resisting Jane's attempt to position her as appropriately sympathetic. At line 56 Jane goes along with the interviewer's move to turn the storytelling interaction away from a sympathetic conversation and back into a research interview, when she answers the question about chapters and when she continues (for a while) to tell her story without any cues that might indicate her current emotional vulnerability.

At this point in the storytelling interaction, then, Jane has swung back and forth between two positions: from cooperative research subject to emotionally vulnerable woman who could use some sympathy and then back to cooperative research subject. Sometimes both Jane and the interviewer treat Jane's story as a piece of data. When the interviewer asks for clarification about "chapters," for instance, she and Jane presuppose that Jane's past experiences are data in this way. Because the interview was in fact taking place as part of a scientific research project, both Jane and the interviewer can and do often presuppose that this scientific type of storytelling event could plausibly be going on. At other points, however, Jane acts vulnerable in the storytelling event. Jane not only describes but later on enacts her vulnerability when she breaks down and cries during the interview. The sections below analyze three instances in which Jane cries because the events she recounts are still painful for her. At these moments the interviewer must take up some position with respect to Jane. The interviewer consistently presupposes only the research interview type of storytelling event, although that one utterance of hers (at line 29) might have been construed as sympathetic. As the storytelling event continues, Jane herself continues to oscillate in and out of a vulnerable position.

Second Institutionalization

In the 20 lines following the last segment, Jane continues to treat the storytelling event as a research interview. She answers the interviewer's question about what chapters the various episodes represent, and she gives a brief (flashback) description of her parents' marriage and divorce and her mother's situation after the divorce. Then she returns to the main story line. After Jane had been in the Academy for 5 years, her mother's health deteriorated so much that Jane's grandparents "sent for" her mother. So Jane and her mother moved to Louisville.

77 J: so: I can remember u:m one- late September day. u:h and it's
        interesting how things
78   are etched in your memory.
79 I: mmhm.
80 J: leaving the Irish Girls Academy, u:m (3.0) when a chi:ld from- I
        mean when half
81   your life, already, at the age of twelve, is spent in an institution,
82 I: mhmm.
83 J: uhm (2.0) it was a shock for me to leave there. [God knows I was
        glad.=
84 I: [mhmm.
85 J: =u:m but- there was no one to talk about it to. u:m there was no
        wa:y of even being in
86   touch with those emotions, it's just that I can look back now. uh
        we're talking forty-
87   five years ago. and remember leaving that place.
88 I: mmhm
89 J: we packed up, m-. Mamma sold most of her possessions, beautiful
        possessions I
90   might add, uh, and left some in storage boxes uh with a woman
        named Melinda
91   who lived upstairs. uh, we never saw those boxes again. so we
        came to Louisville
92   with little or nothing. my grandparents we:re very comfortable.
        my grandfather had
93   been a very successful businessman. so we lived in u:h we moved
        in with my
94   grandparents. uh my mother- once again, had her bedroom that
        she had as a child.
95   and the small bedroom with the adjoining bath, sharing with my
        mother's bedroom
96   which was the maid's room. I want you to know, I got the maid's
        room.
97 I: mhmm.

98   *J:* my grandfather had built this building in 1910, and there was um
         ac<u>com</u>modations fo:r
99   uh, <u>help</u>.
100 *I:* mhmm.
101 *J:* so <u>we</u> lived in Eastside from 1945. (2.0) I- don't even remember
         which- until <u>what</u>
102   year, but anyway that wa:s, a <u>big</u> move. so <u>chap</u>ter one would be
         u:h (3.0) your <u>bas</u>ic
103   everyday (2.0) <u>tod</u>dler, yeah a <u>nor</u>mal toddler stage.=
104 *I:* <u>mm</u>hm.
105 *J:* chapter <u>two</u> would be uh (1.0) the institutionalizing of a- of a
         <u>hu</u>man being, from age
106   seven to twelve, which wa:s u:::nh (3.0) [voice quivering] it <u>still</u>
         bothers me. (11.0) °I'm
107   <u>so</u>rry.°
108 *I:* °it's okay.° (7.0)
109 *J:* [voice quivering] and then <u>Lou</u>isville was another chapter. (2.0) I
         went there (3.0)
110   <u>ne</u>ver having freedom before. (4.0) in the Academy, we went to
         Mass <u>e</u>very week for
111   five years. (2.0) we were <u>ri</u>tualistically, <u>cri</u>ticized and- uh, a<u>bused</u>.
         (1.0) by a bunch of
112   pa<u>the</u>tic women. (2.0) who when- the priest who said the Mass
         would <u>walk</u> into
113   the school you would have thought that Jesus Christ him<u>self</u> had
         entered the
114   premises. (1.0) [sniff] uh (1.0) and so I <u>went</u> to Louisville,

The voicing for Jane and her mother in this segment remains similar to that established in Jane's narration of her first institutionalization. Jane portrays her mother as passive and childlike. In addition to
being "sent for" by her parents, she "once again had her bedroom that
she had as a child" (line 94). Jane herself, despite the fact that she had
been rescued from the institution, continues to be somewhat deprived.
As she says, "I want you to know, I got the *maid's* room" (line 96). Jane
the narrator certainly acknowledges that life with her grandparents was
comfortable—if, as she says later, interpersonally difficult—compared
to the institution. But she nonetheless points out what she considers
the indignity of getting the maid's room.

Note the clause "I want you to know" in line 96. Here Jane steps
out into the storytelling event for a moment, with an implicit plea for
the interviewer to notice her grandparents' alleged mistreatment of her.

This might presuppose the sympathetic or therapeutic type of interactional positioning introduced earlier. Jane's use of "we're talking" at line 86 puts her into a group with the interviewer and thus might also presuppose a more sympathetic relationship (see also the repeated uses of "we're talking" at lines 36, 172, and 230). For most of this segment, however, Jane acts like a cooperative research subject, and she remains distanced from the events she describes. She uses indefinite *you* again (lines 78–81), which distances her from the narrated events. In lines 83–86 she talks analytically about her experience of leaving the Academy. Jane maintains her position as a cooperative research subject up through line 106, where she is summarizing the various chapters of her story so far. But then the distance between narrated and storytelling events abruptly breaks down.

This is the first of three places during the interview where Jane cries. She has said earlier that her experiences in the Academy still haunt her in the present, and here she enacts this when she is unable to get through a summary of that chapter in her life. By her action Jane shows that the trauma of that institutionalization continues to influence her. The interviewer here adopts what might be a sympathetic stance. She says "it's okay" to comfort Jane (line 108). But then she does not say anything else. In most settings an interlocutor would respond to such a painful story and a crying narrator by saying something else sympathetic, or at least by changing the subject. But the interviewer here acts to maintain her position as a research interviewer, and she waits for Jane to collect herself.

This Jane does, and she goes on to finish her summary of chapters. But then Jane returns immediately to further description of the Academy (line 110). Here she reinforces and extends the voicing and ventriloquation of the teachers that she did earlier. Now the teachers are not only mean and vindictive but also engage in "ritualistic" abuse of children. This description implies that the institution was like a cult that does horrible things to vulnerable people. She also describes the teachers as "pathetic" (line 112), for their worship of the officiating priest. The conditional verb tense in lines 112–113 indicates that Jane the narrator herself finds the teachers' worship of the priest irrational and ridiculous. That is, the conditional presupposes that the teachers acted as if the priest were Jesus Christ, while anyone knows that he cannot be, and so Jane concludes that the teachers behave as they do out of some pathetic and irrational motive.

In the storytelling event, Jane's breakdown in this passage clearly takes her out of the position of cooperative research subject and puts her into the vulnerable position of someone sharing a personal story about experiences that both were and are upsetting. For the second time, then, Jane swings into a more vulnerable position in the story-telling event. But from the interviewer's responses—extended silence at lines 106–108 and the request about "chapters" at lines 54–55—Jane realizes that she is not behaving like a cooperative research subject. She acknowledges this when she apologizes at line 107. Later in the interview as well, Jane and the interviewer presuppose that one might do a better or worse job at being a research subject (e.g., at lines 188, 447–448, 564–574). When she breaks down and acts vulnerable in the storytelling event, this might mean that Jane is doing a bad job in the interview. So she apologizes, recovers her position as a co-operative research subject, and goes on to summarize the "chapters" in her life.

After breaking down and crying, Jane gives a brief description of her difficult life in Louisville. Then she goes on to describe her second institutionalization.

124 *J:* (2.0) so: we uh lived with my grandparents for a few years, and u:h that was very

125   difficult. and once again, for some reason, I don't know why, but my mother thought

126   that it would be best that I: (1.0) be placed in a private school again. [sniff] and this

127   time she picked u:h this is u:h age fifteen, she was- it was again recommended, my

128   mother was u:h easily influenced as intelligent as she- she was, she was easily

129   influenced. to a place called Carter's School for Girls, anothe:r, god awful institution.

130   and I was there for a year and a half. and u:h, evidently my u:h character was being

131   developed and- o:r either by: age or by anger, because I ran away in November of '49.

132   I went there in May of '48, and in November of '49, I ran away. and u:h (3.0) I went to

133   the drug store that used to be at the corner of First and Main and I called my mother at

134   my grandparents' house. and I refused to tell her where I wa:s unti- I negotiated with

135   her. I- I look back now-, how I did that at the age of fifteen amazes me. sixteen.

136   and I negotiated with her that I wouldn't come home unless she-
      promised me that I

137   would never go <u>back</u> there. u:m (2.0) they a<u>greed</u>. picked me up,
      and then I-

138   proceeded to- spill out my <u>heart</u> and my <u>guts</u> when I got back to
      my grandparent's

139   house, who were ap<u>palled</u> at all that went on at this girl's school.
      um, I who came

140   from a <u>so</u>-called, you know- <u>good</u> family, uh, <u>proper</u> family, upper-
      middle-class

141   family, was <u>thrown</u> into this uh insti<u>tu</u>tion that- was pre<u>dom</u>inantly
      a dumping ground

142   for the courts, fo:r a <u>lot</u> of young women who u:m fought- that
      <u>couldn't</u>- uh be: put into

143   <u>fos</u>ter homes or their- they were considered in<u>cor</u>rigible and,
      even- even <u>street</u>

144   people. You had this hor<u>ren</u>dous combina[tion.

145 *I:*   [mhmm.

146 *J:* so, I: was u:h sub<u>jec</u>ted to um (2.0) a- a side of- of u:h the <u>human</u>
      race at a very early

147   age without any foun<u>da</u>tion to fend for myself. I was a<u>bused</u>, uh
      my- my- I took all

148   my recor- you know, when you're a <u>young</u>ster you don't know
      anybody, I took my

149   <u>record</u> collection, it wa- de<u>stroyed</u>, <u>stol</u>en, everything was <u>stol</u>en
      from me there. I-

150   didn't know how to <u>fend</u> for myself.

In this passage Jane indexes three familiar voices. Jane's mother was "easily influenced" and again acted on someone's recommendation to institutionalize Jane (lines 127–129). Like the Academy, this institution was "god awful" (line 129). Jane gives the other institutionalized girls a voice similar to the one she gave the teachers at the Academy. These girls "abused" Jane, "destroyed" her belongings and were generally "incorrigible" (lines 143–149). Jane herself, before she ran away, "didn't know how to fend for" herself (lines 149–150), and was passive and vulnerable.

Figure 4.4 depicts these voices. The narrated event contains the same four voices as in Jane's description of her first institutionalization, although this time she does not describe the person who recommended the second institution. Jane hints later in the interview that

FIGURE 4.4 Jane's Second Institutionalization

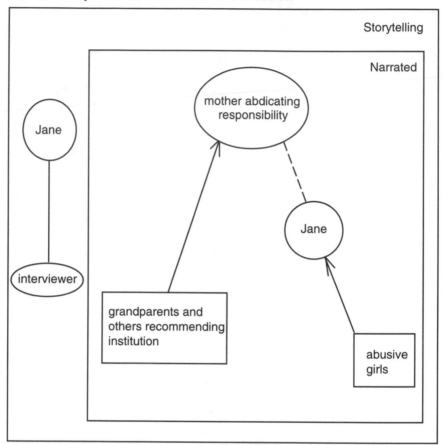

her grandparents might have encouraged her mother to institutionalize her, so I place them in this role in the figure. Once again, Jane's
mother passively acquiesces to someone's advice and subjects Jane to
an abusive institution.

The figure also depicts the storytelling event at this point in the
interview. The solid line from Jane's storytelling self to the interviewer
shows Jane's position as a cooperative research subject who remains
in control and presents her experiences to the interviewer as data. She
describes these events objectively, as would be appropriate for a research
interview. The figure places Jane above the interviewer because she is
no longer vulnerable in the storytelling event. Her actions in the story-

telling event at this point give no indication that her second institutionalization has any continuing negative impact on her.

Jane also does some ventriloquation of her mother and grandparents in this passage. In lines 139–140 she says that she "comes from a so-called, you know, good family." The phrase "good family" here echoes with the voices of people like her grandparents: upper-middle-class people who believe themselves morally superior to other groups in the society. By prefacing this phrase with "so-called," Jane the narrator makes clear that she does not endorse these moral pretensions. In an earlier passage Jane also distances herself from her grandparents' pretensions. In describing her grandfather's building she says: "there was accommodations for uh help" (lines 98–99). Upper-middle-class people from an earlier era, like Jane's grandparents, often used *help* as a euphemism to refer to servants. Jane's hesitation before uttering the word "help," and her tone of voice, indicate that she herself does not comfortably use this word. Thus she distances herself from people like her grandparents who felt comfortable putting themselves above members of the working classes. At lines 139–140 Jane might also be pointing to the irony of her grandparents' pretensions, given that her "so-called good family" was willing to institutionalize her for almost half of her first 16 years.

In addition to mirroring the voicing from Jane's first institutionalization, however, this passage also describes another voice for Jane's narrated self. This time Jane did not passively endure the abusive institution. She ran away. Jane the narrator describes how this assertive narrated self "negotiated" with her mother and grandparents (lines 134ff.). The type of speech event characteristically described as a "negotiation" involves two parties with approximately equal status. Thus Jane voices her narrated self as mature and assertive. Figure 4.5 depicts the changed configuration of narrated roles at this point in the narrative. The thick barrier in the narrated event represents the distance that Jane has placed between herself and the former abusers. The arrow from Jane to her mother and grandparents indicates that she has transformed her situation by asserting herself and forcing her relatives to change their behavior toward her. The voices and relationships within the narrated event in this figure signify the second of the two configurations that recur throughout Jane's narrative. First, Jane was passive and vulnerable. Those who should have cared for her did not, and Jane was subjected to abuse. But now Jane is active and assertive. She acts to protect herself from the abusers, and forces the failed caregivers to acquiesce. I use a new shape, the triangle, to represent Jane when she speaks with this active and assertive voice.

FIGURE 4.5 Jane Acts to Defend Herself

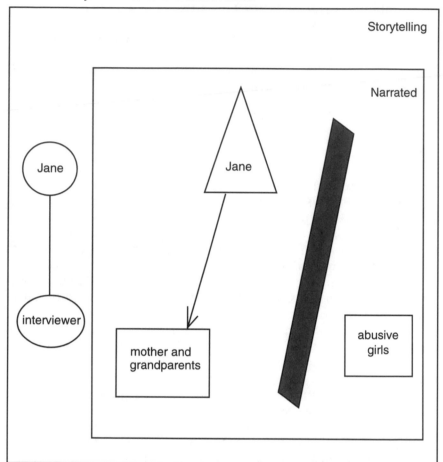

Jane the narrator also indicates the shift from her vulnerable narrated self to her assertive narrated self by shifting her grammatical constructions at the point of transformation in line 131. In the lines immediately preceding 131, Jane almost never presents herself as an agent.

I was regarded as other (117)
I was ostracized (118)
I jumped from one space of being ostracized into another (122–123)
my mother thought that it would be best that I be placed in a
    private school (125–126)

> I was there for a year and a half (130)
> evidently my character was being developed (130–131)

In the lines immediately following her narrated transformation, Jane almost always presents herself as an agent.

> I ran away (131)
> I went there (132)
> I ran away (132)
> I went to the drug store (132–133)
> I called my mother (133)
> I refused to tell her (134)
> I negotiated with her (134–135)

Thus Jane also uses her choice of grammatical constructions to voice the first narrated self as passive and the second as active.

Jane's description of herself at age 16 indicates that she has not fully left behind her more passive and vulnerable self, however. After describing her "negotiation," Jane describes a second speech event between herself and her relatives: She "proceeded to spill out my heart and my guts" to them (line 138). She had the strength to defend herself, but she still wanted support from her caregivers. Neither her mother nor her grandparents ever filled this role adequately, and for most of her life Jane had to assert herself without support. Only later in life, when Jane found a supportive group in the women's movement, did anyone successfully fill the role of caregiver for her. Even then, as I will describe below, Jane still swings back into a passive, vulnerable position at times.

Table 4.3 lists the salient voices from the first three central episodes of Jane's story—her two institutionalizations and her running away from the reform school. This table presents two sets of voices that recur in the narrated events throughout Jane's story. In all Jane describes five episodes—three in addition to the two institutionalizations—in which self-interested recommenders and failed caregivers subject Jane to an abusive institution, which she passively endures. But in three other episodes—two in addition to her running away from the reform school—Jane assets herself against the failed caregivers and selfish recommenders, and she actively protects herself from the institution that has abused her.

In the storytelling event, Jane acts like a research subject while recounting her second institutionalization and her subsequent escape. She has recovered from the earlier breakdown of boundaries between narrated and storytelling events, where she enacted how past experi-

TABLE 4.3 Two Sets of Voices in Jane's Narrative

EPISODE	SELF-INTERESTED RECOMMENDERS	FAILED CAREGIVERS	ABUSIVE INSTITUTIONS	JANE'S VOICE	CAREGIVERS AND RECOMMENDERS, OVERCOME	ABUSIVE INSTITUTIONS, NEUTRALIZED	SUCCESSFUL CAREGIVERS
First institutionalization	Mr. McGee	Jane's mother	Teachers at the Academy	Passive and vulnerable			
Second institutionalization	Jane's grandparents	Jane's mother	Girls at the reform school	Passive and vulnerable			
Running away from reform school				Active and assertive	Jane's grandparents and mother	Girls at the reform school	

ences still haunt her by crying while recounting her first institutionalization. Jane reports her second institutionalization as a good research subject should. She steps out of the narrative briefly while recounting this episode, with comments to the interviewer like: "how I did that at the age of [sixteen] amazes me" (line 135); and "I didn't know how to fend for myself" (lines 149–150). But she maintains her position as a cooperative research subject and shows no sign of breaking down.

Note the partial parallel between narrated and storytelling positions in Jane's descriptions of her two institutionalizations. In her first institutionalization, Jane voices her narrated self as passive and vulnerable. While summarizing this episode Jane herself acts vulnerable in the storytelling event, in a way that shows how the narrated victimization continues to affect her and might entice the interviewer to be more sympathetic. At this point in the narrative, Jane's narrated and storytelling selves are both passive and vulnerable. After her second institutionalization, Jane asserts herself and forces her relatives to treat her better. In the storytelling event at this point, however, Jane is simply positioning herself as a cooperative research subject. Later in the storytelling event, as described below, Jane does assert herself with respect to the interviewer. But at this point the only parallel is between her vulnerable narrated and storytelling selves. In the present, as in the past, she cycles into and out of a passive, vulnerable position.

Note that Jane's recurring enactments of her vulnerable self in the storytelling event show that her autobiographical narrative does not simply describe the established fact of her development into an active and assertive woman. If Jane developed an active, assertive self once and for all when she ran away at age 16, why does she still enact the vulnerable self in the storytelling event at age 57? I argue that the assertive self Jane first showed at age 16 needs to be maintained. She repeatedly enacts the transformation from vulnerable to assertive, in the storytelling event, because it is in these sorts of enactments that her self gets established and maintained.

JANE ENACTS THE TRANSITION FROM PASSIVE TO ACTIVE

Adolescence

After she escaped from the second institution, Jane and her mother moved into their own apartment near her grandparents. For several years after this move, Jane did not experience the sort of abuse she endured during her two institutionalizations. She nonetheless presents herself as ostracized and alone during much of this time, and she continues to be victimized. When she went to high school, for instance, she was unable to get into a quality school.

224 *J:* so we <u>tried</u> to put me into Eastside High School where again, I
            would be with, <u>kids</u>
225   that were, <u>from</u> Eastside, <u>bet</u>ter families and what have you. and
            the <u>boun</u>dary for
226   al<u>low</u>ance to go into Eastside High School was Fifteenth Street,
            and we lived, <u>east</u> of
227   Fifteenth Street.=
228 *I:* mmhmm.
229 *J:* so the <u>only</u> other high school left, was Louisville Vo<u>ca</u>tional at
            Nineteenth Street.
230   once a<u>gain</u>, we are talking, <u>lower</u>-class, <u>un</u>educated, <u>street</u>
            men<u>tal</u>ity. so- <u>once</u> again I
231   was <u>thrown</u> into:, <u>situ</u>ations and sur<u>round</u>ings tha:t was, not
            familiar to me. I <u>still</u>
232   wasn't accepting it. and yet, I- I had no choice. I was <u>put</u> into that
            school, it was the
233   only school that I could <u>go</u> to. (2.0) I made the <u>best</u> of the
            situation. um (1.0) I was
234   one of the <u>top</u> students in the school because I had such a fi:ne
            foundation as an
235   education in New York, that's the <u>one</u> good thing that I got, in
            the Academy was I <u>did</u> get a very fine education from the
236   teachers.
237 *I:* mhmm.
238 *J:* when I came to Louisville, schooling was, so simple, for me because
            I had been <u>used</u>
239   to such <u>disci</u>pline, a:nd I was <u>far</u> ahead of all the other kids. in
            <u>math</u>, in- <u>sci</u>ence, in
240   [<u>his</u>tory,=
241 *I:* [mmhmm.
242 *J:* =<u>e</u>verything. so: chapter four with- my <u>teen</u>age years (1.0) was
            a<u>gain</u> a: a<u>no</u>ther a-
243   a<u>wak</u>ening and- a <u>diffi</u>cult time because I was with, my <u>friends</u>
            were different
244   backgrounds a:nd <u>I</u> didn't fit in. <u>they</u> were either first generation
            European, <u>all</u> blue-
245   collar families. or <u>some</u> of them were from the streets. um. (1.0) so
            <u>any</u>way in high

246   school I'd- I tried to make the <u>best</u> of what I could, I had some
        close friends, as a

247   matter of fact I became a <u>lead</u>er in high school. I uh, I was the
        <u>first</u> girl to wear uh,

248   <u>ny</u>lon stockings. I was even called into the <u>Dean</u>'s office, why
        I(hh) wasn't wearing,

249   <u>bob</u>by socks. and I just said it was more <u>com</u>fortable for me. <u>I</u> was
        the first to wear

250   <u>make</u>-up, and I- put <u>eye</u>liner on my eyes when I was in first year
        of high school. that

251   was because, I guess because my <u>mo</u>ther was- ex<u>treme</u>ly glamorous
        and the<u>at</u>rical and

252   it was an ac<u>cept</u>ed thing in my family that you just, put yourself
        to look <u>prop</u>er and, I

253   was always a little <u>old</u>er than the rest of the girls. I wore <u>lip</u>stick
        and everything

254   before anyone else. (2.0) I had a <u>ve:</u>ry <u>strange,</u> <u>good</u> but a<u>bus</u>ive,
        art teacher. I took

255   com<u>mer</u>cial art in- in high school. I go- I was de<u>ter</u>mined to get a
        good education, out

256   of that <u>school</u> even though, <u>no</u> one bothered to go to hi- go to
        <u>col</u>lege out of that

257   schoo [l.=

258 *I:*   [mmhmm.

259 *J:* =college was just- you just- <u>got</u> your high school degree and you
        went to <u>work.</u> that

260   was <u>blue</u>-collar mentality. (2.0) <u>I</u> wanted to go to college, but got
        no encouragement

261   from my <u>fam</u>ily whatsoever. u:m my <u>grand</u>father wa:s uh (2.0) I
        don't think my

262   grandfather <u>ev</u>er got over the fact that he didn't have a son. my
        mother could never do

263   enough to please him, as <u>bril</u>liant as she was, this woman went to
        uh an elite private

264   school (2.0) uh was a special student of, the best teacher in the city.

265 *I:* this is your mother?

266 *J:* this is my <u>mo</u>ther. that was a well-known school. and she was
        highly educated, but

267   uh, uh not having a <u>boy.</u> and then when I came along, it was
        another <u>girl.</u> so there

268   <u>was</u> this uh re<u>luc</u>tance or (2.0) there was just no need to encourage
        a girl to go to

269   college. and when I was younger and extremely <u>pre</u>tty, there was
           this oh, that's
270   al<u>right</u>, honey. you don't need to go to college. you know, you'll-
           you'll <u>ma</u>rry.
271   some- some good lookin' <u>man</u>'ll hook you up anytime.

Note that Jane the narrator introduces this episode by repeating the phrase "once again" twice (line 230). She seems to be indexing similarities between this episode and her institutionalizations.

Three of the central voices established in earlier episodes recur here. The other students at the vocational high school are "lower-class, uneducated, street mentality" (line 230) and "all blue-collar families, or some of them were from the streets" (lines 244–245). These students seem to speak with the same voice as the abusive girls from Jane's second institutionalization—some of whom she described at lines 143–144 as "street people." Her high school peers do not abuse her in the same way as the institutionalized girls do. But they do offer poor educational role models: "no one even bothered to go to college out of that school" (lines 256–257). Jane herself went to junior college briefly, but she could not sustain the motivation to finish. While her high school peers did not abuse her physically, then, they might have damaged her educational prospects.

Just as Jane's mother and grandparents failed to care for her and allowed her to be abused at the institutions, they also allowed her to be educated at this inferior school. As she says at lines 260–264, her family did not encourage her educational aspirations at all. She largely blames her grandfather for this, because of his attitude that women should be married and not educated. She captures his voice in quoted speech, at lines 269–271. Instead of being concerned for her development, he acted in a way that fit in with his stereotypes and was more convenient for him.

The third familiar voice in this segment is the passive, vulnerable one given to Jane's narrated self. She is "thrown into" an unpleasant situation (lines 230–231) where she "didn't fit in" (line 244), and she simply has to endure. The embedded rectangle in Figure 4.6 presents the voices that Jane represents as part of the narrated event in this episode. The characters speaking with these four salient voices have similar relationships to those established in earlier episodes: Jane's grandfather and mother do not take care of her, and she becomes the victim of an inferior education. The figure also depicts the storytelling event in which Jane speaks as a cooperative research subject (e.g., by giving chapter summaries at line 242).

FIGURE 4.6 Jane in High School

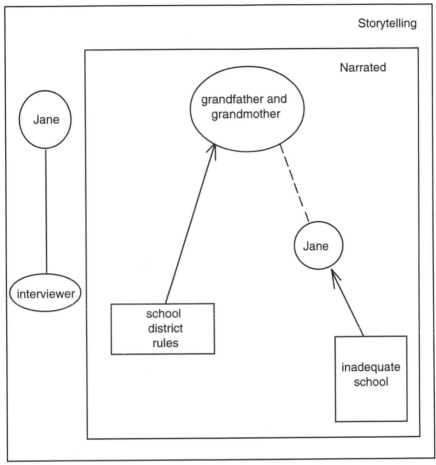

Jane's narrated self does not remain passive and vulnerable through-out this episode, however. Jane also describes her narrated adolescent self as active and assertive at times. She made the best of her situation and even "became a leader" (line 247). Jane describes herself as asser-tive by using quoted speech at line 249. An authority figure (the Dean) challenges her by asking "why I wasn't wearing bobby socks" (lines 248–249). Jane's narrated self responds in a mature, assertive voice: "I just said it was more comfortable for me" (line 249). One would not normally expect an adolescent facing an authority figure to speak so calmly. In describing her experiences during high school, then, Jane presents both the more passive and more active voices that she attributed to herself in earlier episodes. In this episode she tries to make the best of a bad situation, even though she ultimately fails to overcome her family's lack of support and drops out of college.

Adolescence was also the first time that Jane lived with her mother for an extended period and was able to form an impression of her. This is the only point in her story that Jane recounts whole episodes with her mother as the main character (episodes 13–14, as presented in Table 4.1). In these episodes Jane the narrator makes her mother speak with voices similar to those that Jane's own narrated selves speak with. Her mother is at first a passive victim, but then she develops into an active, assertive woman. Jane represents the first of these voices in the following passage.

156 *J:* my <u>mo</u>ther got a job, in the <u>neigh</u>borhood, in a <u>dress</u> shop. (2.0) this in<u>cred</u>ibly
157   in<u>tel</u>ligent woman. (2.0) [heavy sigh] also very <u>phy</u>sically beautiful, extraordinarily
158   beautiful woman. u:m (1.0) was <u>work</u>ing in a dress shop on Fifteenth Street. <u>ca</u>tering
159   to a bunch of very <u>pam</u>pered, insensitive spoiled women. u:m <u>we</u> lived in Eastside
160   there until I was a teenager.

Here Jane presents her mother, despite her talents, as being forced to work in a demeaning job, catering to spoiled women who mistreat her. The two voices here sound similar to those from Jane's own experiences with abusive institutions: Jane's mother is the vulnerable victim, and the spoiled women are the abusers.

As Jane describes it, however, her mother did not remain passive and vulnerable.

174 *J:* um (3.0) <u>while</u> I was in high school my <u>mo</u>ther, <u>an</u>swered an ad in the paper, and she
175   got a <u>top</u>-notch job downtown. sub<u>ser</u>vient position but- nonetheless, u:h it was-
176   somewhat of a: a <u>se</u>cretary <u>not</u> quite a secretary, but an assistant uh upper echelon
177   photography school photogra- not <u>school</u>, photography o:f uh, of men.

178 *I:* m [hmm.
179 *J:*   [from <u>Dal</u>las. the- these were <u>por</u>trait photographers of u:h <u>high</u>ly
        successful
180   businesspeople. <u>men</u> <u>on</u>ly, they did <u>not</u> photograph women. um
        (2.0) and within a
181   certain amount of years, (1.0) she was the <u>mid</u>west <u>man</u>ager, she
        was running the
182   office. Be<u>cause</u> she was u:h, extraordinarily <u>bright</u>, um (2.0) and
        she just knew how to
183   <u>han</u>dle, the gentlemen that came into the- office. whereas the old
        manager was- (1.0)
184   you know, a flash in the pan. really wasn't as- ef<u>fec</u>tive as my
        mo[ther.
185 *I:*   [mmhmm.
186 *J:* so she became an- an ex<u>ec</u>utive.=
187 *I:* wha- what <u>chap</u>ter of, your life would you say this period is? (3.0)
188 *J:* all right, I'm- I'm sorry, I didn't go into <u>chap</u>ters. all right the
        <u>sec</u>ond chapter was in
189   the Academy, the <u>third</u> chapter I would say was, <u>pre</u>-teen and
        being <u>in</u>stitutionalized
190   once again and finally as<u>sert</u>ing myself in November of '49. Um
        (2.0) I- I have to- it's
191   an <u>un</u>derstatement for me to <u>say</u> that I was brought up to be
        extra<u>or</u>dinarily proper and
192   ladylike, <u>not</u> to show anger and um (1.0) to <u>fol</u>low the rules. so
        for <u>me</u> to (1.0)
193   <u>lit</u>erally u:h pra- uh practically <u>black</u>mail my mother and my
        grandparents at the age
194   of fifteen and a half, sixteen, tha- I wouldn't tell them where I was
        unless they
195   promised me that I wouldn't have to go <u>back</u> to that <u>place</u> that to-
        that's a <u>chap</u>ter unto
196   itself. <u>that</u> was really a: a coming into an awareness of my<u>self</u>. so
        (1.0) my <u>teen</u> years
197   and my mother making a- a- a <u>good</u> step to better herself as an
        executive, be<u>come</u> an
198   executive, while I was in high school or as I was ap<u>proach</u>ing high
        school and
199   through<u>out</u> high school, wa:s, was very <u>good</u> for her sense of self
        and- and for <u>my</u>
200   sense of self too. I was very <u>proud</u> of her.

In this new job her mother started out as a "subservient" assistant, but she ended up running the office (lines 175, 180–182). This seems to be a similar developmental transition to the one that Jane represented for herself during her second institutionalization: from passive and vulnerable to active and assertive. Thus Jane has her mother speak with similar voices to those that she assigns to her own narrated selves. (There is, of course, an irony in Jane's mother's success: she overcame her father's sexism by succeeding in a business that catered to men only.)

Because of the similarity of voicing between Jane's past experiences and her mother's, we can learn something about Jane's own position in the storytelling event by examining how she ventriloquates her mother. Jane the narrator appears to align herself with her mother's active, assertive voice. She describes her mother's job as "top-notch" (line 175), and she presents her mother as being in control: "she just knew how to handle the gentlemen that came into the office" (lines 182–183). Jane the narrator uses the term "gentlemen" here, which would have been the way her mother and the company itself described its clients. She does so without any apparent irony, and so she seems to align herself with her mother's active, professional self. Jane also claims that her mother's success was good for her mother's self-esteem, "and for *my* sense of self too. I was very *proud* of her" (lines 199–200). Because Jane the narrator has aligned herself with her mother's active voice, she herself seems to have been positively influenced by her mother's success. She positions herself as someone who admires and benefited from her mother's talent and success.

Throughout this passage, and for some time before, Jane has positioned herself as a cooperative research subject in the storytelling event. She tells the interviewer her story as if it were a piece of data. At line 187, when the interviewer breaks in to ask what chapter Jane is describing, the interviewer might again be presupposing that research subjects can do better or worse jobs. Jane herself ratifies this presupposition when she apologizes at line 188. Then Jane goes on to emphasize her remarkable accomplishment when she asserted herself and "blackmailed" her mother. I argue that this emphasis on her own strengths is part of a larger pattern in the storytelling event. On several occasions Jane acts insecure or apologetic about her quality as a research subject. But then at lines 190–196 she emphasizes her own remarkable characteristics. This pattern complicates the storytelling event. In addition to giving and receiving data objectively, the interviewer might be evaluating Jane's performance and Jane might be trying to impress the interviewer or to justify her performance.

Jane might also be expressing impatience at line 188 with the interviewer's distanced position. When told about Jane and her mother's remarkable accomplishments, most people would express some admiration. But the interviewer sticks so closely to the research interview script that she apparently cares only about what "chapter" these accomplishments go into. By underlining the actions' remarkableness, Jane seems to suggest that the interviewer is inappropriately distanced. Earlier, when she broke down, Jane's actions could have prompted the interviewer to be sympathetic. Here, when she recounts the admirable resolve and talent that she and her mother have shown, the interviewer could have shown some appreciation. In the face of the interviewer's continuing distance, Jane's actions seem to say: "Perhaps you won't act like my therapist, but at least have the decency to acknowledge that I have triumphed over some remarkable adversity." In the storytelling event, then, Jane acts in such a way as to ask the interviewer to acknowledge her competence. At this point in the interview, Jane's positioning still involves some insecurity over her performance as a research subject. Later on, this positioning will become more like self-assertion.

Parenthood

As the storytelling event continues, Jane acts like a good research subject by volunteering to divulge some interesting personal information to the interviewer. She introduces the next episodes by saying: "because I believe in behavioral studies and everything, I will give you information I normally don't talk about" (lines 301–304). She then tells the story of her first pregnancy. After finishing high school, Jane worked during the day and took junior college classes at night. She lacked discipline, however, and had "no leadership" from her family, so eventually she lost the job and dropped out of college. For a while she did not work, and during this time she had a secretive relationship with a man named Robert. He was from a wealthy Armenian family and about 8 years older than Jane. Although Robert was not married, neither of them expected that this relationship would last. Jane does not say why, although it might be because she did not feel a legitimate part of the Armenian community in Eastside. They did not go on dates in public much, but instead met in Jane's apartment and had sex while her mother was at work. Eventually Robert moved out of town and the relationship ended. Jane began to work at a job that she liked. Then she discovered that she was pregnant.

Impending parenthood presents Jane with a choice: will she decide to keep her baby or give it up for adoption? As Jane presents it, this is also a choice about whether to treat her child as her own mother

treated her. Will she abdicate the responsibility to care for her own child
and give her son away to an institution?

340 *J:* I- finally I went to a doctor recommended- by a girlfriend. and uh
        (3.0) end of
341   November, no, it's- yeah, it would be beginning of December
        now I think because I
342   found out that I was pregnant when I was four and a half months
        pregnant.
343 *I:* mmm.=
344 *J:* four and a half months. you're talking about naiveté, you're talking
        about, un- not
345   dealing with reality or an inability to deal with it. so I found out I
        was four and a half
346   months pregnant. I was in shock. (2.0) Abortion in those days was
        u:h rarely talked
347   about. It was done, but it was illegal in Kentucky. I told my
        mother that I was
348   pregnant. and for the rest of my pregnancy I-, first of all, I lied at
        my job. I told them
349   that I had been married, and divorced, and now I was pregnant.
        The man I worked for,
350   his wife could not have children and they had had to adopt so he
        wa:s fascinated with
351   my pregnancy, and very supportive in his own way. I worked
        until I was eight and a
352   half months pregnant, putting my money away. and some time in
        that- four month
353   span, I also had- made the decision to call Robert's mother, and I
        fibbed to her. I told
354   her that I was an old friend of Robert's and that it was- and that
        something u:h of
355   importance came up that I'm sure he would want to know about,
        and- I was very
356   charming and very warm and, I talked her into giving me Robert's
        address or phone
357   number or whatever, how to reach him. he was now in California.
        I: wrote him a
358   letter, and told him that uh (3.0) that I was pregnant and I- I: just
        rem- ironically
359   enough, (2.0) he had- called me at the end of the summer because
        he had been told that

360　he had had a case of syphilis. and he was concerned about <u>me</u>. and asked me if I had

361　any kind of <u>symp</u>toms and I said no, not at <u>all</u>. I said- I haven't had my <u>per</u>iod lately,

362　and he said <u>what</u>? and we <u>joked</u> about the fact that I could　possi bly be pregnant, and

363　<u>god</u> wouldn't we have a <u>hel</u>luva kid. (1.0) this was as a <u>joke</u> said in September. so

364　he:re, the end of November, beginning of De<u>cem</u>ber I find out that I am now four and

365　a half months pregnant. (2.0) <u>Robert</u> came back to Louisville in January (1.0) It was

366　very <u>ve</u>ry cold weather, I- I met him at a ho<u>tel</u> and we <u>talk</u>ed. and he said what are

367　you going to <u>do</u>. I said I don't <u>know</u>. I was being heavily <u>pres</u>sured by, so<u>ci</u>ety, my

368　own <u>thoughts</u>, by Robert, by my <u>mo</u>ther, to give the child up. (6.0) on the night of

369　April 5, I went into <u>lab</u>or, went into the <u>hos</u>pital a:nd at <u>two</u> o'clock in the morning

370　on April 6, 1956– I gave birth to a- <u>beau</u>tiful baby boy. (3.0) <u>while</u> I was in the

371　hospital, I called- a<u>gain</u> by recommendation the city <u>or</u>phanage. (1.0) at the ti:me,

372　there was a <u>shor</u>tage, on <u>good</u> <u>white</u> <u>ba</u>bies. (3.0) and a <u>very</u> <u>vile</u> <u>wo</u>man at the city

373　orphanage, a<u>greed</u> to take my baby until I could make a decision. so I took my- my

374　<u>dar</u>ling Kenny, u:m (3.0) hu::nh (4.0) [Voice quivering] to the orphanage on thirteenth

375　Street (3.0) and <u>left</u> him there for <u>two</u> weeks. (2.0) two of the <u>har</u>dest weeks of my life.

376　(4.0) and when the <u>two</u> weeks were up (3.0) I went <u>down</u> there, and this hor<u>ren</u>dous

377　p- person had these <u>pa</u>pers out for me, to <u>sign</u>. she had a <u>fa</u>mily all lined up. (1.0)

378　there was a- (1.0) there was a <u>shor</u>tage of- like I say they- in <u>those</u> days (2.0) a <u>nice</u>

379　good <u>white</u> <u>ba</u>by, was a- <u>short</u> coming a good <u>heal</u>thy baby. [Sniff] She handed me the

380　<u>pen</u> (2.0) but I <u>could</u>n't do it. (5.0) [voice quivering, crying] I said <u>bring</u> me my <u>ba</u>by.

381   (6.0) I want you to know this woman <u>yelled</u> at me. (2.0) and tried
         to <u>guilt</u>-trip me. she
382   said, how <u>dare</u> you do this to me I made <u>place</u> for your baby. <u>I</u>
         helped you out. you
383   <u>have</u> to sign these papers. I said I don't have to do anything of
         the <u>sort</u>. I <u>want</u> my
384   child [Sniff]. and at first she re<u>fused</u> me. and I said I want my
         <u>baby</u>. (1.0) and she:
385   practically threw a <u>tem</u>per tantrum right there in the office of the
         orphanage, and was
386   <u>scream</u>ing at me, because she had made <u>room</u> for my baby and
         she <u>want</u>ed my baby.
387   they brought- my <u>dar</u>ling baby to me: who ha:d (1.0) his <u>skin</u> on
         his <u>feet</u> and his <u>legs</u>
388   was totally <u>scaled</u>. (1.0) I think they <u>left</u> him a<u>lone</u> for two weeks.
         I mean they- you
389   know how you're supposed to put <u>oil</u> on a newborn's to keep the
         skin pro<u>tec</u>ted
390   because it's <u>tender</u>? <u>my</u> <u>child</u>'s <u>bo</u>:dy was, (1.0) if I hadn't <u>known</u>
         that it was dryness,
391   it looked like it was in<u>fes</u>ted with some di<u>sease</u>. <u>I</u> was ever so glad
         that I got him <u>out</u> of
392   there, got him <u>home</u>, <u>bathed</u> him, rubbed <u>oil</u> on his body, a:nd
         u:h was de<u>ter</u>mined- I
393   didn't know <u>how</u> I was gonna make- make it but- <u>I</u> wanted to
         have my <u>baby</u>. so, I
394   would say that's chapter <u>five</u>. which- de<u>ter</u>mined an <u>aw</u>ful lot of
         the rest of my life.

In this segment of her story Jane presents both sets of salient, recurring voices. First Robert fails to care for her, and she is a passive
victim of the orphanage woman. This set of voices includes a failed
caregiver, an abusive institution, and Jane's passive, vulnerable self.
Then Jane asserts herself against the prejudices of people like her grandparents and against the orphanage woman, and she claims her child.
This set of voices includes Jane's active, assertive self, plus the defeated
institution and self-interested advisors.

In this episode Robert speaks with the voice of a potential caregiver
abdicating responsibility. His only response on seeing her 6 months
pregnant with his child is: "what are you going to do?" (lines 366–367).
A few lines earlier Jane has characterized her relationship with Robert
as a joking one, by describing their lighthearted exchange about the

serious topic of pregnancy (lines 362–363). Because of her physical condition, Jane herself is forced to take the issue more seriously a few months later. Robert apparently stops joking, but he does not take responsibility for the pregnancy.

Jane says that she "was being heavily pressured" to give the child up for adoption (lines 367–368). She also notes that she called, "again by recommendation," an orphanage (line 371). Her use of the word "recommendation," especially with "again," may index her mother's earlier experiences with the two institutions. This time, Jane must make the decision whether to give her child to an institution. She does not say who actually recommended the particular orphanage, but she does list "society," Robert, and her mother as the people pressuring her to give the baby up. "Society," given the voices Jane has presupposed for her grandparents, most likely indexes them. Robert, her mother, and grandparents would all benefit if Jane were to choose adoption. Robert would avoid child support, and her relatives would avoid the scandal of an unwed mother in the family. So these characters all speak with the same voice as Mr. McGee did earlier: self-interested people pressuring her to send her baby to the institution. (Robert thus speaks with two voices in this segment: as a potential caregiver abdicating responsibility and as a self-interested advisor.)

The abusive institution is represented by the "vile," "horrendous" orphanage woman (lines 372, 376). "Horrendous" is a term Jane used to describe the abusers and abusive conditions in her two institutionalizations, and her use of it here helps establish the same voice for the orphanage woman. Like the teachers from Jane's first institutionalization, the orphanage woman is also greedy—as Jane says, "she *wanted* my baby" (line 386). So this passage about the orphanage contains ineffective caregivers, self-interested advisors, and an abusive institution. It also contains both Jane's vulnerable and her assertive narrated voices. Up until the pivotal section of this segment (lines 380ff.), Jane herself speaks in her passive, vulnerable voice. She tells Robert she doesn't know what to do (line 367), and she gives in to her family's pressure and gives her child to the recommended institution.

As she did in the narrative about her second institutionalization, Jane develops from passive to active in the narrated events at the orphanage. This happens in the pivotal section from lines 380–388. These lines accomplish particularly rich voicing and ventriloquation, largely through the dense use of metapragmatic predication and quotation. Jane and the orphanage employee both speak with two distinct voices in the encounter described in these lines. At first (lines 381–383) the orphanage woman speaks like an authority figure: She "yelled," she "tried to guilt-trip" Jane, and she said, "how dare you do this to me." These metapragmatic descriptions presuppose recognizable voices and a recognizable type of narrated event—the woman is like a parent and Jane is like a recalcitrant child. At line 383, however, Jane the narrator switches the characters' voices. From lines 383–388 Jane speaks like an adult. She is rational and even-tempered, saying, "I don't have to do anything of the sort; I want my child," in a controlled, matter-of-fact way. In the narrated event Jane has asserted her rights as a parent, against the prejudices of society and against the evils of the institution, and she steps forward to care for her child. This reversal of Jane's relationship with the orphanage woman is so powerful, and so artfully presented, that the reader or hearer has to admire her resolve and might even share her sense of triumph. In listening to the interview or reading the transcript at this peak moment, one feels that a triumphant development has occurred. Jane seems to have overcome her passive, vulnerable self and developed her active, assertive self once and for all.

Table 4.4 shows how the narrated event during this orphanage episode contains the same voices that appeared in earlier episodes. In the first part of the orphanage episode, before line 380, Robert fails to care for her, and she goes along with her family's wish that she give her baby to the orphanage woman. Here Jane is passive and vulnerable and the orphanage woman takes advantage of her. But then Jane asserts herself against her family and Robert's desire that she give her baby away, and against the orphanage woman, to claim her child.

Jane also moves out of a passive, vulnerable position in the storytelling event as she narrates this episode. The segment begins with Jane the narrator distancing her storytelling self from her "naive" narrated self (by using the device called *epistemic modalization*, described in Chapter 3) at line 344. By calling this past self "naive," Jane positions her current self as able to understand the situation better than her past self could. She presupposes that her current self would never fail to recognize a pregnancy for 4½ months. At this point she is still positioning her storytelling self as a cooperative research subject. Later in this segment, however, the distance between Jane's narrated and storytelling selves breaks down again. By line 371 her narrated self has yielded to pressure and accepted the recommendation to give her baby to the orphanage. Jane the narrator begins to position herself with respect to the orphanage woman here—clearly distancing her storytelling self by describing this woman as "vile." Then Jane stops the narrative and cries. As she did during the description of her first institutionalization, by breaking down in the storytelling event (at line 380)

TABLE 4.4 Two Recurring Sets of Voices in Jane's Narrative

EPISODE	SELF-INTERESTED RECOMMENDERS	FAILED CAREGIVERS	ABUSIVE INSTITUTIONS	JANE'S VOICE	CAREGIVERS AND RECOMMENDERS, OVERCOME	ABUSIVE INSTITUTIONS, NEUTRALIZED	SUCCESSFUL CAREGIVERS
First institutionalization	Mr. McGee	Jane's mother	Teachers at the Academy	Passive and vulnerable			
Second institutionalization	Jane's grandparents	Jane's mother	Girls at the reform school	Passive and vulnerable			
Running away from reform school				Active and assertive	Jane's grandparents and mother	Girls at the reform school	
High School	Jane's grandfather	Jane's mother	Inadequate School	Passive and vulnerable			
Orphanage (1)	Jane's mother and grandparents	Robert	Orphanage woman	Passive and vulnerable			
Orphanage (2)				Active and assertive	Mother, grandparents, and Robert	Orphanage woman	

Jane enacts how much the narrated events still affect her. She no longer dispassionately recounts her story as a piece of data, but instead positions herself in the storytelling event as someone who has been abused and could use some sympathy.

The interviewer, however, does not say anything in response. Although Jane positions herself as someone deserving sympathy the interviewer does not ratify this position. This leaves Jane in a difficult spot. She could intensify her plea for sympathy—by adding painful details or crying harder—or she could return to her position as a cooperative research subject. Jane adopts the latter option. She recovers and goes on to describe how she routed the orphanage woman and displayed her assertive narrated self. In the storytelling event she moves back into her position as a cooperative research subject. At lines 393–394, for example, she voluntarily identifies the "chapter" she has been discussing and thus presupposes that the storytelling event is once again a dispassionate research interview.

Figures 4.7 and 4.8 present the narrated and storytelling events in the two phases of the orphanage episode. Figure 4.7 depicts the storytelling and narrated events right before line 380. The narrated event contains self-interested recommenders, failed caregivers, abusive institutions, and Jane's passive self. The figure places Jane below the interviewer in the storytelling event because Jane positions herself as vulnerable at lines 374ff. Jane enacts how these past experiences still deeply affect her by crying. Figure 4.8 depicts the narrated and storytelling events after line 380. In the narrated event, Jane has shifted into her active and assertive voice. In the storytelling event, she positions herself as a cooperative research subject.

This powerful episode at the orphanage might lead one to interpret Jane's narrative as an explanation of how she came to be the mature self she is now in the storytelling event at age 57. She had to endure abuse passively during her early life, but after claiming her son she has become the mature woman we see in the interview. While perhaps partly true, this explanation does not suffice. Jane at age 57 cannot be simply describing how a *past* passive, vulnerable self has been transformed into a mature, assertive one. This would not explain her repeated enactments of the passive, vulnerable self in the storytelling event itself. She is not simply an active, assertive woman who dispassionately recounts how her passive, vulnerable self was transformed into her current one. Instead, she not only describes her vulnerable self in the narrated events, but she also enacts it in the storytelling events. (The next section will show that Jane also acts assertively in her storytelling interaction with the interviewer.)

FIGURE 4.7 Jane Passive at the Orphanage

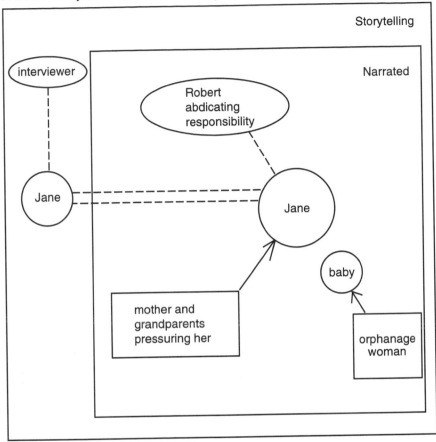

In both the past and the present, then, Jane develops from a more vulnerable to a more assertive self. As I will discuss further in Chapter 5, this happens because the patterns characteristic of the self are regularly re-created through interactional positioning in discursive interaction. This is what Jane does in telling her story. She describes narrated events in which, at first, potential caregivers abandoned her and she was abused. But then she found the strength to assert herself and take control of her own life. In the orphanage segment, for instance, she broke out of the interactional position characteristic of her mother (a passive woman willing to let this passivity damage her child) and began to speak with a more assertive voice. In the interview situation

FIGURE 4.8 Jane Takes Control at the Orphanage

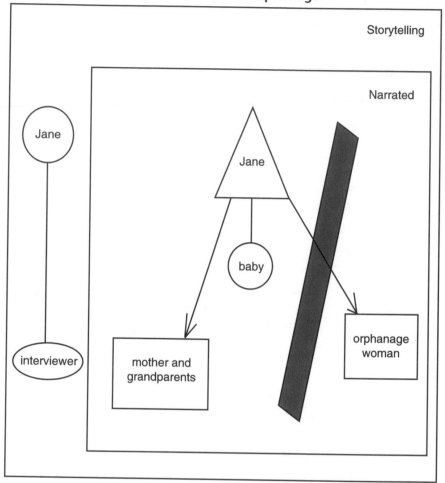

itself, Jane finds herself in a similar position. She recounts difficult and emotional events and breaks down. The interviewer, who is the only person available to support her, does not act sympathetic. In the storytelling event, then, Jane positions the interviewer in the role of absent caregiver. For this reason the various figures depict the interviewer in an oval in the storytelling event, just like other potential caregivers who abdicated responsibility for Jane.[2] When Jane overcomes her vulnerability, despite the interviewer's scientific distance, she recreates in the storytelling event something like the developmental transition that occurs in several narrated events. This parallel between narrated and storytelling events is central to Jane's narrative self-construction. The next central episodes of the narrative show this parallelism more clearly.

JANE ENACTS HER ASSERTIVE VOICE

Child Rearing

At the orphanage Jane triumphs over the evil orphanage woman—not by getting revenge, but by acting mature and assertive. In doing so she might also be overcoming the others who have abused her in the past, when she turns out to be an assertive adult and good mother despite her horrendous early experiences. The interview comes to a conclusion within about 200 lines after this point, in part because the interviewer hurries Jane along. But in these last 200 lines, Jane breaks down once more and also describes two difficult narrated events in which the familiar voices reappear. In the second of these events, Jane finally discovers someone who successfully plays the role of caregiver for her.

After describing her experience at the orphanage, Jane goes on to describe the first few years of her son's life. During this time she stayed home to take care of her baby, and she was financially supported by her mother and informal child support payments from Robert ("seventy-five dollars a month," she says at line 411, "big deal"). Jane stayed home because she "was determined to give my baby a good foundation" (lines 412–413). After her son began school, Jane got a job in the neighborhood, staying close to home in order to care for her son and her by-now-disabled mother. At this point Jane describes her mother's death.

429 *J:* June 30 of 1966 my <u>son</u> went to go- spend the- a- a sleep-over with a
430   friend at an overnight party. and my mother- (2.0) must have had
       a heart attack, I- I-
431   we're not <u>quite</u> sure what happened, but uh (3.0) the night of
       June 30, 1966 my
432   mother died in my arms. (2.0) [crying] (8.0) [voice quivering] and
       so <u>that</u> added another
433   chapter. (5.0) she had <u>lost</u> the will to live, and felt that she was-
       in<u>tru</u>ding on my life
434   with her disability. so I've been <u>left</u> with that guilt t- t- to u:h
       con<u>tend</u> with. we

435   moved <u>out</u> of that apartment within a month, I couldn't- I
      couldn't <u>take</u> the memories.

436   and moved, only about <u>four</u> or five blocks <u>north</u>, <u>still</u> saying in
      Eastside, putting my

437   son in <u>pri</u>vate school. [sniff] I was trying <u>des</u>perately to protect his
      education.

438   (3.0) u:h, the <u>neigh</u>borhood was going throu:gh <u>ver</u>y dramatic
      changes, and my

439   son had been ac<u>cos</u>ted on the street a few times. and <u>all</u> my
      friends were moving

440   out of Eastside and so: in 1966 I- <u>threw</u> in the towel more or less,
      a:nd even though I

441   had gotten a <u>very</u> good job and ha- was the <u>on</u>ly woman, in my
      <u>real</u> estate office which

442   I had- it's <u>in</u>teresting I had gotten a job right- right when my
      <u>mo</u>ther <u>right</u> before my

443   mother died. and <u>pas</u>sed the state license, you know, <u>test</u>. and was
      the: one of the <u>very</u>

444   few, I was the <u>on</u>ly woman in- in the u:h east part of the city that
      was a <u>bro</u>ker for a

445   real estate firm. but I was willing to <u>leave</u> that, or at least <u>trav</u>el,
      and we moved to the

446   <u>sub</u>urbs. and I think that began a different chapter in my life. um
      (1.0) <u>mov</u>ing out of

447   Eastside, making that- that <u>cut</u> with uh- what had <u>al</u>ways been my
      family tie. am I-

448   am I running behind?

449 *I:* u:h no, I'm just- <u>check</u>ing to make sure the tape's still running.=

450 *J:* okay. [sniff] u:h (2.0) we <u>mov</u>ed to the suburbs and I lived there for
      two years where

451   a<u>gain</u> my son, I was pro<u>tec</u>ting his education, so from <u>pri</u>vate
      school to <u>bet</u>ter

452   schools and- um (1.0) the <u>sub</u>urbs. I was <u>try</u>ing to do for my son
      what my family

453   did <u>not</u> do for me. and <u>that</u> was- even though my <u>fam</u>ily was
      <u>high</u>ly intelligent (1.0)

454   and ex<u>treme</u>ly successful in- in almost every line of de- en<u>deav</u>or
      that they had eve:r

455   done, education for <u>me</u> was not encouraged. <u>I</u> was not taken
      seriously at anything that

456   I was interested in. after all, I was <u>pret</u>ty and there was no sense
      in- a woman who's

457   just going to get <u>ma</u>rried, there was no sense in <u>ed</u>ucating her. u:m, we're not <u>tal</u>king

458   about in the dark ages, we're talking- in the fifties and- fifties and sixties I mean

459   that's not that <u>long</u> ago. but that men<u>ta</u>lity was pervasive. u:m (3.0) I had <u>had</u>

460   relationships, off and on, with u:m (2.0) <u>var</u>ious men. <u>two</u> of which were <u>ma</u>rried. and

461   I <u>think</u> the reason I did that, is that that was the <u>safe</u> way of trying to have a

462   relationship (1.0) with<u>out</u>- any <u>fu</u>ture or any <u>ties</u> because my ties to my son, and

463   my disabled mother was <u>pri</u>mary. so: <u>that</u> way I couldn't be u:h, <u>com</u>promised

464   [energy-wise.

465 *I:* [mmhmm.

466 *J:* so it was very <u>eas</u>y for me to have relationships with married men. u:h <u>one</u> of whom

467   was the <u>bro</u>ther of an ex-<u>boy</u>friend. w- as a matter of fact <u>both</u> of them were brothers

468   of ex-b(hh)oyfriends [laugh] and <u>both</u> of them were married.

This segment contains some of the voices familiar from earlier narrated events, but not arranged in the same configuration. I briefly analyze this segment because it contains the third and last occasion of Jane breaking down and crying in the storytelling event (at line 432).

While describing her mother's death Jane breaks down and once again enacts how narrated events still affect her. The interviewer does not respond, and Jane quickly reestablishes distance between her narrated and storytelling selves in two familiar ways: by saying "that added another chapter" (lines 432–433) and by giving a more clinical assessment of why the narrated event still affects her—"I've been left with that guilt . . . to contend with" (line 434). Jane positions herself later in the segment as a cooperative research subject. The interviewer, perhaps inadvertently, ratifies the research interview type of interactional positioning by looking at the tape (lines 447–449). Note that Jane responds, again, in a way that presupposes insecurity about her performance as a research subject when she asks whether she is "running behind."

Jane ends this segment by modifying her position in the storytelling event somewhat. She reiterates that she wanted to do for her child what her own mother had not done for her: provide support and guidance (lines 451–453). Then she flashes back to her own childhood, in which her family had not supported her because of her gender. In this passage she voices her mother and grandparents, by quoting the speech of people like her grandparents: "a woman who's just going to get married, there was no sense in educating her" (lines 456–457). Thus Jane has her family speak with the voice of unsupportive, outdated, sexist people. In the next lines she goes on to position herself, in the storytelling event, as opposed to this sexist voice. By saying "we're not talking about in the dark ages" (lines 457–458), she presupposes that these sexist attitudes do in fact belong in the dark ages (because only unenlightened people would hold such views). Jane herself disdains such views.

In these last lines of the segment Jane also positions herself as a more mature woman than the interviewer, a mature woman who tells a younger woman about the past and present realities of gender relations in this society. When she says "that's not that long ago" (line 459), she presupposes that she herself experienced the bad old days, she implies that the young interviewer didn't, and she suggests that the interviewer should pay attention to the facts about gender that Jane is telling her. In the storytelling event, then, Jane begins to introduce a third type of interactional positioning here.

First, Jane and the interviewer have been engaged in a research interview, as research subject and research scientist. Second, Jane's telling of her personal, traumatic experiences has made her vulnerable in the storytelling event. On several occasions she positions herself as deserving sympathy, but the interviewer does not willingly occupy the position of sympathetic friend or therapist. Jane also occasionally positions herself as somewhat insecure about her performance as a research subject on several occasions. This insecurity might be compounded by the fact that the interviewer is in a position of authority—as indicated by the fact that Jane looks to the interviewer to evaluate her performance—despite the fact that the interviewer is less than half Jane's age. As she finishes narrating her mother's death, however, Jane stops acting insecure and starts acting more assertive with respect to the interviewer. Jane has not only experienced more sexism in her life than the interviewer, but she has also participated in the feminist struggles that have made the interviewer's own experiences as a woman less oppressive. This third type of interactional positioning develops in the next episodes.

First Abortion

Jane next goes on to describe the final two extended narrated events of her story, each of which involves an abortion.

480 J: I <u>don't</u> know what the <u>tie</u> in is- or if there <u>is</u>, I'm sure that psycho-
            logically there could
481   be found a tie. I: uh (2.0) I had <u>two</u> pregnancies after my son. the
            <u>first</u> one was
482   when he was about a <u>year</u> old. a:nd I <u>knew</u> I could not have   an
            other child, this by the
483   way was- I had gotten <u>preg</u>nant by an old boyfriend of mine that I
            had- been going
484   with for years, and he had <u>just</u> come out of the service. and we
            had- uh re<u>sum</u>ed an
485   old relationship that we had had as teenagers. and I found myself
            <u>preg</u>nant again. I
486   couldn't be<u>lieve</u> it. we:ll I, <u>could</u>n't have another child, I could
            <u>bare</u>ly take care of
487   Kenny. so and u:h (1.0) so I <u>called</u> him and he:, made ar<u>range-</u>
            ments. through the
488   <u>syn</u>dicate, at the <u>time</u>, uh the only a<u>bor</u>tion that you could get
            was through the Mob.
489   I'm- <u>ser</u>ious. and you ha:d a <u>choice</u> of what kind of abortion you
            wanted, depending
490   on how much <u>mon</u>ey you had. if you ha:d the <u>bare</u> amount of
            money, which <u>I</u> only
491   had, it was like about <u>three</u> hundred dollars or four hundred
            dollars. <u>they</u> would <u>come</u>
492   and, a<u>bort you</u>, they would <u>not</u> give you a D & C they would
            a<u>bort</u> you i:n some <u>room</u>.
493   if you had a <u>thou</u>sand- and they- and it was interesting, the Mob
            u:sed <u>terms</u>, in those
494   days they made a <u>f:or</u>tune off abortion, a:nd a Chevrolet abortion
            was a <u>three</u> or <u>four</u>
495   hundred dollar abortion. a <u>Ca</u>dillac, if they talked on the phone
            used I've got a
496   Cadillac for you. That meant that they had a woman who had a
            <u>thou</u>sand dollars, and it
497   would be done in the privacy of <u>some</u> place under their, supervi-
            sion. well I couldn't
498   afford a Cadillac abortion. so I <u>rent</u>ed a mo<u>tel</u> room, and they
            showed up, <u>not</u> only did
499   they show up with another young woman in my- to <u>share</u> the
            room with me- to give a
500   <u>teen</u>ager, to give <u>her</u> an abortion, they were going to take ad<u>van</u>-
            tage of the fact that <u>I</u>

501   rented a room. but they <u>al</u>so had this, extra<u>ord</u>inarily ignorant, European woman,

502   who, when she <u>went</u> in<u>side</u> of me, and said, im<u>pos</u>sible, you can't be pregnant,

503   you have a <u>tipped</u> uterus. they w- at the <u>turn</u> of the century, <u>lit</u>erally at the turn

504   of the century, there was a belief that if you had a <u>tipped</u> uterus you could <u>not</u>

505   get pregnant.

506 *I:* mmhm.

507 *J:* believe me I am a testament to the- the <u>opposite</u> [of that fact. and I- and <u>she</u> wasn't=

508 *I:*   [mmhm.

509 *J:* going to give me an abortion. and I: raised holy hell. I said you'll <u>do</u> it. and what they

510   <u>did</u> was, that they put some sort of instrument that clamped <u>onto</u>, the <u>sac</u>, [a:nd=

511 *I:*   [mmhm.

512 *J:* they gave you some uh, I don't know if they gave you <u>Er</u>got, which was whenever-

513 *I:* [mmhmm

514 *J:* [to make it ex<u>pel</u>, a:nd uh, they <u>left</u> you.

515 *I:* mmhm.

516 *J:* so they left me there, and they <u>told</u> me that uh, you know, if I felt any kind of <u>pushing</u>

517   to go into the toilet. and this was e<u>lev</u>en o'clock at night, and the next morning, <u>I</u> went

518   into labor. I was <u>five</u> and a half months pregnant. a:nd I expelled a <u>fetus</u> into the toilet.

519   I was told later that- by the young <u>teen</u>ager that went in and looked and her mother

520   came in- <u>I</u> don't know, but they thought it was a <u>boy</u>. um, which Joe would have <u>loved</u>

521   to have had a boy. uh, and I made my way back to the <u>bed</u>, and I was hemorrhaging. I

522   had left a note for my <u>mo</u>ther who- I didn't give her the <u>details</u> but she figured it out.

523   and I <u>called</u> her, and she was <u>wor</u>ried sick. 'cause I had left her a <u>note</u> that if I- I swear

524   I was- I didn't know if I was going to <u>die</u> that night or not, but- I <u>begged</u> her to take

525   care of Kenny. so I went home. I assured her I was all right, and
        two days later I started

526   hemorrhaging even more, and I was rushed to the hospital, where
        I was given a proper

527   D & C, of a botched abortion.

528 *I:* mmhm.

529 *J:* so this is- you know, this is 19 uh, 57, [uh summer of '57,=

530 *I:*   [mmhm.

531 *J:* beginning of the summer (3.0). you'd have thought I had learned
        my lesson.

The narrated event here contains the voices of failed caregivers and abusers. Jane's boyfriend, as she presents him, shows no signs of sympathy for Jane. He simply "made arrangements" with the Mob for her abortion (lines 487–488). These "arrangements" sound similar to the "recommendations" made earlier to her mother about institutions. Like Mr. McGee, this boyfriend had a motive for turning Jane over to the Mob, namely, evading the responsibilities of parenthood. The Mob itself also benefits from Jane's ordeal, as they "made a fortune off abortion" (line 494).

Jane's mother continues to be weak, and she fails again as a caregiver. Jane reports that, while she was away having the abortion performed, her mother "was worried sick" (line 523). Normally, a mother who is worried sick about her daughter does something to help the child through the trauma. But in this case Jane went home and had to "assure" her mother that she was all right (line 525). The metapragmatic verb "assure" presupposes that Jane was in a more responsible position in the relationship and that it was her mother who needed assurance. Jane, however, makes clear that she could have used some support herself. She "didn't know if she was going to die" (line 524), and later she had to be rushed to the hospital.

In addition to her vulnerable position later in the segment, Jane also describes her narrated self early in this episode as speaking with the passive, vulnerable voice familiar from earlier episodes. She has to go along passively with the arrangements made by her boyfriend and the Mob, and she allows the Mob to "take advantage" of her (line 500). (Jane does also briefly speak in her more active, assertive voice in this episode, at line 509. She generally submits to the arrangements made for her, but she does assert herself at this one key point.) The only Mob-related person Jane describes in any detail is the "extraordinarily ignorant, European woman" who performs the abortion (line 501). Note the similarity between this description and the one Jane used for the teachers in her first institution. She describes them as "extraordinarily oppressed" (line 36), voices them as ignorant (lines 112–114), and also notes that they were European. Like the teachers, this European woman also abuses her, by giving her a botched abortion. Jane voices the abortionists as particularly brutal. She says, for instance, that they would "abort you in some room" (line 492)—a description that presupposes unsanitary, indiscriminate procedures.

Figure 4.9 represents the voices in this first abortion episode. In the narrated event, these four voices recur in the configuration familiar from earlier episodes. In ventriloquating the voices in the passage, Jane dis-

FIGURE 4.9 Jane's First Abortion

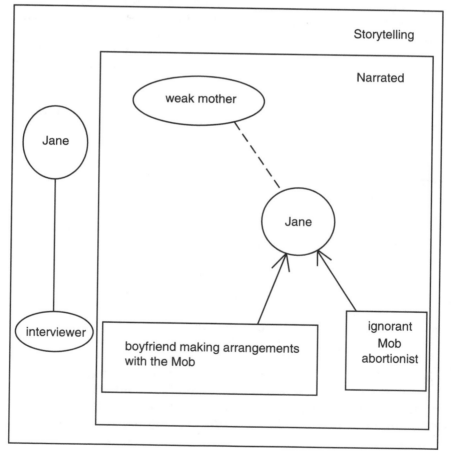

tances her storytelling self from her naive narrated self, as she did above in describing her first pregnancy—for instance, when she says "I found myself pregnant again. I couldn't believe it" (lines 485–486). Note also the last line in the segment: "you'd have thought I had learned my lesson" (line 532). This presupposes that her current self knows more than her naive narrated self (thus accomplishing "epistemic modalization"). Jane positions her storytelling self closer to her assertive narrated self— the one who "raised holy hell" and demanded that the Mob woman proceed (line 509). Evidence for this comes from the similar epistemic position that her storytelling and this assertive narrated self share. Both selves know that despite her "tipped uterus" she could get pregnant.

Jane the narrator clearly distances herself from the "ignorant European woman," in part through evaluative terms like "ignorant" and in part by portraying this woman as less knowledgeable than Jane's storytelling self. The woman had a belief current only "at the turn of the century" (line 503)—by implication, a belief that educated people had not held for 60 years. Even at age 24 Jane knew this was false. She steps into the storytelling event at this point in the story, to address the interviewer directly—"believe me, I am a testament to the opposite of that fact" (line 507)—and this reinforces that her current self is clearly superior (epistemically and perhaps otherwise) to the Mob woman. In this passage Jane does not do much ventriloquation of her boyfriend or mother. Perhaps her storytelling self evaluates them negatively, by presenting them as distanced and weak.

In the storytelling event in this passage, I argue that Jane positions herself as more experienced and less squeamish than the interviewer. She begins the passage by indexing the psychological enterprise represented by the interviewer—"I'm sure that psychologically there could be found a tie" (lines 480–481). This could entail that the interviewer (as a presumed psychological expert) will be able to interpret Jane's experiences better than Jane herself can. This type of relationship does not emerge, however. When Jane begins to describe her abortion, she apparently elicits a nonverbal reaction of shock or disbelief from the interviewer, when she stops and says "I'm serious" at line 489. Jane follows up this reaction of shock by reporting several graphic details that make the narrated events seem even more horrible: "They would abort you in some room" (line 492); "when she went inside of me" (line 502); "they put some sort of instrument that clamped onto the sac . . . to make it expel and they left you" (lines 510–514); "I expelled a fetus into the toilet" (line 518); "I started hemorrhaging even more and I was rushed to the hospital" (lines 525–526). Apart from their contributions to the narrated content, these extremely graphic descriptions might follow up on the interviewer's shock and might position Jane as someone who has survived such a horrible experience and yet does not flinch when recounting it. The density of graphic descriptions even seems to presuppose that she relishes telling this narrative. I argue that this relish is interactional. After positioning herself as insecure and the interviewer as authoritative earlier in the storytelling event, she now relishes the reversal that positions herself as experienced and the interviewer as young. This reversal in the interactional positioning also gets presupposed, in another way, in the next episode.

Second Abortion

   In the next segment Jane describes her second abortion. The second was very different from the first.

533 *J:* uh, so back into the chapter now where I'm with<u>out</u> my mother, and <u>I</u> found myself,

534   uh in 19- in January of '67 I got <u>preg</u>nant again. I couldn't believe I
535   was- so <u>stupid</u>. (3.0) but <u>no:w</u>, there was a thing called uh the <u>wo</u>men's movement,

536   who was, not only trying to get abortion <u>legal</u>ized, but they were <u>fight</u>ing the uh

537   <u>butch</u>er abortions that were going on in back rooms all over the- country. [including=

538 *I:*   [mmhm.

539 *J:* Louisville. there was a- an organization, uh by the name of WO<u>L</u> (1.0) that you

540   would <u>call</u> and you got a recorded message and you would <u>leave</u> your name and they

541   would call you back. and <u>they</u> made arrangements for me to have an abortion. (4.0) I:,

542   the <u>difference</u> between the <u>first</u> abortion and the <u>sec</u>ond abortion is- is <u>day</u> and <u>night</u>.

543   this was a group of <u>wo</u>men that we:re extraordinarily <u>caring</u> and pro<u>tec</u>tive, a:nd they

544   took you to <u>one</u> address and then a<u>noth</u>er, they gave you <u>medica</u>-tion, uh and they gave

545   you antibi<u>o</u>tics in case you got an infection they held your <u>hand</u> throughout the

546   abortion, it you- it- was ex<u>treme</u>ly painful, I have a <u>very</u> sensitive uterus, and uh, it

547 was <u>ve</u>ry very painful, but I had a <u>clean, de</u>cent, <u>car</u>ing abortion. I was so im<u>pressed</u>

548 by these women in '67 that I, joined <u>for</u>ces with them, and I joined the

549 organi<u>za</u>tion. I no sooner <u>join</u>ed than uh they were ar<u>rest</u>ed. they were called- that was

550 the Louisville <u>pro</u>test. um (2.0) e<u>ven</u>tually uh the grand jury dis<u>missed</u> the case, uh

551 but we con<u>tin</u>ued to be an abortion referral service, and a preg- nancy testing service, I

552 <u>join</u>ed them in Eastside Park. a:nd uh, it was a <u>new</u> awareness for me of, of a con<u>cern</u>

553 or women's health, and women's <u>bo</u>dies, and the oppressive <u>laws</u> that I was- <u>to</u>tally

554 unaware of, com<u>plete</u>ly unaware of. <u>all</u> I knew was that abortion was illegal, but I had

555 no idea of the <u>poli</u>tics behind it.

556 I: mmhmm.

557 J: I became <u>ve</u>ry politically <u>ac</u>tive. u:m passed those politics <u>on</u> to my son, whether

558 he l(hh)iked it or not. I uh, don't think it has <u>hurt</u> him, I am very <u>proud</u> of h- to hear

559 nowadays that it is uh, that he's-, he's very a<u>ware</u> of politics, [of political science,=

560 I: [mmhm.

561 J: of personalities, of international affairs [of- of de<u>ci</u>sions that are made in Washington=

562 I: [mmhmm

563 J: that affect all of us so, I'm- I'm glad I in<u>stilled</u> that in him.

564 I: I- I don't mean to <u>rush</u> you

565 J: [no, it's all right

566 I: [um but we've- there are a- <u>bunch</u> of other sections, of this inter- view,

567 J: [okay.

568 I: [so I'm wondering if there's some way that you can try to <u>cap</u>sulize the re<u>main</u> [ing=

569 J: [that

570 was uh- [yeah, that- well that was- yeah- they- the- being poli<u>ti</u>- cally active in the=

571 I: [= chapters so that- that we can get on to the next <u>sec</u>tion.

572 *J:* = '70s wa:s where my life continued, [u:h and I <u>only</u> have been <u>less</u>
          politically=
573 *I:*   [mm<u>hm</u>
574 *J:* active in the last, few years.
575 *I:* mmh [mm.
576 *J:*   [s- simply because of <u>burn</u>out and exhaustion
577 *I:* mmhmm.
578 *J:* and my <u>son</u> growing up (3.0) and <u>try</u>ing to, I- I w- just wanted him
          to have a
579   <u>more</u> complete life,

This second abortion, although obviously a difficult experience, was
"clean, decent, and caring" (line 547) due to the presence of a new voice
in Jane's story: the "extraordinarily caring and protective" women's organization (line 543). These women provided the strong support that
all Jane's other potential caregivers—from her mother to her grandparents to her boyfriends—had failed to give her. They acted like a good
mother and held Jane's hand throughout her trauma (lines 545–546).
Jane's narrated self joins the women's organization. She voices herself
as assertive here, and she joins with these women to fight against mi-
sogynist laws in the larger society. Jane also connects her son to the
values represented by this organization.

Table 4.5 shows how the first and second abortion episodes contain voices that also appeared earlier in Jane's story. The first abortion
episode contains self-interested recommenders, failed caregivers, abusive institutions, and Jane's passive self. The second abortion episode
contains Jane asserting herself against abusive institutions, but it also
contains the new voice of successful caregivers.

In this passage Jane at first distances her storytelling self from her
naive narrated self: "I got pregnant again. I couldn't believe I was so
stupid" (lines 534–535). She also positions her storytelling self alongside the women's organization by, for instance, describing them as
"fighting the butcher abortions" going on across the country (lines 536–
537). The strong negative evaluation connected to "butcher abortions"
places the narrator alongside anyone fighting them, especially given
Jane's graphic description of her first abortion. Toward the end of the
segment, once Jane has described how her narrated self became active
and joined the women's group, the narrated events begin to approach
the present. This becomes clear in her use of "we" at line 551. This
presupposes that Jane the narrator considers herself still a member of
the women's group that her narrated self joined. Note that this breaking down of distance between the narrated and storytelling events does

Table 4.5 Two Recurring Sets of Voices across the Entire Narrative

EPISODE	SELF-INTERESTED RECOMMENDERS	FAILED CAREGIVERS	ABUSIVE INSTITUTIONS	JANE'S VOICE	CAREGIVERS AND RECOMMENDERS, OVERCOME	ABUSIVE INSTITUTIONS, NEUTRALIZED	SUCCESSFUL CAREGIVERS
First institutionalization	Mr. McGee	Jane's mother	Teachers at the Academy	Passive and vulnerable			
Second institutionalization	Jane's grandparents	Jane's mother	Girls at the reform school	Passive and vulnerable			
Running away from reform school				Active and assertive	Jane's grandparents and mother	Girls at the reform school	
High School	Jane's grandfather	Jane's mother	Inadequate School	Passive and vulnerable			
Orphanage (1)	Jane's mother and grandparents	Robert	Orphanage woman	Passive and vulnerable			
Orphanage (2)				Active and assertive	Mother, grandparents, and Robert	Orphanage woman	
First abortion	Boyfriend	Jane's mother	Mob abortionist	Passive and vulnerable		Butcher abortionists	
Second abortion				Active and assertive	Misogynistic society		Women's community

not lead Jane to cry, because she aligns her current self with the assertive narrated self here.

Jane's narration of her second abortion also continues to presuppose a reversal in the interactional positions that she and the interviewer occupy. Jane "joined forces" with the women's organization (lines 548–549). This presupposes a military campaign, one in which Jane and others fought against unjust laws and even got arrested (line 549). In the storytelling event, then, Jane presents herself as a veteran of a moral crusade. Because of her youth, the interviewer could not be a veteran of this crusade. Furthermore, the crusade that Jane fought in has benefited women like the interviewer. Because of women like Jane, the interviewer will never have to endure an ordeal like Jane's first abortion. Thus Jane continues to presuppose the interactional reversal she started earlier. Earlier, Jane positioned herself in the storytelling event as insecure about how the authoritative interviewer might evaluate her performance in the interview. But now Jane positions herself as a veteran of the crusade for women's rights that took place while the interviewer was still a child.

Figure 4.10 represents the narrated and storytelling events during the second abortion episode. In the narrated event, the solid line between the supportive women and Jane indicates that they provided the care that she had needed for so long. In the storytelling event, for the first time Jane asserts herself against the interviewer, by indexing her own higher status. The figure represents this with the triangle and the arrow from Jane to the interviewer in the storytelling event.

At this point Jane has created a more elaborate parallel between the narrated and storytelling events. In the narrated events Jane repeatedly describes a transformation from passive and vulnerable to active and assertive—at the second institution, in high school, at the orphanage, and in her abortion experiences. In the first stage of each sequence Jane describes four voices: potential caregivers who abandon her; self-interested people who recommend an abusive institution; heartless people at the institution who abuse her; and Jane herself with her passive, vulnerable voice. In the second stage, Jane comes to speak with her active, assertive voice. She shields herself or her child from the abusers, and she does not allow the "recommenders" or the failed caregivers to control her life. Furthermore, as she has matured Jane's narrated self has also become more active and assertive over her life, developing from passive victim, to brave child, to high school leader, to aggressive defender of her child, to finding a supportive "other" in the women's movement and passing on these feminist values to her child. So Jane's developmental transformation from passive and vul-

FIGURE 4.10 Jane's Second Abortion

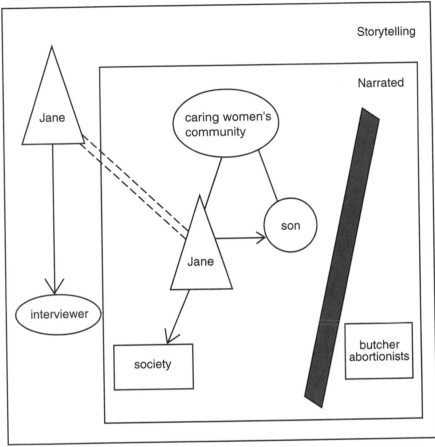

nerable to active and assertive happens in two respects in the narrated event: both *within* several episodes and *across* the entire narrative.

I have argued that Jane enacts an analogous transformation in her relationship with the interviewer in the storytelling event. Jane starts out vulnerable and insecure. She breaks down because the narrated events still haunt her. And she looks to the interviewer both for sympathy and for assurance that she is performing well as a research subject. As she narrates her abortions, however, Jane asserts herself. At the end of the interview she does not look to the interviewer to approve of her past actions or her interview performance. Instead, she positions herself as a veteran of a vital moral crusade for women's rights and the interviewer as a young woman who now benefits from Jane's actions and her experience.

This interactional reversal from passivity to self-assertion is not the only thing going on in the storytelling event. Jane and the interviewer still presuppose that they are engaged in a research interview. At line 564, for instance, the interviewer tries to move the interview along, and Jane complies. Jane has also just narrated very traumatic, personal experiences, and this makes her vulnerable. In fact, her vulnerable storytelling self reenters more than once after she narrates the abortion episodes—perhaps at line 577 where she mentions her "burnout and exhaustion" and certainly later on when she says that her son has gone to college (and beyond) and that this has left her all alone in the present. But the third type of interactional positioning, the one that involves Jane's development from vulnerable and insecure to active and assertive, also takes place over the course of the storytelling event.

Despite the active, assertive self that Jane both represents and enacts at the end of the interview, Jane's *recurring enactments* of her vulnerable self in the storytelling event show that her autobiographical narrative does not simply describe the established fact of her development into an active and assertive woman. The next chapter argues that the assertive self Jane first showed at age 16 needs to be continuously maintained. She enacts the transformation from vulnerable to assertive, in the storytelling event, because it is in these sorts of enactments that her self gets established and maintained.

The final lines of the interview show that Jane continues to face this developmental challenge.

582 *J:* when he left fo:r <u>col</u>lege, and <u>that's</u> a different chapter that- that's
     the <u>next</u> chapter.
583   tha:t, jarred me. first of all I had <u>not</u> been alone, in my life, <u>ev</u>er.
584 *I:* mmhmm.
585 *J:* this was the first time in my life I was a<u>lone</u>. and <u>sec</u>ond of all I felt
     that I had <u>lost</u> him.
586   and <u>he</u> was my only sense of family.
587 *I:* mmhmm.
588 *J:* by <u>now</u> my grandmother had died. my <u>mo</u>ther had died in 1966,
     my <u>gr</u>andmother died
589   in 1966. and <u>she</u> was my only family. u:m, (3.0) that- that's I
     guess that's like a-
590   that's a <u>cur</u>rent chapter. it has taken me the last decade or more
     to: ad<u>just</u> to,

591   my son <u>liv</u>ing, inde<u>pen</u>dent of me. and right now—I'm looking
         forward to him
592   coming home next w(h)eek. [sniff] um (3.0) I guess that pretty
         much you know the-
593   the uh- the <u>first</u> two-thirds of my life were the- <u>had</u> the biggest
         impact, <u>and</u> were
594   the most strenuous, that's why I, <u>seem</u> to have, uh <u>do</u>ted heavily
         on that
595 *I:* mmhmm.
596 *J:* because, I was- <u>fen</u>ding without, any- any <u>road</u>, I mean I was just-
         and <u>now</u> uh, I have
597   a- a <u>clear</u>er concept of who I am and what I want. as a re<u>sult</u> o:f
         all this that is be<u>hind</u>
598   me,
599 *I:* mm<u>hmm</u>.
600 *J:* and now that my son is grown.

After her son left for college, Jane found herself in a familiar position: she has been abandoned by someone she cares about and now must fend for herself. In narrating this event, Jane herself might be speaking in her more vulnerable voice. Despite her claim to "have a clearer concept of who I am" (line 597), the distance between her (lonely) narrated and storytelling selves seems about to break down and she may be about to speak with her vulnerable voice once again. If she stays in character, she will go on to enact her active, assertive voice in response to this developmental challenge.

CHAPTER 5

Narrative Self-Construction and the Nature of the Self

The first chapter argued that a more sophisticated analysis of autobiographical narrators' interactional positioning helps explain how they can partly construct themselves while telling their stories. Chapters 2 and 3 introduced tools for analyzing positioning in narrative, especially the concepts of dialogue, mediation, emergence, voicing, and ventriloquation. Chapter 4 illustrated how this approach can uncover both interactional positioning and parallelism between positioning and represented content in an autobiographical narrative. To complete the argument, this chapter explores further how interactional positioning and parallels between represented content and interactional positioning can contribute to narrative self-construction. With reference to the detailed consideration of Jane's autobiographical narrative in the last chapter, we can sketch a clear picture of how narrative self-construction works and what the self might be.

As described in the last chapter, Jane's autobiographical narrative has three central aspects: (1) In the narrated events, she describes two recurring sets of voices: first, negligent caregivers, self-interested recommenders, heartless abusers, and her own passive and vulnerable self; then, an active and assertive self that shields herself from failed caregivers and abusers. Jane establishes these two configurations of voices in a mediated way, by creatively deploying indexical cues. The configurations presuppose preexisting patterns, but the full structures emerge in and are tailored to Jane's particular story. (2) In the storytelling event, Jane positions herself first as passive and vulnerable, then as active and assertive. This interactional positioning emerges over the course of the storytelling event, as Jane positions herself with respect to the voices in the narrative and with respect to the interviewer. (3) Sometimes Jane speaks with the same voices in the narrated event that she uses in the storytelling event. The represented content and interactional positioning are partly parallel, such that Jane both represents and enacts the development from passive and vulnerable to active and assertive. This chapter explores how several theories of the self would explain these three patterns in Jane's autobiographical narrative. I combine aspects of these different theories into a picture of the self that not only accounts for these three patterns in Jane's autobiographical narrative but also describes how interactional positioning in autobiographical narrative can partly construct the self.

I argue that narrative self-construction can depend in particular on the *interrelation* of representation and enactment. By definition, autobiographical narratives involve the doubling of roles for the narrator. As Stahl (1989) and most others define the genre, an autobiographical narrative presupposes the biographical identity of the narrator (in the storytelling event) and the main character (in the narrated event). Bruner (1987), Crites (1986), Mishler (1986), and others argue that the connection between narrated and storytelling selves gives autobiographical narrative its power for constituting the self. As Crites puts it, autobiographical narrative artistically bridges the gap between past and current selves, and thus it helps construct a coherent identity for the narrator.

Bakhtin's approach helps show how the interrelation between narrated and storytelling selves works. An autobiographical narrator voices and ventriloquates himself. In voicing his own narrated selves, a narrator identifies those past selves as recognizable types of people engaged in recognizable relationships with narrated others. Then the narrator ventriloquates those voiced selves, taking some evaluative stance with respect to them. Jane, for instance, positions herself at the orphanage as moving from passive and victimized to active and assertive, when she takes her child back from the cold, self-interested orphanage bureaucrat. Later in the narrative she also positions her storytelling self as more mature than both the orphanage woman and the interviewer.

This voicing and ventriloquation of the self yields a trajectory for the narrator, as the positions of past selves lead toward the self narrating the story here and now. Jane's past, victimized self has become the active, assertive woman telling her story in the storytelling event. Note how the creation of such a trajectory depends on the interrelationship between represented content and enacted positioning. The voicing of past selves is represented, even though much of it is presupposed indexically and not denoted explicitly. But positioning the storytelling self with respect to those past selves is often enacted without ever being explicitly represented, in the same way as Rather and Braver's mock trial of Bush (see chapter 3) was enacted without being explicitly represented.

Furthermore, in the storytelling event the narrator positions himself not only with respect to past selves but also with respect to the interlocutors. Thus Jane positions herself not only with respect to represented voices like her past selves and the orphanage woman but also with respect to the interviewer in the storytelling event. This interactional positioning can sometimes depend on what Silverstein (1998) and Irvine (1996) call a "mapping" from represented content to enacted positioning. Voices and relationships that get *represented* by the narrator can come to organize the storytelling event itself, as narrator and interlocutors act out relationships partly analogous to those represented in the narrative.

Represented content and enacted positioning, therefore, can interrelate in two ways so as to construct the self. First, represented voices presupposed for the narrator's past selves can lie on a trajectory that leads toward the storytelling self that is ventriloquating these voices—by positioning herself in characteristic ways through this ventriloquation the narrator can partly create herself. Second, represented voices can be mapped onto and thus organize the interaction between narrator and interlocutors. If the positioning in this interaction gets repeated and becomes habitual, it can shape the narrator's self. In other words, we are to some degree the kind of people we position ourselves as when we narrate ourselves, especially when we represent and enact parallel positions for our narrated and storytelling selves.

THE STABLE PSYCHOLOGICAL SELF

Most theories of the self try to explain why people often appear to others and experience themselves as relatively coherent individuals. One common kind of psychological answer is provided by Damon and Hart (1988), who argue that a person has a coherent self insofar as she has an *organized self-understanding*. The pattern that characterizes a self comes from "the cognitive representation of personal identity" (p. 13), not from interpersonal or emotional patterns. From this perspective, Jane's self would centrally include her coherent understanding of herself as an active and assertive woman who has developed through difficult times into her current mature state.

Damon and Hart propose seven aspects of self-understanding that together constitute a person's organized self-representations. The self as represented object contains the physical self, the active self, the social self, and the psychological self. The self as representing subject involves representations of continuity, distinctness, and agency. For each of these seven aspects, Damon and Hart propose a set of four developmental stages: from categorical identifications, to comparative assessments, to interpersonal implications, to systematic beliefs and plans. Damon and Hart claim that the resulting 28-cell matrix (seven aspects of self-understanding, each with four developmental levels) captures all possible types of self-understanding. When faced with an actual person talking about himself, Damon and Hart interpret which of the 28 types of self-understanding the subject's self-description represents. For instance, Jane remarks on the clarity of her memory about leaving the Academy at age 12. Damon and Hart might see this as indicating a systematic, highly developed (i.e., at the stage of late adolescence and beyond) sense of her own distinctness as a subject, because she shows an awareness of her own unique subjective experience.

Thus Damon and Hart, claiming that self-understandings come in 28 rigidly defined types, identify an individual's type of self by coding the representational content of his self-descriptions into the 28 categories that describe different types of organization for the self-concept. As argued in Chapters 2 and 3, this sort of unmediated approach cannot explain evolving, emergent types of narrated self-descriptions created by narrators like Jane. In autobiographical narratives, narrators often use indexical cues creatively to establish unexpected, nonnormative patterns, like the two sets of voices described in the last chapter. Damon and Hart's reliance on 28 rigidly defined categories restricts their ability to appreciate context-specific patterns that involve multiple voices for self and for relevant others. Fitting the configurations of voices in Jane's story into rigidly defined categories would miss substantial details of these voices.

Their emphasis on (representational) self-understanding also makes Damon and Hart's account of self a *monologic* one. Just as a monologic interpretation of speech focuses on represented content and ignores how the utterance positions the speaker interactionally, Damon and Hart focus on cognitive representations of self and ignore how the self gets positioned in social action with respect to others. A *dialogic* theory of self would also take into account the positioning of the individual with respect to others in actual practice, just as a dialogic account of speech goes beyond the narrated content of speech to analyze how speech positions the speaker with respect to others in the storytelling event. Damon and Hart appear to be uninterested in these interactional patterns, because they believe that interactional patterns are not essential to Jane's true psychological self or are simply a manifestation of her underlying self-understanding.

Theories of self that rely on rigidly defined categories cannot describe how any of the three central patterns in Jane's autobiographical narrative might contribute to constructing her self. First, because they offer an account in terms of a few rigidly defined categories of self-understanding, Damon and Hart cannot account for the particular configurations of voices Jane describes in the represented content of her narrative. Their categories might capture some broad aspects of Jane's repeated development from passive to active, but any limited set of categories must ignore most of the voicing—for example, Jane's repeated victimization by and triumph over heartless institutions. Second, Damon and Hart cannot account for the interactional positioning in Jane's narrative because their method relies solely on the represented contents of self-descriptions, and they show no interest in how autobiographical narrative might position the narrator dialogically in relationships with others. Third, because they ignore the interactional positioning accomplished through autobiographical narration, Damon and Hart would miss the parallel between represented content and interactional positioning, such as the fact that Jane positions herself in her interaction with the interviewer in a similar relational configuration to the one she describes for her narrated selves.

Although theories like Damon and Hart's cannot explain how the three central aspects of Jane's narrative might contribute to constructing her self, that fact does not disprove these theories. They might argue that their categories capture the essence of Jane's self. And they could argue that the positioning done in any autobiographical narrative simply manifests an underlying psychological self. The last section of this chapter gives reasons for preferring a different account, but I do not claim to have conclusive arguments. Given the rich and pervasive interactional patterns created in autobiographical narrative, however, theories of self that can account for interactional patterns would seem to be stronger.

THE NARRATED SELF

McAdams (1985, 1993, 1997) and Freeman (1993) do not use rigidly defined categories in their theories of the self, yet they still claim to explain the apparent coherence of many selves. These two theories come from different traditions; McAdams comes from the personological tradition in personality psychology and Freeman from hermeneutic philosophy and developmental psychology. But they agree that the coherence of a self is best understood in narrative terms. They do not mean that a self consists of nothing more than the particular stories a person tells about herself. They argue instead that real selves, which provide unity and purpose to people's lives, should be analyzed as one would analyze the coherence of a narrative. Self is best understood as an evolving life story.

Selves cohere because individuals construct coherent stories out of their particular actions and experiences. Just as an indeterminate number of stories could be written about a life, one could imagine an indeterminate number of coherent selves. McAdams (1993) argues that so many different yet coherent lives are possible that no one could ever generate a universal typology to capture every one. Freeman (1993) argues, further, that the process of interpreting any particular life is indeterminate. Any individual's actions and experiences could fit more than one coherent story.

Interpreters foreground certain actions and experiences as most salient and emplot these into an overall narrative pattern that gives coherence to the self. One might, for instance, emphasize Jane's first "institutionalization" as the key experience in her life. This might lead an interpreter to conclude that she does not have much of a "foundation" and to emphasize her passive, vulnerable self. This interpretation would construe Jane's life as a tragedy, with her potential undermined by the early institutionalization. On the other hand, one could emphasize Jane's resourcefulness in "blackmailing" her mother at age 16. By foregrounding this event an interpreter could read the story as more heroic and highlight Jane's active, assertive self.

According to McAdams and Freeman, the establishment of self-coherence is a back-and-forth or dialectic process, from elements to whole and back again. The overall plot of one's life does not determine the meaning of the parts, because some elements demand that interpreters modify their construal of the whole. But neither can an interpreter compute a coherent self from the elements, because elements only have clear meaning as they are construed within the whole. An act or experience begins the interpretive process, by leading an interpreter to construe the overall life in a certain way. For instance, emphasizing Jane's first institutionalization would lead one to interpret her as vulnerable and without foundation. This interpretation makes other events salient, such as Jane's inability to confront the father of her child. But this element brings along others that do not fit neatly with the first interpretation. Despite Robert's absence, for instance, Jane did end up being a good parent. Then an interpreter must reconsider the whole life in light of this new evidence and infer the coherence of the life by constructing a context of salient life events.

Self-coherence emerges in a life as a set of salient elements come to fit together in a plausible story line for the life. With this narrative theory of self, McAdams and Freeman can account for the first central aspect of Jane's autobiographical narrative—its presentation of two particular sets of voices. McAdams and Freeman expect contingent, context-specific configurations like this to emerge in the interpretive process of giving structure to a life. Instead of fitting a life into rigidly specified categories, McAdams and Freeman describe an inferential process through which the coherence of the self emerges as elements of the life get emplotted into a narrative whole.

McAdams and Freeman's emergent narrative structure, however, has a different nature than the type of emergent structure discussed in Chapter 2. The narrative structures that McAdams and Freeman describe are emergent but not interactional. Neither of them discusses the context outside the individual in any systematic way. They both acknowledge that cultures provide ways of interpreting particular events as well as models of normative selves. But they do not offer dialogic accounts of the self that would attend to how the self gets positioned as part of interactional events. For McAdams and Freeman, self-coherence involves representation and not enactment. They move beyond Damon and Hart's list of rigidly specified structures to an account of how contingent patterns of voices and relationships can emerge and organize particular lives. But they focus on representations of the narrated event and ignore positioning in the storytelling event. Thus McAdams and Freeman would not attend to the interactional positioning in autobiographical narratives like Jane's. Their theories of the self cannot explain how the self might get partly constructed through positioning in autobiographical narrative.

McAdams and Freeman also rely heavily on individual psychology to explain how one coherent self emerges from the ongoing process of interpretation. Freeman is particularly concerned to rebut what he calls "the skeptical challenge," the claim that no real, coherent self exists. In the face of the indeterminate number of possible construals of any person's life, he argues, people must "have faith" that a real self does exist. "Autobiographical texts do not and cannot reveal the past 'as it was' . . . [but] these texts, far from *necessarily* falling prey to illusion, may in fact be quite real and (dare I say?) true" (1993, p. 31). The coherent "text" that people make out of a life can become really true, not just an illusion designed to make oneself feel better. Freeman argues that the narrative coherence of a self represents a real psychological phenomenon that people must have faith in. To be sure, this self changes over time and people only access it through fallible inference. But the indeterminate process of constructing narrative coherence for the self yields a definite interpretation when people take a leap of faith that some version is true to their selves at this moment. Like Freeman, McAdams also ends the interpretive process inside the individual—in his case, in a more stable version of the story that *is* the self. He describes "the *central* story," as "there all along, inside the mind" (1993, p. 20).

For both McAdams and Freeman, then, self-coherence is ultimately accomplished inside the individual. Freeman supports his argument here with several convincing examples. The examples that Freeman gives of "truer" versions of the self all rest on a developmental intuition. He argues that people can have faith in certain versions of themselves when these interpretations show those selves developing a more "comprehensive and expansive" view (1993, p. 32)—a type of self-understanding that allows one to reflect on and take some control over one's life. Freeman favors examples in which people move from being objects to being creators, in which coming to awareness of previously unconscious patterns can dissolve the power of these patterns over one's life. He praises the self that attempts a "serious and probing attempt at self-understanding" (1993, p. 24), and he admires the power "to become conscious enough of my world to shape my destiny" (p. 217). So people can have faith in a particular interpretation of their selves when that interpretation shows the self reflecting on itself and using that reflection to take some control. Freeman argues that, while there are and have been places and times in which this narrative of self-awareness and agency was not powerful, it does capture a real possibility for contemporary Western selves. And to doubt the existence of a true self would be to deny ourselves the power of this sort of developmental life story. Thus Freeman argues for a privileged developmental path which is preferable to others, at least in this time and place. He does not claim that all lives have the same trajectory, and he admits pluralism in people's goals. But he does favor one abstract type of life trajectory over others.

McAdams also argues that people in Western cultures strive for unity and agency in their autobiographical narratives. Both McAdams and Freeman acknowledge that selves are not necessarily unified or in control and that people in other times and places might strive for different narratives of the self. But they argue that modern Westerners should have faith in a coherent psychological-level self, one that strives for unity and resists endless and fickle rereadings of a life. This faith will allow people to overcome the indeterminate number of possible accounts of their selves and settle on provisional but solid construals of those selves.

I cannot disprove this preference for reflective, psychological selves. I can point out, however, many arguments to the effect that even contemporary Western selves need not be independent (e.g., Gilligan, 1986) or reflective (e.g., Rorty & Wong, 1990) to be coherent. I would also argue that Freeman finds skepticism such a threat largely because of his more representational, psychological approach. If self-coherence comes primarily from representations, interpreters will always face worries about whether those representations correspond to underlying realities (cf. K. Gergen, 1982). But the best argument against a primarily psychological account of the self will be to develop a plausible alternative account of self-coherence. I suggest that perhaps self-coherence is in substantial part an interactional accomplishment, something that happens when a set of characteristic positions for self and relevant others emerge and solidify. If so, one might worry less about whether self-representations correspond to real selves and focus instead on how people's actions reinforce or re-create their selves. Thus a self would come to cohere in significant part because of enacted interactional patterns, as coherent ways of positioning emerge in autobiographical narratives and other types of interactions with others. Bakhtin and some contemporary social constructionists offer accounts of self along these lines—theories that can account for the interactional positioning in Jane's autobiographical narrative.

THE DIALOGIC SELF

McAdams and Freeman move beyond rigidly specified, universal categories of the self, to describe how self-coherence can emerge in particular lives. Thus they can account for one central aspect of Jane's autobiographical narrative—the particular configurations of voices that emerge in her life story. Any adequate account of narrative self-construction will have to give some similar description of how particular patterns of voicing emerge. McAdams and Freeman also make the important point that selves cohere relatively well in most cases. Fragmented and anomic selves do exist, but postmodern accounts tend to overstate the degree of fragmentation. Jane, for instance, both describes and enacts more than one self. But the passive and active aspects of her self relate in a coherent way, in both narrated and storytelling events.

Although I agree with McAdams and Freeman that relatively coherent selves exist, I find their explanation for self-coherence incomplete. Because they do not attend to interactional positioning, McAdams and Freeman cannot account for the interactional accomplishment of self-coherence. They cannot account for how the second and third central aspects of Jane's narrative—her systematic interactional positioning with respect to the interviewer and the parallel between the storytelling and narrated events—might contribute to her narrative self-construction. This section draws on more dialogic theories of self, including Bakhtin's, which focus on interactional positioning in autobiographical narrative. Such accounts of the self can explain how Jane's interactional positioning might play a role in her narrative self-construction.

In this section I will refer to a group of contemporary theories in theoretical, clinical, and social psychology, collectively, as *social constructionist* (K. Gergen, 1991, 1994; Hermans & Kempen, 1993; Schafer, 1992; Shotter & K. Gergen, 1989). Like McAdams and Freeman, these social constructionists all use narrative as a metaphor for self. They argue that a coherent self emerges from the various events of a life as a narrative organization for that life emerges. Unlike McAdams and Freeman, social constructionists argue that the self gets constructed through relationships with others, especially in discourse. By this they mean, in part, something that McAdams and Freeman agree with: people rely on typical "texts" (Shotter & K. Gergen, 1989) or "story lines" (Schafer, 1992) from the culture to organize themselves. But the social constructionists emphasize the interactional aspects of this process. While interacting with others, people often talk about themselves. Within the interaction this talk functions "performatively" (K. Gergen, 1989). That is, talk about oneself positions people with respect to others. Talk about the self, according to the social constructionists, should not be assessed for truth or falsity with respect to an independently existing self. Instead, this talk is "constitutive of our actual relations to one another, and, to the extent that we constitute ourselves in our relations to others, constitutive of ourselves" (Shotter, 1989, pp. 136–137). In talking about themselves with others, people can develop coherent selves. This happens as the person positions himself or herself in characteristic ways with respect to others.

According to the social constructionists, people can constitute and reconstitute their selves by positioning themselves with respect to others in actual interaction. McAdams and Freeman would agree with the description of ongoing reconstruction stressed in this account, but they would focus on self-interpretation instead of interactional positioning. The difference between social constructionist and more psychological accounts of self can be understood in terms of the distinction between monologic and dialogic. For McAdams and Freeman, the life story is best understood as a monologic event. Any references to others and positioning of the self occur *within the narrated event*. The picture of self-creation that one gets from Freeman involves a person sitting alone, reflecting on himself and perhaps writing an autobiography. Freeman acknowledges that the autobiographer uses language and categories drawn from the culture and that the autobiographer reflects on his relations with others. But he does not describe self-construction as happening *within the storytelling event*, as the social constructionists do.[1] For the latter, the self emerges not primarily from self-reflection but instead from participation in verbal practices that position narrators in various ways. According to the social constructionists, the self is not "narrated" into being. It is, instead, "positioned" into being in interactional events like those enacted by Jane and the interviewer.

This social constructionist approach to self can account for the second central aspect of Jane's autobiographical narrative. If self-coherence gets established in important part through interactional positioning, then Jane becomes the kind of person she is partly by positioning herself with respect to people like the interviewer. When Jane positions herself as alternately vulnerable and assertive in the storytelling event, she is (re-)creating characteristic positions that partly constitute her self. If she consistently positions herself as accomplishing this developmental transition in many interactional events, she can become this type of person, one who has developed from passivity and vulnerability to self-assertion. Whatever her representations of self are, consistent interactional positioning like this can partly construct or transform her self.

Bakhtin's suggestive comments about the self serve to articulate how the self might be positioned into being as the social constructionists suggest. Bakhtin presents the self not as a bounded territory but as what Morson and Emerson call a "boundary phenomenon" (1990, p. 51). The self exists only on the boundary between self and other. It does not contain or develop inner regions, but instead exists only in dialogue with the other (cf. Mead, 1934, p. 91, for a similar view). When Bakhtin discusses a dialogic self, he writes about the self as if it were one big speech event. He intends this only partly as a metaphor, because social life does in fact consist largely of speech events. As described in Chapters 2 and 3, all speech events place participants in social positions with respect to others. A good portion of one's life is a series of speech events, in which the self gets positioned and repositioned with respect to others. Insofar as these speech events position the self in characteristic ways over time, the self can develop coherence. With respect to the self, then, *dialogic* has the same meaning as it does with respect to a speech event. A speech event comes to have meaning as analysts and participants construe the speaker's position with respect to relevant others. Similarly, one develops a coherent self by consistently positioning oneself with respect to others over time.

Bakhtin describes this positioning with respect to others as the "ventriloquation" of others' "words." "The ideological becoming of a human being, in this view, is the process of selectively assimilating the words of others" (1935/1981, p. 341). Particular words index the social positions and associated ideological views of those who habitually use those words. To become a self one must speak, and in speaking, one must use words that have been used by others. In using words that echo with the voices of others, one must take a position with respect to those others. Expanding this analysis metaphorically from the level of the speech event to the level of a whole life, Bakhtin argues that becoming a self involves positioning oneself with respect to other speakers whose words (and relational stances, characteristic acts, and viewpoints) one ventriloquates. Of course, people in some social positions may have more latitude in this ventriloquation than others. Bakhtin would not deny the constraining power of social organization. But he would resist rigid accounts of monolithic groups locked into one position or another and point instead to the complexity, the inevitable loopholes, and the flexibility in the system.

On Bakhtin's account, then, a person cannot become a self alone. Just as a novelist most often articulates her own position by speaking through others' voices, a person only articulates herself by ventriloquating others. The self has unique experiences and a unique trajectory because any particular self gets positioned with respect to the others it happens to encounter and ventriloquate. But this individual uniqueness gets fashioned only by ventriloquating others. In this way, as K. Clark and Holquist (1984) argue, Bakhtin attempts to capture both the uniqueness and the dialogic character of the self.[2]

This puts the (Western) self in an ironic position: struggling to articulate its own individual voice but able to do so only by speaking through others. Bakhtin sometimes talks of this tension between the individual and the collective in terms of the inevitable tension between "centripetal" and "centrifugal" forces (1935/1981, pp. 271ff.). The centripetal forces push for a monologic self—an essence, located in and articulated by the individual and resistant to change. The centrifugal forces encourage the proliferation of other voices that both speak through and get ventriloquated by the self. By presenting the self as existing in the tension between centripetal and centrifugal forces, Bakhtin offers neither a social nor a psychological account of the self (cf. Hermans & Kempen, 1993, for a useful articulation of this point). Against social determinism, he does not reduce the self to social categories. On the contrary, Bakhtin casts the creative self, ventriloquating others and creating complexity, as the hero in the struggle against official monologic discourse. He praises romanticism for elaborating this aspect of the self: "Romanticism made its own important discovery—that of the interior subjective man with his depth, complexity, and inexhaustible resources" (1965/1984b, p. 44). But he complicates this view by locating the self within a dialogic process.

Bakhtinian and social constructionist accounts of the self can describe how the interactional positioning Jane does while telling her autobiographical narrative might partly construct her self. She first positions herself as passive and vulnerable, as a victim of traumatic early experiences whom the interviewer might want to console. But when the interviewer does not ratify this positioning, Jane repositions herself as a cooperative research subject. As the storytelling interaction continues, she slips into and out of a passive and vulnerable position with respect to the interviewer. These cycles continue until, at the end, Jane positions herself as self-assertive with respect to the interviewer. Note that, because she is telling an autobiographical narrative, Jane has the opportunity to ventriloquate both others and herself. Her position with respect to her earlier selves—as when the distance between narrated and storytelling breaks down suddenly and she falls into her vulnerable voice—shows how the opportunity to position oneself with respect to one's own past selves makes autobiographical narrative a particularly rich site for positioning and creating the self.

So a constructionist, Bakhtinian theory of self can account for how the first two aspects of Jane's autobiographical narrative might partly construct herself. Because Bakhtin and some of the social constructionists describe how narrators creatively deploy cues to represent particular configurations of voices, such an account can capture the particular configurations of voices that Jane presents. Bakhtin and the social constructionists also can explain how Jane's interactional positioning in the storytelling event can contribute to her self-construction. Jane develops from vulnerable to assertive as she positions herself in these ways with respect to interlocutors like the interviewer. Neither Bakhtin nor the social constructionists, however, account for the third central aspect of Jane's autobiographical narrative—the parallel between represented content and interactional positioning. If all three central aspects of Jane's autobiographical narrative play a role in her narrative self-construction, the constructionist account of self needs to be elaborated.

THE ENACTED SELF

Jane both describes and enacts similar configurations of voices for herself and relevant others while telling her autobiographical narrative. She describes her narrated selves moving through a cycle from passive and vulnerable to active and assertive and back again. While giving these descriptions to the interviewer she goes through a parallel cycle, first positioning herself as passive and vulnerable with respect to the interviewer and then as active and assertive. Neither Bakhtin nor the social constructionists describe this sort of parallel between narrated and storytelling voices in any detail. Bakhtin and the constructionists present the self as emerging through interactional positioning in everyday action. If some everyday actions—for instance, some events in which a narrator tells a story about his or her own past experiences—involve both the description and the enactment of parallel configurations of roles for self and others, these actions might play an important role in the construction of self.

This section argues that the interrelations between represented content and interactional positioning in autobiographical narrative can play an important role in constructing the self. In order to capture these interrelations, an account of narrative self-construction must not *oppose* the representational and interactional functions of narrative discourse. Interactional positioning is crucial to the construction of self in autobiographical narrative. But autobiographical narrators also represent things about themselves. Without naively assuming that these representations correspond to underlying psychological reality, an account can still describe how the represented content of autobiographical narratives can combine with interactional positioning to construct the self.

Transference

The striking parallel between represented content and interactional positioning in Jane's narrative seems to demand a psychological explanation, however. In his theory of *transference* Freud (1900/1965a) notes that patients often enact, in their relationship with the analyst, interactional patterns that match key relationships from their past. While they describe their past relationships to the analyst as the narrated events discussed in therapy, patients also enact similar relationships with the analyst in the therapeutic storytelling event. His psychological theory leads Freud to *expect* patients both to describe and to enact similar patterns. According to Freud, neurotics get stuck in relational patterns they experienced with important others, and their reenactment of these patterns can lead to pathology. In therapy the analyst asks patients to describe past events, and because patients are stuck in relational patterns that originated in the early experiences they describe, they will often both describe and enact the same patterns. In Jane's case, Freud might argue that she was so traumatized by her relationships with a negligent mother and abusive caretakers that she sometimes continues to position herself just as her passive, vulnerable 7-year-old self did. It should come as no surprise, then, that while describing these narrated events Jane positions her storytelling self in a parallel vulnerable role and projects the complementary role of negligent caretaker onto her interlocutor.

Freud's (1900/1965a) observations about transference are brilliant. He was able to describe the type of interactional positioning exemplified in Jane's autobiographical narrative, without access to the methodological tools that now allow us to uncover such positioning systematically. The ubiquity of transference, both in therapeutic and in other types of discursive interactions (cf. Wortham, 1994, 2001), also demands an explanation. But Freud's own explanations for transference rest on problematic assumptions. Like Damon and Hart (1988), Freud (1933/1965b) posits a small set of rigidly specified types of self and interprets both narrated and storytelling patterns by fitting them into his taxonomy. This approach glosses over the mediated process through which indexical cues help establish particular configurations of voices. Like McAdams and Freeman, Freud also explains self-coherence by positing an underlying psychological entity. For him, both the narrated description and the enactment in an autobiographical narrative like Jane's derive from the subject's psychological self, a self that has been structured through past experiences with significant others.

Transference as Interactional Positioning

I propose an alternative, partly cultural explanation for the parallel between represented content and interactional positioning in autobiographical narratives like Jane's. A more sociocentric account can incorporate Freud's extraordinary insights about transference without adopting his metapsychology. Crapanzano (1992) argues that Freud's concept of transference can be understood in constructionist terms as a matter of interactional positioning and not of psychological structure. Crapanzano argues that "the 'self' is an arrested moment in the ongoing dialectical movement between self and other" (p. 72). This dialectical movement happens in the everyday practice of positioning oneself with respect to others, just as Jane does in her interaction with the interviewer. People constitute themselves by positioning themselves with respect to others—by "casting the other to cast oneself" (p. 82). Interactional positioning is "ongoing" because in everyday life individuals position themselves in response to how others position them, then the others reposition themselves in response to this positioning, and this process has no end. People bring order to the flow of reciprocal positioning in everyday life by "arresting" it "through desired characterizations and typifications of the other (and therefore the self)" (p. 91). The self has structure, then, largely as cultural typifications are enacted, and sometimes amended, in everyday interactional events. This process involves desire as well as cognition: People not only know how to speak in particular configurations of voices, but they also express and experience desire toward certain roles or configurations. The emotional aspects of this process do not necessarily provide evidence for underlying psychological structures; emotional display might also be explained as part of salient cultural positioning, such as the sort one often sees in important ritual events.

By foregrounding cultural and not psychological patterns in his account of transference, Crapanzano moves toward a sociocentric account of the parallel between represented content and interactional positioning. The social world offers typical positions and events, and in practice people tend to enact particular configurations of these types over and over. In this view, the parallel between representation and enactment in autobiographical narrative results from the salience of certain socially typical positions and events. Jane does not both describe and enact her development from passive and vulnerable to active and assertive only because of something in her psychology, but also because of the ubiquity of these as cultural patterns.

The Ritualized Construction of Self

Crapanzano shows how the Freudian concept of transference can be interpreted in a more cultural and less psychological way. He gives only an abbreviated account of the parallel between representation and enactment in autobiographical narratives like Jane's, however. What function could the parallel have, if it is not simply manifesting some psychological structure? A fuller answer to this question can be found in the linguistic anthropological theory implicit in much of Crapanzano's analysis. This pragmatic theory of language and culture has been developed by Michael Silverstein (1976, 1993, 1996) and many of his colleagues (cf. the collections in Lucy, 1993; Mertz & Parmentier, 1985; Silverstein & Urban, 1996) and is usefully reviewed by Parmentier (1997). One aspect of this theory focuses on cultural events, often ritual events, that include the same type of parallel between representation and enactment that occurs in Jane's autobiographical narrative. Silverstein and his colleagues argue that rituals often involve a parallel between storytelling and narrated events because this sort of parallel helps reproduce cultural patterns. Analogously, I argue that the parallel between storytelling and narrated events in autobiographical narratives like Jane's helps reproduce the self.

In order to make this argument, I must briefly summarize Silverstein's cultural account of *ritual parallelism*. Social categories are maintained in discursive practice as people enact characteristic events and adopt types of positions within those events (Silverstein & Urban, 1996; Urban, 1996). Members of any society explicitly and implicitly recognize many types of events. When confronted with empirical evidence of an ongoing event, these members will generally come to understand the event as coherent when the (largely indexical) signs that compose the event come increasingly to presuppose that a particular type of event is going on (Silverstein, 1992). Ritual events play a particularly important role in maintaining particular types of events as salient within a given culture. Parmentier (1997), Silverstein (1981,1993), and others offer a semiotic account of how this works. Ritual does not merely represent or symbolize salient concepts and social patterns. In addition, ritual participants also enact relationships among themselves that signal these patterns. Ritual has particular power to re-create ways of understanding social events when it both describes and instantiates the same patterns. In other words, participants in ritual events often describe what they enact in the process of (re-)creating their culture. I argue that Jane's autobiographical narrative can usefully be interpreted as a ritualized event in this respect.

An autobiographical narrative like Jane's involves both representation and enactment of the same relational configuration. At the level of a social group, Silverstein (1993) and Urban (1996) describe how this sort of parallel helps reinforce cultural patterns. But autobiographical narratives can also partly establish the selves of particular individuals. For Jane, telling a story about herself that both describes and enacts a powerful set of voices allows her to establish herself as a certain kind of person. When autobiographical narratives involve a parallel between described and enacted voices, they can be ritualized events that reproduce or re-create the self.

It may be that Jane establishes and maintains her active, assertive self by simultaneously representing and enacting this pattern in everyday life. By representing and enacting her development from passive child to active adult, Jane accomplishes that development. Her story illustrates how this sort of parallel in autobiographical narrative can maintain the characteristic position of the self in presupposed cultural patterns. Just as ritual events often center around simultaneously represented and enacted patterns, and thus maintain central ways of organizing social events, autobiographical narratives can center around such parallels and maintain the self. I am arguing that the theory of culture developed by Silverstein (1976), Urban (1996), and their colleagues provides a more cultural, less psychological account of the parallel between represented content and interactional positioning in Jane's autobiographical narrative. Such parallels do not occur primarily because of underlying psychological structure that manifests itself in both action and representation. Instead, enacted autobiographical narratives are ritualized events for constructing or maintaining the self. The configuration of voices in Jane's autobiographical narrative recurs in both representation and enactment because this is how semiotic processes of cultural reproduction work. People position themselves whenever they speak, whether in autobiographical narrative or other discourse. Self-positioning in any context, whether it involves parallelism between representation and enactment or not, can potentially contribute structure to the self. But autobiographical narratives in which narrators both represent and enact analogous patterns can make particularly salient contributions to self-construction. Autobiographical narratives that both describe and enact the same configuration of voices for self and other seem particularly likely to provide robust structure to the self. Jane's autobiographical narrative, then, illustrates a particularly rich type of narrative self-construction.

THE MULTILAYERED SELF

I am not arguing that a parallel between representation and enactment in autobiographical narrative is the primary mechanism of narrative self-construction. It is more plausible that various aspects of autobiographical narration can each help maintain or transform the self—emergent patterns of narrated voices for the self and salient others, the ventriloquation of these voices by autobiographical narrators, the positioning of the narrator's self with respect to interlocutors in the storytelling event, and in some cases a parallel between represented and enacted patterns.

While describing narrated events, a narrator represents salient voices from the social world. The narrator arranges these voices in some configuration and positions her narrated self with respect to those salient voices and their associated ideological commitments. This aspect of autobiographical narration by itself can contribute some structure to the self. By positioning her own narrated self in a recognizable trajectory—say a heroic one, with the self moving from passive to active and overcoming unjust treatment—a narrator can characterize her self as being in fact heroic (Freeman, 1993; Gergen & Gergen, 1983; Sarbin, 1997).

Such an emphasis on represented content in narrative self-construction, while an important aspect of a full account, misses the power that interactional positioning can have. In addition to positioning their narrated selves with respect to salient voices, autobiographical narrators also ventriloquate these voices and thus position their storytelling selves (Hill, 1995; Schiffrin, 1996). By positioning their storytelling selves with respect to the voices represented in the narrative, autobiographical narrators can identify with some voices and distance themselves from others. Jane clearly identifies her narrating self with the women's movement, against both the sexism of her grandparents and the ineffectiveness of her mother. This sort of positioning through ventriloquation adds power to narrative self-construction.

But even such an account of ventriloquation does not fully capture the power that interactional positioning in autobiographical narration can have to construct the self. As part of the represented content, autobiographical narrators do invoke and position their narrated selves with respect to salient voices from the social world. And autobiographical narrators do position their own storytelling selves with respect to these voices through ventriloquation. But narrators also use this voicing and ventriloquation to position themselves with respect to their interlocutors in storytelling events. By positioning themselves and their audiences in characteristic ways in storytelling events, narrators also contribute structure to their selves. Jane enacts her development from passive and vulnerable to active and assertive over the course of the storytelling event, and this enactment may help maintain her self.

In cases like Jane's, all three types of narrative self-construction reinforce each other. The voicing that Jane does as part of the represented content, plus the ventriloquation and the enactment that she does as part of the storytelling event, all position her in parallel ways.

Autobiographical narratives that involve this sort of parallel across represented content and interactional positioning can be powerful, ritualized events for constructing and maintaining the self. Jane's narrative self-construction, as first vulnerable and then assertive, has particular force because she both describes and enacts the same pattern. But Jane's story is in some ways a special case, of course. In general, narrative self-construction can be accomplished in various ways, with at least the four types of mechanisms illustrated here able to work together, or separately, to maintain or transform the self.

If the self is something that can be partly constructed through autobiographical narrative in these various ways, what can we conclude about the nature of the self? Bickhard and Christopher (1994), Csordas (1994), Dennett (1991), Penuel and Wertsch (1995), and others argue convincingly that the self is not an object but a process. The self appears to be an object, but in fact its stability is accomplished through processes in which individuals interact with the social and physical environment. Theorizing the self as an object, on this view, presupposes what needs to be explained.

So a convincing account of the self must describe the processes through which partial integration of the self can be accomplished. I would argue that any account must describe how individual, social, and interactional factors together contribute to the ongoing processes of self-construction. This book has provided an empirical argument that social and interactional patterns play an important role in the processes of self-construction. Most psychological accounts of self would miss some of the interactional positioning that demonstrably does occur in autobiographical narrative. Showing how interactional patterns emerge through autobiographical narrative, as I have done, should make it clear that interactional structure plays some role in maintaining the self.

Just because self-coherence can be accomplished in interaction does not make it insubstantial. Jane's self is tied into powerful and enduring patterns from the social world, which give it solidity. And if she enacts these sorts of positions regularly, she can establish considerable coherence in her habitual orientations toward the social world. Just as Freeman (1993) shows that the move from a static to an emergent self need not make the self unreal, the move from a psychologically represented self to a socially enacted self need not make it unreal either.

Of course, I cannot prove that the self gets constructed, and not simply manifested, through interactional positioning in autobiographical narrative. Sass (1998) points out that any attempt to explain a psychological phenomenon in terms of discursive patterns might encounter the following counterargument: Patterns in discourse, like Jane's positioning as first vulnerable and then assertive in the storytelling event, do not constitute but instead manifest a psychological self. No matter how sophisticated the linguistic analysis and no matter how robust the discursive pattern, these patterns can always be interpreted as manifestations of underlying psychological structure (see also Fisher, 1995; Scheibe, 1995). While I resist such an attempt to reduce social and interactional patterns to underlying psychological ones, I do not claim that the sorts of interactional positioning described here exhaust the self. There undoubtedly exist partial structures at other levels— perhaps including the neurological, psychological, cultural, and macro-social—that also contribute to the self.

The self itself, then, is the virtual or absent center of many over-lapping processes (Dennett, 1991). I have described this as "the het-erogeneously distributed self" (Wortham, 1999). Others have articu-lated similar views. Hermans and Kempen (1993) present the self in Bakhtinian terms as a "centripetal force," as something that holds to-gether and draws other things to it, but which is also always subject to centrifugal forces as well. Thus there is no final unification, just ongo-ing activities of synthesis and dissolution. An adequate account of the self must take into consideration processes that cover several levels of explanation at once and not limit itself to patterns at one level or an-other. It would be most productive at this point not to claim the en-tire self for one favored level of explanation, but instead to explain how partial structures at several levels interact to produce the self. I argue in this book that interactional positioning provides one relevant type of structure.

CHAPTER 6

Implications

Many have argued that autobiographical narration can provide coherent direction and even transform a life. The opportunity to tell stories about their lives can help autobiographical narrators establish a coherent sense of who they are. Most accounts explain autobiographical narratives' power with reference to their representational functions. This explanation undoubtedly has some truth. The power of autobiographical narrative to represent a self within a coherent plot likely contributes some structure to the self. But this explanation remains incomplete because it disregards the interactional positioning accomplished through autobiographical narrative. In this book I have argued that interactional positioning in autobiographical narrative also contributes to self-construction. Autobiographical narrators can partly construct themselves as they interactionally position themselves in characteristic ways while telling stories. Autobiographical narrators do more than understand themselves differently by representing their lives; they also learn how to act in characteristic ways with respect to others by enacting characteristic positions as they narrate their lives.

In studying interactional positioning, however, we must not set the represented content in opposition to the interactional positioning accomplished through speech. In autobiographical narratives like Jane's, the interrelation of representational and interactional patterns contributes to the narrative's power. I have argued that autobiographical narratives have particular power to construct the self when the represented content and enacted positioning run parallel, such that narrators both represent and enact analogous patterns. Not all autobiographical narratives involve this sort of parallel, and there are undoubtedly other mechanisms of narrative self-construction. But the simultaneous representation and enactment of parallel events is one powerful mechanism through which autobiographical narration can partly construct the self.

I agree with advocates of an interactional approach to speech who insist that representation and emplotment are not the essence of narrative self-construction (e.g., K. Gergen, 1989). Any adequate approach to autobiographical narrative—indeed, any adequate approach to language use in general—must attend to the interactional positioning done through speech. But, in our enthusiasm at discovering the interactional aspects of autobiographical narrative, we should not lose sight of the important role that representation plays. The essentialization of representation should not be met with an equally implausible essentialization of interaction.[1]

Humans engage in many types of complex behavior simultaneously. The structures and processes that facilitate these complex behaviors often interconnect, either because it was most efficient for the same structures and processes to serve multiple functions or because they coevolved. For instance, the vocal tract was initially an instrument for eating, but in humans it has also evolved the capacity to produce the complex sounds required for speech. The capacity to produce speech evolved as another layer, taking advantage of and modifying structures that had earlier evolved for the purpose of eating.

The interactional and the representational functions of language may be analogous to this in some respects. Language use both represents states of affairs and accomplishes socially consequential interactional positioning. The linguistic structures and processes that evolved to allow the representational and interactional functions are not accomplished by completely separate systems, but sometimes interconnect. Further study should focus on how represented content and interactional positioning can interrelate in autobiographical narrative and other verbal genres. This book contributes by describing how parallelism between represented and enacted patterns can have particular power for constructing the self.

STUDYING INTERACTIONAL POSITIONING IN OTHER CONTEXTS

The account of narrative self-construction developed here can do more than help explain the power of autobiographical narrative. Suitably elaborated, it could also contribute to broader projects in the human sciences. For example, the foregoing chapters make constructionist and practice-based accounts of self more empirically specific, by specifying how the self can get positioned in the details of verbal interaction. Many others have argued that the self gets important structure from habitual positioning in everyday interaction (e.g., Bourdieu, 1972/1977; Csordas, 1994; K. Gergen, 1991). This book has provided a systematic approach to interactional positioning, which makes constructionist and practice-based accounts more specific.

The approach to language use described in this book also yields conceptual and methodological tools that can be applied to other important topics in the human sciences. Chapters 2 through 4 illustrate a dialogic, mediated, and emergent approach to language use. I have described how verbal cues index relevant aspects of the context and how patterns of cues coalesce into emergent structures that provide relevant background for interpreting language use. I have sharpened the central Bakhtinian concepts of voicing and ventriloquation in order to make such a dialogic approach to language use more precise. My analyses show how a focus on mediating indexical cues and emergent structures can yield empirically warranted interpretations of interactional positioning.

I have given three detailed examples of how such analyses work: the Spartan babies class, the CBS News coverage of the elder George Bush, and Jane's autobiographical narrative. These extended examples illustrate how the conceptual and methodological tools developed in this book might facilitate a dialogic approach to other important questions in the human sciences. In the Spartan babies class analyzed in Chapter 2, for instance, a dialogic, mediated, and emergent approach showed how students and teachers enact a salient conflict from the larger society at the same time as they discuss an ancient Greek text. A representational approach to language, or an approach less sensitive to complex interactional patterns that emerge in context, would have missed this covert conflict.

Interactional positioning of this sort in classroom conversation might contribute to the development of social identities among young people. If these lower-class black students characteristically get positioned as parasitic and undeserving, they might internalize this voice as part of their more enduring identities. Systematic study of interactional positioning like this could facilitate research on the maintenance and transformation of identity in various contexts. Studies of interactional positioning in family conversations, for example, could follow the approach developed here to explore how the characteristic positioning of children and parents influences children's social and moral development.

I would argue that the interactional positioning done by teachers and students in the Spartan babies class also contributes to social reproduction, namely, the reproduction of subordinate social positions for children from certain social groups (Wortham, 1992, 1994). By positioning the Asian students as deserving and the lower-class black students as undeserving, for instance, the teachers reinforce the social division between "model" and other minorities. Thus systematic study of interactional positioning like that illustrated here can also support research on how the status of social groups gets maintained and transformed.

Studying how minority clients get positioned in interactions with lenders or other service providers, for instance, might show one way in which race-based differential treatment gets accomplished in practice.

In the mock trial of the elder George Bush discussed in Chapter 3, a dialogic, mediated, and emergent approach showed how newscasters evaluate political candidates by positioning themselves interactionally. It turns out that positioning of this sort occurs regularly in broadcast news (Locher & Wortham, 1994; Wortham & Locher, 1996, 1999). In fact, such positioning contributes to a subtle but widespread form of media bias: By positioning themselves and their subjects interactionally, members of the media can take political and moral positions without making explicit evaluative statements. Similar positioning in other contexts would allow a wide range of speakers tacitly to communicate evaluative attitudes about others. The tools developed here could facilitate further studies of how media and other institutions express political and moral views without explicitly representing them. Systematic study of interactional positioning in advertising, for instance, could uncover how some powerful but tacit messages are communicated.

Despite these tools' promise to facilitate work on the interactional construction of identity, on social reproduction, and on the communication of evaluative stances in institutionalized discourse, the interactional positioning accomplished through speech provides only one relevant set of tools. Just as interactional positioning in autobiographical narrative does not constitute the entire self, positioning in other contexts will not fully explain identity development, social reproduction, or other important processes. The tools developed in this book can help subsequent research explore exactly how interactional positioning in speech interrelates with other types of processes to constitute important human phenomena.

A DIALOGIC APPROACH

The systematic approach to interactional positioning developed here also helps make a dialogic approach to the human sciences more precise and more plausible. Calls for a more dialogic approach have come from several directions. Many have described both conceptual and practical problems with monologic approaches—that is, dualist approaches which separate the individual from others and the world (e.g., Haroutunian-Gordon, 1983; Sampson, 1993; Shotter, 1993a; Taylor, 1977/1985b; Wertsch, 1991). These conceptual and practical problems cannot be solved without developing a more adequate overall picture of human functioning, and a dialogic approach offers a more promising alternative.[2] Sampson (1993) and Shotter (1993a, 1993b) argue that human scientists must stop focusing on self-contained individuals, who allegedly construct boundaries to distinguish themselves from others and the world, because in fact people become human only by participating in practices where their relationships with others are prior to representations of them. Taylor (1985a, 1991) argues that paradigmatically human acts do not involve disengaged, objective consideration or manipulation of others and the world, but instead involve ethically laden engagement with others in shared practices.[3]

Bakhtin provides a compelling alternative to monologic approaches, built around the central theme of dialogue (cf. K. Clark & Holquist, 1984; Morson & Emerson, 1990). For this reason he has appealed to many human scientists who are searching for more dialogic alternatives. But Bakhtin's own writing is complex and difficult, and none of his interpreters has worked out the details of a dialogic approach to the human sciences, especially with respect to Bakhtin's theory of language. I have tried to show why a Bakhtinian approach does indeed show substantial promise, by developing a more precise Bakhtinian approach to language use.

The dialogic approaches to the human sciences developed so far (e.g., by Sampson, 1993, Shotter, 1993b, Taylor, 1985a, and Wertsch, 1991) need elaboration because they do not explore the linguistic details of dialogic practices as deeply as they might. These approaches explicitly rely on verbal action as their paradigmatic case of human action. Instead of the lone thinker, they describe people acting within ongoing practices, especially verbal practices. Instead of relying on self-contained representations and identities, they describe understanding and self as emerging within multivoiced conversations. As Sampson says, the key to a dialogic account is "language as communication in action" (1993, p. 97). But none of these accounts goes as deeply as Bakhtin himself into the details of how language functions dialogically. This book has supplemented Bakhtin with contemporary work on language, in order to develop more precise tools for conceptualizing and applying the central concepts of dialogue, mediation, and emergence. These conceptual and methodological tools should complement dialogic approaches to the human sciences, by showing in more detail how speakers engage in multivoiced verbal action and how these engagements partly constitute speakers' selves. The tools provided here are resources for looking at the human world in a dialogic way, not a complete theory. Nonetheless, I hope that this demonstration of the analyses possible with more precise tools will make a dialogic approach to the human sciences more plausible.

Notes

Chapter 1

1. I have changed many details of Jane's life in order to disguise her identity.

2. I have simplified the transcription here because the details are not crucial in this introductory chapter. An underlined syllable indicates stress. Commas indicate brief pauses, and periods indicate falling intonation. The pauses marked in parentheses, "(pause)," range from 1 to 6 seconds. More exact durations for each pause are given in the more detailed transcript of this segment presented in Chapter 4.

3. At the same time, however, some narrators do benefit from foregrounding more univocal senses of themselves at certain points in their lives. As Joy (1993) argues, despite their acceptance of fragmentation and multiplicity, many feminists want to maintain the option of speaking as a univocal self at times. Such a univocal voice, thought not foundational, can be useful to overcome chaotic personal experiences and to provide a stance for critique.

Chapter 2

1. Bakhtin argues that all linguistic meaning—whether that involves represented content (i.e., meaning communicated through reference and predication) or interactional positioning—is dialogic. He claims that analysts cannot grasp even simple narrated content without including various aspects of the storytelling context. Hanks (1990, 1996), Silverstein (1976, 1992, 1993), Verschueren (1999), and others argue plausibly that Bakhtin is mostly correct in his claim that reference and predication are best analyzed as dialogic phenomena. That is, an adequate account of how language refers and predicates must include aspects of the storytelling context in its analysis. Bakhtin is wrong, Hanks and Silverstein argue, only in ignoring the relatively small but important role that decontextualized grammatical categories play in establishing meaning. In this book I elaborate Bakhtin's claim about the inevitably dialogic aspects of all utterances—that is, that all speech places speakers in some position with respect to other speakers—and I go beyond Bakhtin to develop a framework for analyzing how language positions narrators interactionally. My account inevitably analyzes both the representational content and the interactional positioning accomplished through speech, because these

are interdependent. Because I plan to extend Bakhtin's framework primarily in order to analyze the interactional positioning accomplished by autobiographical narrators, I focus in this chapter and the next on his claims about interactional positioning. But Chapter 3 also uses Bakhtinian concepts to discuss the interrelation between represented content and interactional positioning.

2. Note here that Bakhtin does not deny two important aspects of traditional monologic accounts: He does not deny that individual speakers sometimes *communicate what they intend*. He claims that, for individuals to accomplish this, they cannot simply express monologic content. They must also take up a social position with respect to other speakers. Nor does Bakhtin deny that utterances can *communicate the truth*. He claims that any adequate explanation for the meaningful and sometimes truthful use of linguistic forms must rest partly on relations between speakers. Unlike many people concerned to emphasize the plurality of relevant viewpoints, Bakhtin was particularly concerned with truth and moral standards. He did not think we should conclude from the fact of plurality that the true and the good are completely relative to particular times and places. However, he did insist that the importance of truth and moral standards should not make us retreat into monologism. "It is quite possible to imagine and postulate a unified truth that requires a plurality of consciousnesses, one that cannot in principle be fitted into the bounds of a single consciousness, one that is, so to speak, by its very nature *full of event potential* and is born at a point of contact among various consciousnesses" (1963/1984a, p. 81). Bakhtin seems to point here toward an interesting middle ground between realism and relativism. See Shweder (1991) for a slightly different version of this middle ground: Shweder defends a position that is simultaneously relativist and realist, by elaborating the idea of "multiple objective worlds." Bakhtin emphasizes the ongoing open-endedness of judgment more than Shweder does, but both integrate aspects of realism and relativism.

3. This obviously summarizes thirty minutes of interactional work coarsely. See Wortham (1994, 2001) for more detailed analysis. One might argue that this is overdrawn and that the teachers are merely teasing again. The students themselves contribute to the discussion of Asians' talents, and they even laugh about the teachers' comments (at line 31). It seems to me, however, too uncomfortably close to salient issues to be a joke. White taxpayer complaints about Black welfare recipients are too real in the contemporary United States to laugh about. And lower-class Blacks' social position is too similar to Helots for this to be merely a joke. The fuller analysis of this and subsequent segments in Wortham (1994) also shows how the students actively resist the teachers, and this resistance provides further evidence that the students do not interpret the teachers as merely joking.

4. K. Clark and Holquist (1984), among others, argue that Bakhtin himself probably wrote most of the text attributed to Vološinov (1929/1973). Morson and Emerson (1990) disagree. Final resolution of this dispute is unlikely, but all agree that Bakhtin and Vološinov were members of the same intellectual circle. Thus Vološinov's (1929/1973) ideas about quoted speech were at least well-known to Bakhtin, and they clearly complement Bakhtin's overall project.

Chapter 3

1. I should also note that, during the 1988 interview Rather refers to, Rather and Bush had a strained, argumentative interaction. Bush put Rather on the defensive—apparently as part of a strategy to enhance Bush's own image with the public—and Rather struggled to regain his stature throughout the interview. Rather might have felt that the 1988 Bush campaign took advantage of him to score political points. This would provide a motive for CBS's mock trial of Bush in 1992. By mentioning this 1988 event, Rather is also noting the reversal of roles that he is likely enjoying, with Bush the "accused" and thus (at least during this broadcast) subordinate to Rather. See also Clayman and Whalen (1988/ 1989) and Schegloff (1988/1989) on the 1988 Rather-Bush confrontation.

2. Various cognitive psychologists have begun to move toward such a dialogic focus, claiming that we must take into account the position of the narrator in the narrating event. Bruner (1996), for instance, argues that narrative involves a larger point, beyond a mere sequence of events: the narrator's "implied evaluation of the events recounted" (p. 121). In a similar vein, Nelson (1996) argues that, in addition to recounting a chain of events, narratives contain cues "that project the narrator's attitude toward the events" (p. 189). These do not represent fully adequate accounts of interactional positioning in narratives, but they do move in a more dialogic direction.

3. Labov (1972, 1982; Labov & Waletsky, 1967) provides an account of narrative that is both dialogic and mediated. He makes clear that narratives always do more than represent past events in sequence. Narratives also contain *evaluation*, "the means used by the narrator to indicate the point of the narrative" (1972, p. 366). Labov's primary example of evaluative structure (1972, pp. 367–368) makes clear that evaluation involves the *positioning* of the narrator in the storytelling event. In addition to being dialogic, his analysis is also mediated, because he accounts for evaluation by describing various "devices" narrators use to indicate the overall point of the story and how it affects their own position in the storytelling event. Polanyi (1989) expands Labov's theory by giving a more comprehensive list of the evaluative devices (or cues) through which narrators make certain aspects of a narrative and its context salient.

4. Bakhtin spends considerable time analyzing the historical development of the novelistic genre. He concludes that this genre emerges in modernity because at this historical point many social groups start to come into closer contact with one another. As he puts it, an ordinary person living in modern times can no longer avoid contact with multiple languages that contest each other's accounts of the world. "The ideological systems and approaches to the world that were indissolubly connected with these languages contradicted each other and in no way could live in peace and quiet with one another" (1935/ 1981, p. 296). Novelists were the first to recognize and artistically express this more dialogic or "polyphonic" social world. This polyphony has, of course, become a central concern in contemporary accounts of the postmodern world (e.g., K. Gergen, 1991; Shweder, 1991).

5. In more complex literary narrative, double voicing is often more complicated. Contemporary novels often make finer distinctions between the various points of view involved. Throughout this section, I use *author* and *narrator* interchangeably. In most analyses of everyday speech this suffices, as the narrator presents himself or herself as an integral person adopting some social position or other. In literary narrative, however, there are generally the distinguishable perspectives of the author and the narrator (Scholes & Kellogg, 1966). Bal (1985) describes yet another perspective sometimes used in literary narrative, the "focalizer." Sometimes literary narratives are written by authors, spoken by narrators, but present events from the point of view of a focal character. In such a case the narrative is written as if the narrator is speaking, but it is also written from the point of view of the focal character. Thus there could be three distinct perspectives to contend with, in addition to the characters'. The analysis here ignores such complexity for the sake of getting clear about the positioning of narrators in simpler oral narratives.

6. One might argue that Bakhtin deliberately does not systematize his approach. He insists that voicing and ventriloquation happen in ongoing dialogue with a live other, not with an object that can be evaluated once and for all. "The consciousness of other people cannot be perceived, analyzed, defined as objects or as things—one can only *relate to them dialogically*. To think about them means to *talk with them; otherwise they immediately turn to us their objectivized side*: they fall silent, close up, and congeal into finished, objectivized images" (1963/1984a, p. 68). Doesn't this preclude objectifying analyses of the sort I am proposing? I would respond to this problem with a distinction that Morson and Emerson (1990) make between two senses of *dialogue*. First, all utterances take their shape partly from other speakers' utterances, and all are addressed to others, as described in Chapter 2. Second, novelists like Dostoevsky are able to represent multiple voices without privileging any of them. Bakhtin affirms the second sense of dialogue in order to take a moral stand. He celebrates heteroglossia (1935/1981) and carnival (1965/1984b) to resist totalitarianism and celebrate creativity. But on my reading, Bakhtin does not claim that objectification never happens in novels or in real life. Instead, there is a continuum of authors and speakers and genres, with some more prone to dialogue in the second sense and others less so. Canonization and finalization always exist in tension with heteroglossia and polyphony, and a systematic approach can help us analyze firmly established interactional positioning when it happens.

Chapter 4

1. This number could be raised or lowered, depending on the purposes of the analysis. In one sense, every use of a first-person pronoun introduces a slightly different narrated self. In another sense, they could all be condensed into a few narrated selves. Here I mean to avoid the question of exactly how many narrated selves there might be and simply give a rough overview of these

narrated selves, in order to introduce Jane's story. Note also that three episodes are missing from Table 4.2: Episode 1 gives the setting of Jane's parents' marriage before she was born, so she does not appear as a character; Episode 4 alludes to Jane's childhood before her first institutionalization, but she does not explicitly include herself as a character; and Episode 15 summarizes the preceding episodes, and so it contains references to several of the narrated selves introduced up to that point.

2. To be fair to the interviewer, one must note that she was in a difficult position. She was supposed to collect dispassionate data as part of her job as a research assistant, but she finds herself confronted with a subject crying about past trauma. Because she had been instructed to keep data from all the interviews comparable, by not intervening except as dictated by the interview protocol, the interviewer stuck to her script.

Chapter 5

1. Those I have grouped as social constructionists locate the self primarily at the level of the storytelling event for various reasons. Hermans and Kempen (1993) draw on Bakhtin and move toward a dialogic account in the Bakhtinian sense. K. Gergen (1989), at least in part, works to undermine the authority of traditional psychological accounts, and thus he analyzes the interactional situations in which everyday actors rely on psychological talk. Shotter (1989) shares this project with K. Gergen, but has also himself drawn extensively on Bakhtin (e.g., Shotter, 1993a). Both Gergen and Shotter also draw on what one might call a "dialogic" instinct in Wittgenstein (1953).

2. At times Bakhtin presents the emergence of a self as a teleological process, as when he argues that "consciousness awakens to independent ideological life precisely in a world of alien discourses surrounding it, and from which it cannot initially separate itself; the process of distinguishing between one's own and another's discourse, between one's own and another's thought, is activated rather late in development" (1935/1981, p. 345). The self comes to have a voice of its own as it comes to ventriloquate others in distinctive ways. Bakhtin argues that not all people make this developmental step. Some people simply parrot what Bakhtin calls "authoritarian enforced discourse" and abdicate from the task of articulating a self. Such people speak in "calcified" ways. They speak in monologue, not dialogue. It is crucial to see that Bakhtin is not essentializing the self with this apparently developmental account. Most developmental accounts have an endpoint, which has a presupposed "natural" value—as if it captured the essence of or the best in human nature. Bakhtin is, instead, making a political point: Given the tendency of political systems to promote authoritarian, monologic discourse (a tendency particularly salient in the Stalinist system Bakhtin endured in Russia), we must favor dialogic practices that promote multiple, open-ended possibilities. In favoring the dialogic over the monologic self, then, Bakhtin argues that dialogic practice allows the continual growth of the self, while monologic practice closes off

growth. Unlike most developmental theories, Bakhtin proposes no endpoint for growth. In fact, in his love for unfinalizability he explicitly opposes endpoints. Thus his quasi-developmental account is not a theory of "internalization," in which the self develops an interior region by borrowing and modifying the words of others. The self remains "on the boundary," because it involves no nondialogic realm. The self remains a matter of ongoing positioning with respect to others, using words that have been used by others. The dialogue continues, unless the self "calcifies," and the self grows through continuous ventriloquation.

Chapter 6

1. Interestingly, the conflict between action and representation is also something that Jane struggles with. Her active, assertive voice often adopts a more disengaged, academic approach to the world. Her vulnerable voice is more involved with others in the world. Jane's experience illustrates some of the practical consequences of the choice between action and representation. A stance that favors distanced representation can protect a person, but it seems to offer limited opportunity for relational connection. A stance that involves a person more fully in the relational world exposes vulnerability. Jane herself, as described above, moves back and forth between these two types of stances. At times she seems to present the more distanced stance as a developmental advance. The larger society values distance in many contexts, like educational ones, but it is not clear that a thoroughly distanced stance is either conceptually or practically preferable.

2. All these critiques of monologic approaches to the human sciences trace the problematic monologic assumptions back to the Enlightenment. The Cartesian ideal of distanced individual contemplation, the rejection of anthropocentric properties in favor of naturalistic ones, the celebration of individual autonomy, the neglect of historical change, and the affirmation of a common human core and the rejection of differences as superficial all come to the contemporary human sciences from the Enlightenment. No one wants to return to premodern times, but all want to overthrow these increasingly counterproductive Enlightenment assumptions. The dialogic project remains unfinished, however, because it is not clear how one could retain some Enlightenment innovations—for example, the celebration of justice and emancipation—while rejecting others. This book does not claim to solve the grand problem of how theorists might preserve the best and eliminate the worst of the Enlightenment. I intend simply to provide a more precise, lower-level formulation of how analysts might go about pursuing a dialogic alternative to some Enlightenment assumptions. I hope that the tools provided here can push forward the search for dialogic alternatives to Enlightenment assumptions, but they do not in themselves constitute a full dialogic theory. As Shotter (1993b) suggests, we should perhaps give up the search for grand theoretical systems in any case.

3. These critics do not argue that all work done under monologic assumptions is worthless. Shotter (1993b) and Wertsch (1991), for instance, agree that the human sciences have produced many plausible interpretations of particular phenomena. But they argue that these successes will represent only fragments, until they are organized under a more compelling overall picture of human functioning. Such a picture, they argue, must be dialogic, that is, it must describe the essential interrelations between individual and relational processes.

References

Anderson, H. (1997). *Conversation, language and possibilities*. New York: Basic Books.

Bailkey, N. (1987). *Readings in ancient history*. Lexington, MA: D.C. Heath.

Bakhtin, M. (1981). Discourse in the novel (C. Emerson & M. Holquist, Trans.). In M. Bakhtin, *The dialogic imagination* (pp. 259–422). Austin: University of Texas Press. (Original work published 1935)

Bakhtin, M. (1984a). *Problems of Dostoevsky's poetics* (C. Emerson, Trans.). Minneapolis: University of Minnesota Press. (Original work published 1963)

Bakhtin, M. (1984b). *Rabelais and his world* (H. Iswolsky, Trans.). Bloomington: Indiana University Press. (Original work published 1965)

Bakhtin, M. (1986a). The problem of speech genres (V. McGee, Trans.). In C. Emerson & M. Holquist (Eds.), *Speech genres and other late essays* (pp. 60–102). Austin: University of Texas Press. (Original work published 1953)

Bakhtin, M. (1986b). The problem of the text in linguistics, philology, and the human sciences (V. McGee, Trans.). In C. Emerson & M. Holquist (Eds.), *Speech genres and other late essays* (pp. 103–131). Austin: University of Texas Press. (Original work published 1961)

Bal, M. (1985). *Narratology*. Toronto: University of Toronto Press.

Bamberg, M., & Marchman, V. (1991). Binding and unfolding. *Discourse Processes, 14,* 277–305.

Bickhard, M., & Christopher, J. (1994). The influence of early experience on personality development. *New Ideas in Psychology, 12,* 229–252.

Bloom, L. (1998). *Under the sign of hope*. Albany: State University of New York Press.

Bourdieu, P. (1977). *Outline of a theory of practice* (R. Nice, Trans.). New York: Cambridge University Press. (Original work published 1972)

Bower, G., & Morrow, D. (1990). Mental models in narrative comprehension. *Science, 247,* 44–48.

Bruner, J. (1987). Life as narrative. *Social Research, 54,* 11–32.

Bruner, J. (1996). *The culture of education*. Cambridge, MA: Harvard University Press.

Butler, J. (1990). *Gender trouble*. New York: Routledge.

Cain, C. (1991). Personal stories. *Ethos, 19,* 210–253.

Clark, H., & Gerrig, R. (1990). Quotations as demonstrations. *Language, 66,* 764–805.

Clark, K., & Holquist, M. (1984). *Mikhail Bakhtin.* Cambridge, MA: Harvard University Press.

Clayman, S., & Whalen, J. (1988/1989). When the medium becomes the message. *Research on Language and Social Interaction, 22,* 241–272.

Cohen, J. (1996). Rewriting our lives. *Journal of Narrative and Life History, 6,* 145–156.

Cohler, B. (1988). The human studies and the life history. *Social Service Review, 62,* 552–575.

Crapanzano, V. (1984). Life-histories. *American Anthropologist, 86,* 953–960.

Crapanzano, V. (1992). *Hermes' dilemma and Hamlet's desire.* Cambridge, MA: Harvard University Press.

Crapanzano, V. (1996). "Self"-centering narratives. In M. Silverstein & G. Urban (Eds.), *Natural histories of discourse* (pp. 106–127). Chicago: University of Chicago Press.

Crites, S. (1986). Storytime. In T. Sarbin (Ed.), *Narrative psychology* (pp. 152–173). New York: Praeger.

Csordas, T. (1994). *The sacred self: A cultural phenomenology of charismatic healing.* Berkeley: University of California Press.

Culler, J. (1975). *Structuralist poetics.* London: Routledge & Kegan Paul.

Damon, W., & Hart, D. (1988). *Self-understanding in childhood and adolescence.* New York: Cambridge University Press.

Davies, B. (1993). *Shards of glass.* Cresskill, NJ: Hampton Press.

Davies, B., & Harré, R. (1990). Positioning. *Journal for the Theory of Social Behaviour, 20,* 43–63.

Dennett, D. (1991). *Consciousness explained.* Boston: Little Brown.

Errington, J. (1988). *Structure and style in Javanese.* Philadelphia: University of Pennsylvania Press.

Ervin-Tripp, S., & Küntay, A. (1997). The occasioning and structure of conversational stories. In T. Givón (Ed.), *Conversation* (pp. 133–166). Philadelphia: J. Benjamins.

Fisher, H. (1995). Whose right is it to define the self? *Theory and Psychology, 5,* 323–352.

Flax, J. (1990). *Thinking fragments.* Berkeley: University of California Press.

Fludernik, M. (1993). *The fictions of language and the languages of fiction.* New York: Routledge.

Freeman, M. (1993). *Rewriting the self.* New York: Routledge.

Freud, S. (1965a). *The interpretation of dreams* (J. Strachey, Trans.). New York: Avon Books. (Original work published 1900)

Freud, S. (1965b). *New introductory lectures on psychoanalysis* (J. Strachey, Trans.). New York: Norton. (Original work published 1933)

Garfinkel, H. (1967). *Studies in ethnomethodology.* New York: Polity Press.

Garfinkel, H., & Sacks, H. (1970). On the formal structure of practical actions. In J. McKinney & E. Tiryakian (Eds.), *Theoretical sociology* (pp. 337–366). New York: Appleton-Century-Crofts.

Georgakopoulou, A. (1997). *Narrative performances.* Philadelphia: J. Benjamins.

Gergen, K. (1982). *Toward transformation in social knowledge.* New York: Springer-Verlag.

Gergen, K. (1989). Warranting voice and the elaboration of the self. In J. Shotter & K. Gergen (Eds.), *Texts of identity* (pp. 70–81). London: Sage.

Gergen, K. (1991). *The saturated self.* New York: Basic Books.

Gergen, K. (1994). *Realities and relationships: Soundings in social construction.* Cambridge, MA: Harvard University Press.

Gergen, K. (1997). The place of the psyche in a constructed world. *Theory and Psychology, 7,* 723–746.

Gergen, K., & Gergen, M. (1983). Narratives of the self. In T. Sarbin & K. Scheibe (Eds.), *Studies in social identity* (pp. 254–273). New York: Praeger.

Gergen, K., & Kaye, J. (1992). Beyond narrative in the negotiation of therapeutic meaning. In S. McNamee & K. Gergen (Eds.), *Therapy as social construction* (pp. 166–185). London: Sage.

Gergen, M. (1994). The social construction of personal histories. In T. Sarbin & K. Scheibe (Eds.), *Constructing the social* (pp. 19–44). London: Sage.

Gerhardt, J., & Stinson, C. (1994). The nature of therapeutic discourse. *Journal of Narrative and Life History, 4,* 151–192.

Gilligan, C. (1986). Remapping the moral domain. In T. Heller, M. Sosna, & D. Wellberg (Eds.), *Reconstructing individualism* (pp. 237–252). Stanford, CA: Stanford University Press.

Goffman, E. (1976). Replies and responses. *Language in Society, 5,* 257–313.

Goodwin, C. (1984). Notes on story structure and the organization of participation. In J. Atkinson & J. Heritage (Eds.), *Structures of social action* (pp. 225–246). New York: Cambridge University Press.

Goodwin, M. (1990). *He-said-she-said.* Bloomington: Indiana University Press.

Goossens, L. (1982). Say: Focus on the message. In R. Dirven, L. Goossens, Y. Putseys, & E. Vorlat (Eds.), *The scene of linguistic action and its perspectivization by speak, talk, say and tell* (pp. 85–131). Philadelphia: J. Benjamins.

Grumet, M. (1987). The politics of personal knowledge. *Curriculum Inquiry, 17,* 320–329.

Gubrium, J., & Holstein, J. (1994). Grounding the postmodern self. *The Sociological Quarterly, 35,* 685–703.

Gumperz, J. (1982). *Discourse strategies.* New York: Cambridge University Press.

Gumperz, J. (1992). Contextualization revisited. In P. Auer & A. DiLuzio (Eds.), *The contextualization of language* (pp. 39–53). Philadelphia: J. Benjamins.

Hanks, W. (1990). *Referential practice.* Chicago: University of Chicago Press.

Hanks, W. (1996). *Language and communicative practices.* Boulder, CO: Westview Press.

Harding, S. (1992). The afterlife of stories. In G. Rosenwald & R. Ochberg (Eds.), *Storied lives* (pp. 60–75). New Haven, CT: Yale University Press.

Haroutunian-Gordon, S. (1983). *Equilibrium in the balance.* New York: Springer-Verlag.

Haviland, J. (1991). "That was the last time I seen them, and no more." *Ethos*, *18*, 331–361.

Havránek, B. (1955). The functional differentiation of the standard language (P. Garvin, Trans.). In P. Garvin (Ed.), *A Prague School reader* (pp. 1–18). Washington, DC: Washington Linguistics Club. (Original work published 1932)

Heidegger, M. (1962). *Being and time.* (J. Macquarrie & E. Robinson, Trans.). New York: Harper. (Orginal work published 1927)

Hensel, C. (1996). *Telling our selves.* New York: Oxford University Press.

Hermans, H., & Kempen, H. J. G. (1993). *The dialogical self.* New York: Academic Press.

Hill, J. (1995). The voices of don Gabriel. In D. Tedlock & B. Mannheim (Eds.), *The dialogic emergence of culture* (pp. 97–147). Urbana: University of Illinois Press.

Irvine, J. (1996). Shadow conversations. In M. Silverstein & G. Urban (Eds.), *Natural histories of discourse.* Chicago: University of Chicago Press.

Jakobson, R. (1960). Closing statement: Linguistics and poetics. In T. Sebeok (Ed.), *Style in language* (pp. 350–377). Cambridge: Massachusetts Institute of Technology Press.

Jakobson, R. (1971). Shifters, verbal categories, and the Russian verb. In R. Jakobson, *Selected Writings* (Vol. 2, pp. 130–147). The Hague, The Netherlands: Mouton. (Original work published 1957)

Jefferson, G. (1978). Sequential aspects of storytelling in conversation. In J. Schenkein (Ed.), *Studies in the organization of conversational interaction* (pp. 219–248). New York: Academic Press.

Jelinek, E. (1980). *Women's autobiography.* Bloomington: Indiana University Press.

Johnson-Laird, P. (1983). *Mental models.* Cambridge, MA: Harvard University Press.

Joy, M. (1993). Feminism and the self. *Theory and Psychology, 3*, 275–302.

Kerby, A. (1991). *Narrative and the self.* Bloomington: Indiana University Press.

Labov, W. (1972). The transformation of experience in narrative syntax. In *Language in the inner city* (pp. 354–396). Philadelphia: University of Pennsylvania Press.

Labov, W. (1982). Speech acts and reaction in personal narrative. In D. Tannen (Ed.), *Analyzing discourse* (pp. 219–247). Washington, DC: Georgetown University Press.

Labov, W., & Waletsky, J. (1967). Narrative analysis. In J. Helm (Ed.), *Essays on the verbal and visual arts* (pp. 12–44). Seattle: University of Washington Press.

Lather, P. (1991). *Getting smart: Feminist research and pedagogy with/in the postmodern.* New York: Routledge.

Levinson, S. (1981). The essential inadequacies of speech act models of dialogue. In H. Parret, M. Sbisà, & J. Verschueren (Eds.), *Possibilities and limitations of pragmatics* (pp. 473–492). Amsterdam: J. Benjamins.

Linde, C. (1993). *Life stories.* New York: Oxford University Press.

Locher, M., & Wortham, S. (1994). The cast of the news. *Pragmatics, 4*, 517–534.

Lucy, J. (Ed.). (1993). *Reflexive language.* New York: Cambridge University Press.

Mayes, P. (1990). Quotations in spoken English. *Studies in Language, 14,* 325–363.

McAdams, D. (1985). *Power, intimacy and the life story.* Homewood, IL: Dorsey Press.

McAdams, D. (1993). *The stories we live by.* New York: William Morrow.

McAdams, D. (1997). The case for unity in the (post)modern self. In R. Ashmore & L. Jussim (Eds.), *Self and identity* (pp. 46–78). New York: Cambridge University Press.

Mead, G. (1934). *Mind, self and society from the standpoint of a social behaviorist.* Chicago: University of Chicago Press.

Mertz, E., & Parmentier, R. (Eds.). (1985). *Semiotic mediation.* New York: Academic Press.

Miller, P., Potts, R., Fung, H., Hoogstra, L., & Mintz, J. (1990). Narrative practices and the social construction of self in childhood. *American Ethnologist, 17,* 292–311.

Mishler, E. (1986). *Research interviewing.* Cambridge, MA: Harvard University Press.

Mishler, E. (1995). Models of narrative analysis. *Journal of Narrative and Life History, 5,* 87–123.

Morson, G., & Emerson, C. (1990). *Mikhail Bakhtin: Creation of a prosaics.* Stanford, CA: Stanford University Press.

Nelson, K. (1996). *Language in cognitive development.* New York: Cambridge University Press.

Ochs, E. (1994). Stories that step into the future. In D. Finegan & F. Biber (Eds.), *Perspectives on register* (pp. 106–135). New York: Oxford University Press.

Ochs, E., & Capps, L. (1996). Narrating the self. *Annual Review of Anthropology, 25,* 19–43.

O'Connor, P. (1994). "You could feel it through the skin." *Text, 14,* 45–75.

Parmentier, R. (1997). The pragmatic semiotics of cultures. *Semiotica, 116,* 1–115.

Peirce, C. (1955). Logic as semiotic. In J. Buchler (Ed.), *Philosophical writings of Peirce* (pp. 98–119). New York: Dover. (Original work published 1897)

Penuel, W., & Wertsch, J. (1995). Vygotsky and identity formation. *Educational Psychologist, 30,* 83–92.

Personal Narratives Group. (1989). *Interpreting women's lives.* Bloomington: Indiana University Press.

Polanyi, L. (1989). *Telling the American story.* Cambridge, MA: MIT Press.

Polkinghorne, D. (1988). *Narrative knowing and the human sciences.* Albany: State University of New York Press.

Pynchon, T. (1959). Mortality and mercy in Vienna. *Epoch, 9,* 195–213.

Ricoeur, P. (1980). Narrative time. In W. J. T. Mitchell (Ed.), *On narrative* (pp. 165–186). Chicago: University of Chicago Press.

Rorty, A., & Wong, D. (1990). Aspects of identity and agency. In O. Flanagan & A. Rorty (Eds.), *Identity, character and morality* (pp. 19–36). Cambridge, MA: MIT Press.

Rosenwald, G., & Ochberg, R. (Eds.). (1992). *Storied lives.* New Haven, CT: Yale University Press.

Sacks, H. (1978). Some technical considerations of a dirty joke. In J. Schenkein (Ed.), *Studies in the organization of conversational interaction*. New York: Academic Press.

Sampson, E. (1993). *Celebrating the other*. Boulder, CO: Westview Press.

Sarbin, T. (1997). The poetics of identity. *Theory and Psychology, 7*, 67–82.

Sass, L. (1998). The grammar of panic. *Theory and Psychology, 9*, 274–277.

Schafer, R. (1992). *Retelling a life*. New York: Basic Books.

Schegloff, E. (1988/1989). From interview to confrontation. *Research on Language and Social Interaction, 22*, 215–240.

Schegloff, E., & Sacks, H. (1973). Opening up closings. *Semiotica, 8*, 289–327.

Scheibe, K. (1995). *Self studies*. Westport, CT: Praeger.

Schiffrin, D. (1996). Narrative as self-portrait. *Language in Society, 25*, 167–203.

Scholes, R., & Kellogg, R. (1966). *The nature of narrative*. New York: Oxford University Press.

Searle, J. (1969). *Speech acts*. New York: Cambridge University Press.

Shotter, J. (1989). Social accountability and the social construction of "you." In J. Shotter & K. Gergen (Eds.), *Texts of identity* (pp. 133–151). London: Sage.

Shotter, J. (1993a). *Conversational realities*. London: Sage.

Shotter, J. (1993b). *Cultural politics of everyday life*. Toronto: University of Toronto Press.

Shotter, J., & Gergen, K. (Eds.). (1989). *Texts of identity*. London: Sage.

Shweder, R. (1991). *Thinking through cultures*. Cambridge, MA: Harvard University Press.

Silverstein, M. (1976). Shifters, linguistic categories, and cultural description. In K. Basso & H. Selby (Eds.), *Meaning in anthropology* (pp. 11–55). Albuquerque: University of New Mexico Press.

Silverstein, M. (1979). Language structure and linguistic ideology. In P. Clyne (Ed.), *The elements* (pp. 193–247). Chicago: Chicago Linguistic Society.

Silverstein, M. (1981). *Metaforces of power in traditional oratory*. Unpublished manuscript, University of Chicago, Anthropology Department.

Silverstein, M. (1992). The indeterminacy of contextualization: When is enough enough? In A. DiLuzio & P. Auer (Eds.), *The contextualization of language* (pp. 55–75). Amsterdam: J. Benjamins.

Silverstein, M. (1993). Metapragmatic discourse and metapragmatic function. In J. Lucy (Ed.), *Reflexive language* (pp. 33–58). New York: Cambridge University Press.

Silverstein, M. (1996). The secret life of texts. In M. Silverstein & G. Urban (Eds.), *Natural histories of discourse*. Chicago: University of Chicago Press.

Silverstein, M. (1998). The improvisational performance of "culture" in real-time discursive practice. In K. Sawyer (Ed.), *Improvisation* (pp. 265–312). Norwood, NJ: Ablex.

Silverstein, M., & Urban, G. (Eds.). (1996). *Natural histories of discourse*. Chicago: University of Chicago Press.

Somers, M. (1994). The narrative constitution of identity. *Theory and Society, 23*, 605–649.

Sperber, D., & Wilson, D. (1986). *Relevance*. Cambridge, MA: Harvard University Press.

Stahl, S. (1989). *Literary folkloristics and the personal narrative,* Bloomington: University of Indiana.

Stewart, K. (1996). *A space on the side of the road.* Princeton, NJ: Princeton University Press.

Stromberg, P. (1993). *Language and self-transformation.* New York: Cambridge University Press.

Taylor, C. (1985a). The concept of a person. In *Human agency and language* (pp. 97–114). New York: Cambridge University Press.

Taylor, C. (1985b). What is human agency? In *Human agency and language* (pp. 15–44). New York: Cambridge University Press. (Original work published 1977)

Taylor, C. (1991). The dialogical self. In D. Hiley, J. Bohman, & R. Shusterman (Eds.), *The interpretive turn* (pp. 304–314). Ithaca, NY: Cornell University Press.

Toolan, M. (1988). *Narrative.* New York: Routledge.

Urban, G. (1996). *Metaphysical community.* Austin: University of Texas Press.

Verschueren, J. (1995). The pragmatic return to meaning. *Journal of Linguistic Anthropology, 5,* 127–156.

Verschueren, J. (1999). *Understanding pragmatics.* London: Arnold.

Vološinov, V. (1973). *Marxism and the philosophy of language* (L. Matejka & I. Titunik, Trans.). Cambridge, MA: Harvard University Press. (Original work published 1929)

Waugh, L. (1995). Reported speech in journalistic discourse. *Text, 15,* 129–173.

Wertsch, J. (1991). *Voices of the mind.* Cambridge, MA: Harvard University Press.

Wertsch, J. (1998). *Mind as action.* New York: Oxford University Press.

White, H. (1987). *The content of the form.* Baltimore: Johns Hopkins University Press.

White, M., & Epston, D. (1990). *Narrative means to therapeutic ends.* New York: Norton.

Witherell, C., & Noddings, N. (Eds.). (1991). *Stories lives tell.* New York: Teachers College Press.

Wittgenstein, L. (1953). *Philosophical investigations* (3rd ed.) (G. E. M. Anscombe, Trans.). New York: Macmillan.

Wortham, S. (1992). Participant examples and classroom interaction. *Linguistics and Education, 4,* 195–217.

Wortham, S. (1994). *Acting out participant examples in the classroom.* Philadelphia: J. Benjamins.

Wortham, S. (1999). The heterogeneously distributed self. *Journal of Constructivist Psychology, 12,* 153–173.

Wortham, S. (2001). Interactionally situated cognition: A classroom example. *Cognitive Science, 25,* 37–66.

Wortham, S., & Locher, M. (1996). Voicing on the news: An analytic technique for studying media bias. *Text, 16,* 557–585.

Wortham, S., & Locher, M. (1999). Embedded metapragmatics and lying politicians. *Language and Communication, 19,* 109–125.

Zuss, M. (1997). Contesting representations. *Theory and Psychology, 7,* 653–673.

Index

Active/assertive voice
  example of, 80, 119–135
  transition from passive voice,
    101–119
Alcoholics Anonymous (AA), 10–11,
    13–14
Anderson, H., 5, 6
Anthropology, 12
Authoring (Bakhtin), 63

Bailkey, N., 24
Bakhtin, Mikhail, xii, 15–16, 17–23,
    37–40, 42–43, 48, 63–67, 146–
    149, 159, 161, 163–164 n. 1–2,
    166 n. 6, 167–168 n. 1–2
Bal, M., 166 n. 5
Bamberg, M., 58
Bickhard, M., 155
Bloom, L., xiii, 7
Boundary phenomenon, 146
Bourdieu, P., 158
Bower, G., 58, 59
Braver, Rita, 51–55, 58, 59, 60, 61,
    66, 67, 68–70, 72
Bruner, J., 137, 165 n. 2
Bush, George, 48–55, 57, 58, 60, 61,
    68–69, 73, 74, 159–160, 165
    n. 1
Butler, J., 12

Cain, C., 6, 10–11, 13–14, 15
Capps, L., 15
CBS Evening News example, 48–62,
    67, 68–70, 72, 74, 159–160
Christopher, J., 155

Chunking, in dialogic approach to
    discourse, 44–46
Clark, H., 72, 73
Clark, K., 63, 147, 161, 164 n. 4
Clayman, S., 165 n. 1
Clinton, Bill, 48–49, 55, 57
Cohen, J., 6
Cohler, B., 5, 6
Contextualization, 42–44
  context-specific patterns, 139
  cues for, 36–37
  indeterminacy of, 23, 43
Conversation analysis, 40–41
Crapanzano, V., 12, 77, 150–151
Crites, S., 137
Csordas, T., 12, 155, 158
Culler, J., 58

Damon, W., 138–140, 142, 150
Davies, B., 7–8
Dennett, D., 155, 156
Dialogic approach, xii, 15–16, 17–
    46, 139
  to autobiographical narrative, 76–
    135
  chunking in, 44–46
  emergence in, 40–44
  and interactional positioning,
    160–161
  mediation in, 35–37
  monologic approach and, 18–23,
    139, 161
  Spartan babies example of, 24–37,
    159
  voicing in, 37, 38–40

Dialogic self, 144–148
Dickens, Charles, 64–66
Disjunct markers, 61
Dostoevsky, Fyodor, 63–64, 68
Double voicing (Bakhtin), 62–66,
    70–74
Doubling of roles, 13, 137

Early speech act theory (Searle), 35
Emergence
    concept of, 40–44, 62
    in dialogic approach to discourse,
        40–44
    in narrative approach, 59–62, 142
Emerson, C., 23, 43, 146, 161, 164
    n. 4, 166 n. 6
Emplotment, 6–7
Enacting self, 149–153
    interrelations in, 13–14
    nature of, 9–12
Epistemic modalization, 74, 114–
    116
Epston, D., 5, 6
Ervin-Tripp, S., 57
Essentialism
    essentialist account of self, 12
    essentialization of representation,
        158
Ethnomethodology, 40–41
Evaluative indexicals, 73–74
Event of speaking (Jakobson), 19

Feminist theory, 12
Fisher, H., 156
Flax, J., 12
Fludernik, M., 57, 73
Freeman, M., 140–146, 150, 154,
    155
Freud, S., 149–150

Garfinkel, H., 36, 40–41, 43
Georgakopoulou, A., 57
Gergen, Kenneth J., vii–viii, xii, 6,
    8–9, 12, 62, 144, 145, 154, 157,
    158, 165 n. 4, 167 n. 1
Gergen, M., 6, 7–8, 62, 154

Gerhardt, J., 15
Gerrig, R., 72, 73
Gilligan, C., 143–144
Goffman, E., 36
Goodwin, C., 60
Goodwin, M., 60
Goossens, L., 72
Gore, Al, Jr., 57
Grumet, M., 8, 9
Gubrium, J., 12
Gumperz, J., 36, 37, 59

Hanks, W., 163 n. 1
Harding, S., 9–10, 11, 13–14, 15
Haroutunian-Gordon, S., 160
Hart, D., 138–140, 142, 150
Havránek, B., 36
Heidegger, M., 23
Hensel, C., 15
Hermans, H., 62, 145, 147, 156, 167
    n. 1
Hermeneutic circle (Heidegger), 23
Heteroglossia (Bakhtin), 38
Hill, J., 154
Holquist, M., 63, 147, 161, 164 n. 4
Holstein, J., 12

Indeterminacy of contextualization
    (Silverstein), 23, 43
Indexical signs (cues), 37–40, 44–46,
    69
Interactional function of
    autobiographical discourse, xi–
    xiv, 7–9
Interactional positioning, 8–9
    chunking in, 44–46
    clues about, 30
    in complex narrative, 51–52, 59–
        62, 65–66
    and dialogic approach, 160–161
    emergence and, 40–44
    example of, 24–35
    mediation in, 35–37
    monologic approach and, 18–23
    and multilayered self, 154
    in other contexts, 158–160

represented content and, 22–23, 136
in speech, 157–158
transference as, 150–151
voicing in, 37, 38–40
Irvine, J., 138

Jakobson, R., 19, 45
Jane (narrative), 23, 76–135, 136–142
active/assertive voice, 80, 119–135
adolescence, 101–109
child rearing, 119–122
and dialogic self, 144–148
and enacted self, 149–153
episodes and characters in life of, 78–79
first abortion, 122–128
first institutionalization, 81–90
and multilayered self, 154–156
and narrated self, 141–144
overview, 1–5, 76–81
parenthood, 109–119
passive voice, 80, 81–101
recurring voices, 100, 131
second abortion, 128–135
second institutionalization, 90–101
and stable psychological self, 139–140
transition from passive to active voice, 101–119
Jefferson, G., 60–61, 62
Jelinek, E., 7
Johnson-Laird, P., 58
Joy, M., 12, 163 n. 3

Kaye, J., 8–9
Kellogg, R., 166 n. 5
Kempen, H. J. G., 62, 145, 147, 156, 167 n. 1
Kerby, A., 5
Küntay, A., 57

Labov, W., 49, 77, 165 n. 3
Lather, P., xiii

Levinson, S., 36
Lewis, Anthony, 51–53, 54, 57, 58, 69
Life of Lycurgus (Plutarch), 24–27
Linde, C., 77
Linguistic analysis, 17–18
Little Dorrit (Dickens), 64–66
Locher, M., 39, 48, 49, 51, 53, 70, 74, 160
Lucy, J., 151–152

Mapping, 138
Marchman, V., 58
McAdams, Dan, ix, 140–146, 150
Mead, G., 146
Media bias, 160
Mediated approach, 62
Mediation
concept of, 35–37
in dialogic approach to discourse, 35–37
in narrative approach, 57–59
Mertz, E., 151–152
Metaprogrammatic descriptors, 71–72
Mishler, E., 47, 137
Monologic approach, 18–23, 139, 161
Morrow, D., 58, 59
Morson, G., 23, 43, 146, 161, 164 n. 4, 166 n. 6
Multilayered self, 153–156

Narrated events, 19–21, 30–31
Narrated self, 140–144
Narrative approach, 47–75
CBS Evening News example of, 48–62, 67, 68–70, 72, 74, 159–160
double voicing and, 62–66, 70–74
emergence in, 59–62, 142
mediation in, 57–59
ventriloquation and, 66–74, 90, 97, 137, 147–148
voice in, 62–66, 70–74
Nelson, K., 165 n. 2

Nixon, Richard, 74
Noddings, N., 6
Novel, theory of, 63

Ochberg, R., 6
Ochs, E., 15
O'Connor, P., 15
Organized self-understanding, 138–140

Parmentier, R., 151–152
Participant examples, 24–35
Passive voice
  example of, 80, 81–101
  transition to active/assertive voice, 101–119
Peirce, C., 36, 37
Penuel, W., 155
Performative account of self, 12
Performative function of talk, 145
Perot, Ross, 48, 49, 55, 57
Personal Narratives Group, 6
Plutarch, 24–27
Poetic structure, 44–46
Polanyi, L., 60, 165 n. 3
Polkinghorne, D., 6, 58
Predication, 70–71
Pynchon, T., 73–74

Quotation, 72–73

Rather, Dan, 48–60, 61, 67, 68–71, 165 n. 1
Reagan, Ronald, 48, 52, 54
Reference, 70–71
Relevance (Sperber & Wilson), 23
Representation
  essentialization of, 158
  in interactional positioning, 22–23, 136
  representational foregrounding, 6
  representational function of autobiographical discourse, xi–xiv, 5–7
  in self-construction, 5–7, 13–14
Ricoeur, P., 58

Ritualized construction of self, 151–153
Ritual parallelism, 152
Romanticism, 148
Rorty, A., 144
Rosenwald, G., 6

Sacks, H., 36, 40–41, 60, 62
Sampson, E., 160, 161
Sarbin, T., 62, 154
Sass, L., 155
Schafer, R., 62, 145
Scheibe, K., 156
Schiffrin, D., 154
Schlegloff, E., 40–41, 165 n. 1
Scholes, R., 166 n. 5
Searle, J., 35
Self-assertion, 148
Self-coherence, 141–144, 150, 155
Self-construction, 1–16, 136–156
  analyzing autobiographical discourse in, 14–16
  and dialogic self, 144–148
  enacting self in, 9–12, 149–153
  interrelation in, 7–9, 13–14
  and multilayered self, 153–156
  and narrated self, 140–144
  representation in, 5–7, 13–14
  and stable psychological self, 138–140
Self-reflection, 146
Shotter, J., xii, 145, 160, 161, 167 n. 1, 168 n. 2, 169 n. 3
Shweder, R., 164 n. 2, 165 n. 4
Silverstein, M., 23, 36, 37, 43, 45, 46, 70, 71–72, 74, 138, 151–152, 153, 163 n. 1
Social constructionism, 145–148
Social determinism, 147–148
Social psychology, 12
Sociology, 12
Somers, M., 12
Spartan babies example, 24–37, 159
Sperber, D., 23
Stable psychological self, 138–140
Stahl, S., 137

Stewart, K., 7, 8, 12
Stinson, C., 15
Storytelling events, 19–21, 30–31
Stromberg, P., 6, 15

Taylor, C., 160, 161
Toolan, M., 58
Transference, 149–151
  concept of, 149–150
  as interactional positioning, 150–
    151

Unfinalizability (Garfinkel), 43
Urban, G., 151–152, 153

Ventriloquation
  in narrative approach, 66–74, 90,
    97, 137, 147–148
  tools for identifying, 70–74
Verschueren, J., 163 n. 1
Voice (Bakhtin)
  active/assertive, 80, 119–135
  in dialogic approach to discourse,
    37, 38–40
  double voicing, 62–66, 70–74

in narrative approach, 62–66, 70–
    74
passive, 80, 81–101
tools for identifying, 70–74
transition from passive to active,
    101–119
Vološinov, V., 38, 72, 164–165 n. 4

Waletsky, J., 49, 165 n. 3
Waugh, L., 73
Weinberger, Caspar, 48–52, 54–56,
    71
Wertsch, J., 155, 160, 161, 169 n. 3
Whalen, J., 165 n. 1
White, H., 58
White, M., 5, 6
Wilson, D., 23
Witherell, C., 6
Wittgenstein, L., 167 n. 1
Wong, D., 144
Wortham, S., 14, 24, 28, 29, 39, 48,
    49, 51, 53, 70, 74, 150, 156,
    159, 160, 164 n. 3

Zuss, M., 6, 8

About the Author

Stanton E. F. Wortham is Associate Professor and Chair of the Educational Leadership Division at the University of Pennsylvania Graduate School of Education. His doctorate is from the Committee on Human Development at the University of Chicago. He is a linguistic anthropologist of education whose work explores how the sociocultural aspects of language use can facilitate learning and identity development in educational settings. He has also developed discourse analytic methods for studying the interactional functions of language use. His first book, *Acting Out Participant Examples in the Classroom*, analyzes the use of examples in urban high school English and history classrooms. He has also studied media bias, through detailed examination of network news coverage of U.S. Presidential campaigns, and the narrative construction of identity. All of his work explores how speech both represents content and establishes interactional positions for speakers, and how these two functions interrelate.